CARDIFF
CAERDYDD

LOBBYING IN THE EUROPEAN UNION

Lobbying in the European Union

Interest Groups, Lobbying Coalitions, and Policy Change

HEIKE KLÜVER

OXFORD
UNIVERSITY PRESS

OXFORD
UNIVERSITY PRESS

Great Clarendon Street, Oxford, OX2 6DP,
United Kingdom

Oxford University Press is a department of the University of Oxford.
If furthers the University's objective of excellence in research, scholarship,
and education by publishing worldwide. Oxford is a registered trade mark of
Oxford University Press in the UK and in certain other countries

© Heike Klüver 2013

The moral rights of the author have been asserted

First Edition published in 2013
Impression: 1

British Library Cataloguing in Publication Data
Data available

ISBN 978-0-19-965744-5

Printed in Great Britain by
MPG Books Group, Bodmin and King's Lynn

To Frederik

Preface

Why can some interest groups influence policy-making in the European Union while others cannot? I remember well when, for the first time, I asked myself the question that this book seeks to answer. I was an exchange student at the Sciences Po in Grenoble and was taking a class called Interest Groups in the European Union, taught by Sabine Saurugger. We were talking about the classical theories of interest representation, interest groups' lobbying strategies, and the population of interest groups that lobby the European institutions. Although I was passionate about interest group politics, I was always wondering to what extent interest groups actually *influence* policy-making outcomes. Given that influence is usually the first thing that people think about when you ask them about interest groups and considering the important normative implications of lobbying, I was surprised to see very little research on this topic. Therefore, when starting my PhD, I did not have to look for a research question for very long. Interest group influence in the European Union quickly became the research agenda that I pursued for the next five years and this book brings together the findings of that academic endeavor.

This book would have not been possible without the help, support, and inspiration of many colleagues and friends. First and foremost, I am deeply grateful to my supervisor, Berthold Rittberger, for his encouragement, advice, and guidance during my PhD and beyond. He has been an excellent supervisor who has given me enough space to independently develop my own research project, but who has provided guidance whenever needed and inspired me to become a better political scientist. Without his encouraging words, academic guidance, and personal counsel I would have not been able to write this book. He made me believe in my qualities as a researcher and encouraged me to pursue an academic career. I will always be grateful for his invaluable support.

Similarly, I would like to thank my co-supervisor, Sabine Saurugger, who has supported me ever since my Erasmus stay in Grenoble. Her course on Interest Groups in the European Union inspired me to investigate this topic later on in my Master's and PhD thesis. Her valuable comments, criticism, and suggestions have played an integral part in the writing of this book, and I am very grateful for her continuous support over the past years. My gratitude also goes to Thomas Gschwend, who has provided indispensable advice on methodological questions. He always had an open door for me and his counsel has significantly improved the quality of this book.

When writing this book, I have benefited from the excellent and stimulating research environment at the University of Mannheim. The exchange with colleagues from the Graduate School of Economic and Social Sciences, the Mannheim Centre for European Social Research and the School of Social Sciences provided me with important insights and inspirations for my work. This book would not have been the same without the excellent feedback and encouragement from my friends and colleagues who have repeatedly commented on my work and who made my time in Mannheim an intellectually stimulating and enjoyable experience. In particular, I would like to thank Doreen Allerkamp, Christian Arnold, Hanna Bäck, Patrick Bayer, Simona Bevern, Thomas Bräuninger, Tanja Dannwolf, Lisa Dellmuth, Thorsten Faas, Nathalie Giger, Iris Glockner, Gesine Götze, Stefan Götze, Marcelo Jenny, Sebastian Köhler, Beate Kohler, Thomas Meyer, Susanne Michalik, Sven-Oliver Proksch, Christine Quittkat, Ellen Schneider, Stefan Seidendorf, Daniel Stegmülller, Michael Stoffel, Bettina Trüb, and Arndt Wonka. Above all, I am grateful to Gema García Albacete and Oshrat Hochman for their intellectual support and invaluable friendship throughout the entire PhD program.

I extended this research project into a book manuscript during my Postdoctoral Fellowship at Nuffield College at the University of Oxford. Nuffield College provided an outstanding and intellectually stimulating environment for the challenging task of converting my thesis into a book manuscript. I am grateful to my colleagues and friends for the fruitful discussions, the support, and the great time I have had throughout my postdoc years. Most importantly, I would like to thank Elias Dinas, Theresa Kuhn, Eline de Rooij, Iñaki Sagarzazu, Daniel Stegmüller, and Adam Ziegfeld for their helpful comments and suggestions. Raymond Duch and Sara Binzer Hobolt have also provided valuable advice and guidance throughout my Postdoctoral Fellowship.

In addition, I have benefited enormously from the Graduate School of Economic and Social Sciences and the Excellence Initiative of the German Science Foundation that provided an exceptional academic environment, generous financial support, and an excellent infrastructure for the completion of my thesis. I am furthermore grateful for financial support provided by the German Academic Exchange Service and the State of Baden-Württemberg. My Postdoctoral Fellowship was generously funded by the Volkswagen Foundation through the Anglo-German State of the State Program. This fellowship program has been coordinated by the University of Oxford, the University of Bremen, and the University of Göttingen and I am very grateful for this outstanding opportunity.

Audiences at several workshops and conferences have provided valuable comments, criticism, and suggestions that have helped to improve this book. In particular, I would like to thank Frank Baumgartner, David Coen, David Lowery, and Christine Mahoney for their excellent comments on my work.

In addition, I am indebted to Christine Mahoney for hosting me as a visiting research fellow at the Maxwell School of Citizenship and Public Affairs at Syracuse University. Additionally, I am grateful to all the interest group representatives who took the time to participate in the survey conducted for this study. Without their participation, this research project could not have been realized.

I would like to thank Dominic Byatt and his colleagues at Oxford University Press who have worked with me on this book as well as the five anonymous reviewers for their insightful and encouraging remarks. Chapter 3 constitutes a revised and much extended version of "Measuring Interest Group Influence Using Quantitative Text Analysis" which was published in *European Union Politics* 10(4) 2009. Chapter 2 partly draws on ideas developed in "Lobbying as a Collective Enterprise: Winners and Losers of Policy Formulation in the European Union," *Journal of European Public Policy* 20(1) 2013. I thank both journals as well as Sage and Taylor & Francis for allowing me to use that material in this book.

Finally, I am eternally grateful for the loving support of my parents, Renate and Otto Klüver, who have always believed in me and are always there for me when I need them. Above all, I thank Frederik Adriaenssens for his love, encouragement, and enduring patience. Without his support throughout the ups and downs of this academic endeavor, this book would not have been the same. With gratitude, I dedicate this book to him.

Heike Klüver

Oxford, May 2012

Contents

List of Figures

List of Tables

List of Abbreviations

ACEA	European Automobile Manufacturers' Association
ADTS	Associação per la Divulgação de les Tecnologies Sostenibles
AEGPL	European Liquefied Petroleum Gas Association
AIC	Akaike Information Criterion
AVELE	Spanish Association for the Promotion of Electric and Non-Contaminant Vehicles
AVERE	European Association for Battery, Hybrid, and Fuel Cell Electric Vehicles
BEUC	European Consumer Organization
BIC	Bayesian Information Criterion
BVRLA	British Vehicle Rental and Leasing Association
CAP	Common Agricultural Policy
CECED	European Committee of Domestic Equipment Manufacturers
CEO	Chief Executive Officer
CMP	Comparative Manifesto Project
COGECA	General Committee for Agricultural Cooperation in the European Union
COMM	European Commission
CONECCS	Consultation, the European Commission and Civil Society
COPA	Committee of Professional Agricultural Organisations
DE	Germany
DemoCiv	Democratic Legitimacy via Civil Society Involvement
DG	Directorate General
EBB	European Biodiesel Board
EC	European Community
ELC	European Lamp Companies Federation
ENGVA	European Natural Gas Vehicles Association
EP	European Parliament
ESPRIT	European Strategic Programme for Research and Development in Information Technologies
ETRMA	European Tyre and Rubber Manufacturers' Association
ETS	Emissions Trading Scheme
ETSC	European Transport Safety Council

ETUC	European Trade Union Confederation
EU	European Union
FAEP	European Federation of Magazine Publishers
FANC	Finnish Association of Nature Conservation
FOEIT	Friends of the Earth Italy
FOEUK	Friends of the Earth UK
GM	General Motors
IG	Interest Group
JAMA	Japan Automobile Manufacturers' Association
KAMA	Korea Automobile Manufacturers' Association
LTI	LTI Vehicles
MEP	Member of the European Parliament
NGO	Non-governmental Organization
NL	Netherlands
OECD	Organisation for Economic Co-operation and Development
OLS	Ordinary least squares
QM	Qualified majority voting
RAI	RAI Vereniging – Rijwel and Automobiel Industrie
REACH	Registration, Evaluation, and Authorization of Chemicals
RSPB	Royal Society for the Protection of Birds
SMMT	Society of Motor Manufacturers and Traders
SQ	Status quo
T&E	Transport and Environment
UK	United Kingdom
UKAA	UK Advertising Association
VDA	Verband der Automobilindustrie
VW	Volkswagen
WWF	World Wide Fund For Nature

1

Introduction

The study of politics is the study of influence and the influential
                                                        Lasswell (1936)

The question of who wins and who loses lies at the heart of the study of politics. Understanding why some interest groups win and others lose should be of central concern to scholars: Since one of the major aims of interest groups is to influence policy-making, any analysis that tries to explain the emergence of policy outcomes should naturally take into account interest group pressure. In addition, interest group influence and the distribution of influence among groups have important normative implications: If public policy is systematically biased in favor of some interests while others are constantly losing, the democratic legitimacy of policy outcomes is greatly undermined (Dahl 1989, 322–326). What determines interest group influence is therefore one of the central puzzles in the study of politics. However, understanding why some interest groups win and others lose is still an area of confusion (Baumgartner and Leech 1998, 13).

Interest group influence should be of particular concern to scholars of European politics since the European Union (EU) constitutes a promising political opportunity structure for organized interests (Richardson 2000). The multiple layers of government together with the high fragmentation of the European institutions provide a plurality of access points to the decision-making process. The institutional provisions facilitating interest group access have been supplemented by an increasing openness of the European institutions towards interest groups. Due to the constant criticism of the democratic deficit, the European institutions have started to consider interest group inclusion as a means to compensate for the representational deficit often associated with the European polity (e.g. Weiler, Haltern, and Mayer 1995; Follesdal and Hix 2006). Since the beginning of the 1990s, the Commission has therefore taken various initiatives to increase the participation of interest groups such as the White Paper on Governance or the Transparency Initiative (Kohler-Koch and Finke 2007).

Even though the Commission initiatives have provided broad access to all sorts of interest groups, recent empirical evidence shows that the ability to exploit this access varies between groups. In his case study of the consultation on the Commission proposal for a new European chemicals policy, Persson (2007) demonstrates that business interest groups were considerably better represented than non-governmental organizations (NGOs). Similarly, Dür and De Bièvre (2007*a*) find that business groups were more successful in influencing European trade policy than NGOs. Even though NGOs managed to gain *access* to European decision-makers by establishing formal or informal contacts with them (Eising 2007*b*, 331), they were not able to translate their *access* into *influence* over policy outcomes. What is more, lobbying success does not only vary across different types of interest groups, but even the same interest groups sometimes successfully lobby the European institutions in one debate whereas they largely fail to shape the policy process in other debates. For instance, Warleigh (2000) demonstrated in an analysis of the legislative debate on the Auto Oil package adopted in 1998 which regulated fuel quality and vehicle emission standards that environmental groups successfully shaped the policy outcome. By contrast, Klüver (2009) showed that the environmental lobby largely failed to influence the Commission proposal on the reduction of CO_2 emissions from cars. How can this be explained? Why can some interest groups influence policy-making in the European Union while others cannot? And even more puzzling, why do the same interest groups sometimes win and sometimes lose?

Despite the central importance of interest group influence in the European Union, only few have studied it. What is more, the few existing studies are usually limited to specific group types and to one or just a few policy issues and are therefore characterized by contradictory findings (e.g. Dür and De Bièvre 2007*a*; Michalowitz 2007; Woll 2007). The lack of research is surprising because studying interest group influence does not only contribute to the scholarly literature on interest groups, but it also has major implications for two ongoing debates in European politics. First, investigating interest group influence can help us to better understand policy outcomes in the European Union. Whereas scholars of EU policy-making have mostly concentrated on explaining policy outcomes with reference to the formal institutions, the role of interest groups has largely been ignored (e.g. Steunenberg 1994; Tsebelis 1994; Crombez 1997). However, if we explain policy outcomes solely drawing on the preferences and bargaining power of the three major European institutions, we disregard how the preferences of these institutions have actually come about (see also Hörl, Warntjen, and Wonka 2005). Moravcsik (1993, 1998) for instance argues that member states in the Council function as a transmission belt for interest group preferences dominant on the domestic level. Supranationalists furthermore suggest that interest groups also get active on the European level and that they have an important direct impact on supranational institutions and European policy-making (Stone Sweet and Sandholtz 1997; Sandholtz and Stone Sweet 1998). Accordingly, the number of interest groups lobbying the European institutions has increased considerably over the past decades (e.g. Stone Sweet and Fligstein 2002, 1221). Thus, ignoring the increasing pressure of interest groups constitutes an oversimplification of the policy-making processes at the European level. Taking into account interest group influence can therefore help us to significantly improve our understanding of how policy outcomes emerge in the European Union.

Even more importantly, an empirical analysis of interest group influence on European policy-making can shed light on the debate on the democratic legitimacy of the European Union. The increasing openness of the European institutions towards interest groups is driven by the intention to bridge the gap between citizens and the European Union (see e.g. Kohler-Koch 2007; Saurugger 2010). Similarly, democratic theory has debated the democratic potential of interest group participation in policy-making (Hirst 1994; Cohen and Rogers 1995; Schmalz-Bruns 1995). It has been argued that interest groups can enhance the democratic legitimacy of a political system by ensuring the participation of citizens and by simultaneously enhancing its problem-solving capacity (Saurugger 2008, 1276). The inclusion of interest groups must, however, be treated with caution from a normative standpoint. Interest group participation can only enhance the democratic quality of supranational policy-making if influence is not systematically biased in favor of some interests while others are constantly losing (Dahl 1989, 322–326). Thus, in order to evaluate the democratic potential of interest group participation in European policy-making, an empirical assessment of interest group influence and the distribution of influence among groups is necessary. This book therefore aims at solving the presented puzzle by explaining why some interest groups are able to influence policy-making in the European Union while others are not.

In order to explain interest group influence in the European Union, this books develops a comprehensive theoretical model for understanding lobbying success. Lobbying is conceptualized as an exchange relationship in which the European institutions trade influence for information, citizen support, and economic power. However, it is argued that it is not sufficient to only look at the supply of these goods by individual interest groups, but that it is necessary to acknowledge that lobbying takes place in coalitions. There is hardly any policy debate on which only one single interest group mobilizes; lobbying is instead a collective process in which a plurality of interest groups simultaneously lobby decision-makers. As a result, it is not the information supply, citizen support, and economic power of individual interest groups that make the difference, but it is the aggregated amount of goods provided by entire issue-specific lobbying coalitions that matters. In order to test this theoretical claim, this book introduces a new approach to measure interest group influence which draws on recently developed quantitative text analysis techniques to analyze online consultations launched by the European Commission.[1] By extracting the policy preferences of interest groups from their consultation submissions and comparing them to the policy outcome, conclusions about the winners and the losers of the decision-making process are drawn.

Even though the empirical focus of this book is the European Union, the analysis presented here has important implications for the study of interest group lobbying more generally. Interest group influence is an important and recurring theme in the study of politics. Studying what makes an interest group a winner or a loser is crucial for our understanding of how democracy works. The European Union functions as the empirical example in this book, but the theoretical claim and the methods introduced to measure influence apply to interest group lobbying in any political system. The idea that lobbying is a collective process is not specific to the European Union. Lobbying in any other political system is similarly a collective exercise in which multiple interest groups mobilize. Interest groups that share the same policy objective are pulling decision-makers in the same direction independent of the political system under study. Hence, the argument that issue-specific lobbying coalitions are the decisive unit of analysis is a universal claim that applies to lobbying anywhere in the world. Similarly, the methodological approach that draws on a quantitative text analysis of legislative consultations is also not limited to the European Union. This technique can be used in any political system in which interest groups release position papers on policy initiatives. Hence, this books does not only provide insights for the study of interest group influence in the EU, but it has important theoretical and methodological implications for the study of interest group lobbying more generally.

In the ensuing sections, I first define the key concepts of this study. I then proceed to discuss briefly the state of the literature on interest group influence on policy-making in the European Union and point out its shortcomings. The next section contains a summary of the theoretical argument followed by an illustration of the methodological approach employed in this book. Finally, I present a short overview of the successive chapters.

---

[1] In the course of this book, the expressions "consultations," "legislative consultations," and "public consultations" will be used exchangeably to denote online consultations conducted by the European Commission.

1.1 KEY CONCEPTS: INTEREST GROUPS
AND INFLUENCE

In this section, I define the central concepts of this study. First, I make clear what makes an actor an "interest group" and what kind of actors are covered by the term. Second, I elaborate on the concept of "influence."

1.1.1 Interest groups

The study of interest group politics has been plagued by a wide variety of terms that were used to denote organized interests. When looking at the literature you find that scholars use terms like interest associations, pressure groups, interest organizations, civil society organizations, non-governmental organizations, or public interest groups. The use of different terminologies goes hand in hand with what Beyers, Eising, and Maloney (2008, 1108) call a "balkanization" of the field into numerous branches that are characterized by little communication between the different strands of the literature. For instance, there is a long-standing divide between scholars studying "special interest groups," that is, interest groups which represent economic interests and scholars studying so-called "civil society organizations," that is, interest groups which represent public interests. Even though these researchers share a common ground and are studying similar phenomena, they are still largely divided (Beyers, Eising, and Maloney 2008; Eising 2008). This study aims to bridge the gap between the different strands in the literature by analyzing a wide variety of different actors. I use the conventional term *interest group*, but employ a very broad definition in order to cover a large range of actors.

According to Beyers, Eising, and Maloney (2008, 1106–1109) three features must be present to define an actor as an "interest group": organization, political interests, and private status.[2] In order to qualify as an interest group, political actors must draw on some sort of *organization*. Organization relates to the nature of the group and excludes unorganized broad movements and waves of public opinion. For instance, the broad women's movement does not qualify as an interest group because it does not dispose of any organizational structure. By contrast, the European Women's Lobby, which is the European federation

---

[2] Beyers, Eising, and Maloney (2008) use the term "informality" to denote private status. However, interest groups can also draw on formal channels such as obligatory hearings to realize their interests which makes the term "informality" somewhat misleading. In addition, I go beyond the mere office-seeking argument that lies behind the informality notion suggested by Beyers, Eising, and Maloney (2008) by also excluding public institutions from the interest group definition. I therefore refrain from using the term "informality" and use "private status" instead.

Table 1.1 Features of social and political organizations

	Organization	Political interest	Private status
Political parties	X	X	
Social movements		X	X
Leisure associations	X		X
Interest groups	X	X	X

of women's associations in the European Union, qualifies as an interest group because it has a clear organizational structure with formal membership status and a permanent secretariat responsible for its administration. The second feature that must be present in order to define actors as interest groups is *political interest*. Actors must pursue the objective to influence political decision-making and to shape policy outcomes. This feature distinguishes interest groups from leisure associations. For example, a sports club usually does not have a political interest and therefore does not qualify as an interest group. Finally, the last characteristic that must be present so that actors are classified as interest groups is *private status*. Private status refers to the fact that interest groups are not seeking public office and that they are not public institutions which are funded and subject to the state. Interest groups do not compete in elections, but instead seek to realize their interests by informal and formal contacts with legislators or by using demonstrations or protests to pressure political decision-makers. Private status therefore distinguishes interest groups from political parties. In addition, private status also distinguishes interest groups from public institutions such as hospitals or universities. Public institutions dispose of an organization and they can have a political interest, but they depend on public funding and are subject to the state.[3] Table 1.1 summarizes how interest groups differ from other organizations.

There are, however, different types of interest groups. A wide variety of actors have an organization, have a political interest, and do not strive for public office. This definition for instance applies to employers' associations, trade unions, environmental groups, companies, or professional associations. For analytical reasons, I further distinguish between two major types: associations and companies. The crucial difference between these two interest group types is membership. Whereas associations are membership organizations which have individuals, companies, or public institutions as members, companies are corporate actors which do not have any members.

---

[3] Chambers are also classified as interest groups as they are organizations with political interests that do not compete for public office. Even though they often perform public or quasi-public functions, they are usually funded by member contributions which grants them considerable independence from the state.

1.1.2 Influence

The second key concept which has to be defined is "influence." Influence is understood as the ability of an actor to shape a political decision in line with his preferences (Dür 2008c, 561). Thus, this book focuses on the analysis of the first *face of power* by examining who wins and who loses regarding a collectively binding decision over public policy (Dahl 1957).[4] Interest groups are considered to be influential if they are able to shape political decisions so that policies converge with their policy preferences. Hence, a necessary condition for influence is the coincidence of the policy preferences of an actor with the output of the political decision-making process (see figure 1.1).

However, winning on a policy issue does not mean that interest groups are in fact influential. The convergence of policy preferences of actors with policy outputs is only a necessary, not a sufficient condition for influence. A pure convergence of policy preferences of interest groups and political decisions does not necessarily imply influence. It can for instance be the case that interest groups simply get what they want since other actors with the same policy goal were influencing the European institutions. Thus, if the distance between the

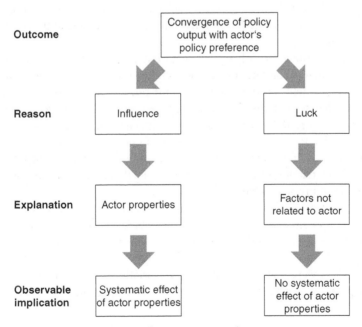

Fig. 1.1 Influence conceptualization

---

[4] The second *face of power* focuses instead on an actor's ability to set the agenda (Bachrach and Baratz 1962) whereas the third *face of power* refers to an actor's ability to prevent other actors from recognizing their genuine interest (Lukes 1974).

ideal point of an interest group and the policy position of a decision-maker decreases over the course of the legislative process, it does not necessarily mean that the policy outcome can be attributed to the policy preference of this particular interest group. This interest group might just be lucky to get what it wants (Barry 1980*a,b*).[5] Hence, convergence can emerge since an actor influenced the political decision-making process or because an actor was simply lucky.

To empirically disentangle influence and luck, I draw on the observable implications illustrated in figure 1.1. The crucial point that distinguishes influence from pure luck is a causal link between the policy preferences of an actor and the output of the policy-making process (Nagel 1975, 29). If an interest group is able to influence a political decision, there must be a causal connection between the attributes of this interest group and the political decision. Hence, there must be a systematic association between actor properties and the policy output. These properties could for instance be bargaining power, information provided by interest groups, or demonstrations that interest groups organize in order to pressure legislators. What kind of actor properties account for the ability of an interest group to influence policy-making has to be specified theoretically (see chapter 2). If an actor is indeed able to influence political decisions which bring about the policy output, one can observe a systematic, that is, statistically significant effect of actor properties.

If an actor is, however, only lucky to get what he wants, then the policy output can be attributed to factors that are not related to the actor and no systematic pattern can be detected that connects actor properties and the outcome of a legislative debate. For instance, a policy change that is favored by an actor might have occurred due to a focusing event that has triggered a swing in public opinion or due to a change in the partisan composition of the government. If the coincidence of an actor's policy preference with the policy output cannot be linked to attributes of the actor, a systematic, that is, statistically significant effect of actor properties cannot be detected.

However, one needs to note that a statistically significant effect does not exclude the possibility of luck. As long as a statistical model cannot account for the entire variance in the data, there can also be luck involved in addition to the systematic pattern that links interest group properties with the policy output. If, however, at least part of the variation is explained by interest group properties, one can conclude that interest groups at least exerted

---

[5] The initial arguments put forward by Barry (1980*a,b*) have led to a vibrant debate about the nature of power and luck between Barry (1980*a,b*, 2002) on the one hand and Dowding (1991, 1996, 2003) on the other hand. However, for the purpose of this analysis, it is sufficient to make the classic distinction between influence defined as the ability of an actor to shape a decision in line with his preferences and luck understood as "getting what you want without trying" (Barry 1980*a,b*).

some influence. In addition, if no systematic pattern between observed actor properties and the policy output can be detected, it can still be the case that unobserved actor properties account for the coincidence of actor preferences with the policy output. Thus, whereas the failure to find a systematic effect that connects actor properties with the policy output does not exclude the possibility of influence since there might be unobserved actor properties at play, the detection of a systematic pattern that links actor characteristics with the policy output provides empirical evidence for the hypothesis that actors indeed exerted influence.

To sum up, influence is understood as the ability of interest groups to shape political decisions in line with their policy preferences. The necessary condition for detecting interest group influence is the convergence of policy preferences of interest groups with the policy output. Convergence is, however, not a sufficient condition for influence. It is important to causally link interest groups' policy preferences with the policy output in order to distinguish influence from pure luck. This can be done by empirically analyzing whether actor properties have a systematic, that is, statistically significant effect on convergence. If there is a statistically significant association between actor properties and the policy output that is based on convincing theoretical reasoning, one can conclude that interest groups indeed influenced the policy-making process.

1.2 THE STUDY OF INTEREST GROUPS AND ITS SHORTCOMINGS

Despite its central importance, scholarly attention to interest group influence in the European Union has been surprisingly limited. Whereas the number of interest group studies has flourished in the past years, researchers have usually avoided the question of influence. A number of textbooks and edited volumes present a general account of European Union lobbying without systematically dealing with interest group influence on European policy-making (Mazey and Richardson 1993; Schendelen 1993; Wallace and Young 1997; Aspinwall and Greenwood 1998; Balme, Chabanet, and Wright 2002; Greenwood 2002; Warntjen 2004; Eising and Kohler-Koch 2005; Greenwood 2007*a*; Coen and Richardson 2009*b*; Coen, Grant, and Wilson 2010*a*). Several other studies are concerned with measuring the interest group population at the European level (Berkhout and Lowery 2008; Messer, Berkhout, and Lowery 2010; Wonka et al. 2010) or attempt to classify the European interest group system as pluralist, corporatist, statist, or network-like (Kohler-Koch and Eising 1999; Eising 2007*a*, 2009). Other scholars focus on explaining lobbying strategies employed by interest groups in the European Union (Coen 1997, 1998; Beyers 2002, 2004;

Eising 2004; Bouwen and McCown 2007; Mahoney 2007*a*; Bernhagen and Mitchell 2009). Another prominent topic in European interest group research has been the impact of European integration on national interest groups and domestic interest intermediation patterns (Schmidt 1996; Richardson 2000; Cowles 2001; Coen and Dannreuther 2003; Saurugger 2003; Quittkat 2006; Beyers and Kerremans 2007; Klüver 2010; Beyers and Kerremans 2012).

In order to gain some leverage on the question of influence, some researchers have opted to work on interest group access to European institutions rather than focusing directly on influence (Bouwen 2004*a,b*; Eising 2007*b*, 2009). They consider access as a precondition for influence and claim that studying access is therefore likely to be a good indicator for influence (Bouwen 2002, 366). Dür and De Bièvre (2007*a*), however, demonstrated that access does not necessarily imply influence. Not all interest groups are equally able to translate their *access* into *influence*. Others have preferred to address the question of interest group influence on European policy-making in purely theoretical terms (Henning 2000; Crombez 2002).

Many hypotheses exist that stress potential determinants of interest group influence on policy-making (for reviews, see Smith 1995; Potters and Sloof 1996; Baumgartner and Leech 1998; van Winden 2003; Dür and De Bièvre 2007*b*; Dür 2008*b*). However, only very few scholars have empirically dealt with interest group influence on European policy-making and empirical tests of these hypotheses for the case of the European Union are therefore scarce (see also Dür and De Bièvre 2007*b*; Dür 2008*b*). Even in the United States, where interest group research draws on a long-standing tradition, the question of interest group influence still remains an area of confusion (Baumgartner and Leech 1998, 13). What is more, the small number of empirical studies on interest group influence in the European Union are characterized by contradictory findings due to focusing only on a specific group type or on one or just a few policy issues (see also Dür 2008*b*). Below, I summarize the hypotheses and the empirical findings for the case of the European Union and outline the shortcomings of the literature that this book aims to overcome. Following Dür and De Bièvre (2007*b*), I classify the factors that are expected to explain interest group influence into three broad categories: the institutional context, issue-specific factors, and interest group properties.

The institutional context defines the opportunities for getting in touch with decision-makers and therefore plays a crucial role in the analysis of interest group influence (Kitschelt 1986; North 1990; Marks and McAdam 1996; Mahoney 2004, 2007*a*; Naoi and Krauss 2009). It is particularly helpful to take into account the institutional context when comparing interest group influence in different political systems (Mahoney 2007*a*, 2008). However, when solely examining interest group influence in one particular political system, the institutional context alone cannot account for variation in interest group influence since it is held constant and all interest groups face the same institutions. However, thoroughly analyzing the institutional context is helpful in understanding the sources for variation in interest group influence. Accordingly, several studies conceptualize lobbying as an exchange relationship between decision-makers and interest groups (Pappi and Henning 1999; Bouwen 2002; Michalowitz 2004; Hall and Deardorff 2006). According to these works, the European institutions demand certain goods from interest groups and the ability to influence political decisions varies with the ability to provide these goods. What is more, several scholars demonstrated that the European Commission even actively supports the creation and maintenance of certain interest groups in an effort to extract goods from them such as legitimacy or information (Bauer 2002; Broscheid and Coen 2003, 2007; Sánchez-Salgado 2007; Mahoney and Beckstrand 2011). In addition, following historical institutionalist reasoning, one could argue that historically grown networks between the European institutions and interest groups could explain variation in interest group influence (e.g. Hall and Taylor 1996, 941). However, the underlying reason for privileging certain interest groups over others is their ability to provide goods that the European institutions require. The European Commission, the Council, and the European Parliament (EP) would not have engaged in long-standing networks with interest groups if these had not been able to provide incentives to the European institutions. Hence, it is crucial to identify the demands of the European institutions to comprehend which properties interest groups have to exhibit to be able to influence policy-making in the European Union. In order to understand variation in interest group influence, it is therefore necessary to identify the demands of political institutions from which explanatory factors for interest group influence can be deduced.

Scholars have furthermore pointed out the importance of issue-related factors for interest group influence (Lowi 1964; Mahoney 2007*a*, 2008; Baumgartner et al. 2009; Klüver 2011). According to the features of the policy issue in question, interest group influence has been expected to vary across issues. Mahoney (2007*a*, 2008) argued that the salience, the degree of conflict, and the scope of an issue have a negative effect on the chance of interest groups to influence policy-making. She reasoned that the more salient an issue, the more actors are active on this issue and the more attentive the general public. Thus, interest groups should find it difficult to exert influence since policy-makers cannot listen to one single advocate. The degree of conflict over an issue was expected to affect the ability to influence policy-making in a similar way: the higher the degree of conflict, the more opposing groups are trying to lobby the decision-makers and the harder it is to shift the policy output in one particular direction. Finally, she expected that the scope of an issue is also negatively associated with interest group influence since large scope issues should involve a larger number of interests and decision-makers therefore cannot follow a single special interest. Her empirical results, however, only supported the negative effect of issue scope on interest group influence on European policy-making. Some scholars have also stressed that interest groups have more influence on technical and highly complex policy issues since public decision-makers require interest group expertise (Smith 2000; Woll 2007). This hypothesis, however, still lacks empirical support. In addition, Dür and De Bièvre (2007*a*) and Dür (2008*b*) argued that interest group influence should also vary depending on whether the policy issue is distributive, redistributive, or regulatory in nature. Up until now, there is, however, also no study that systematically tests this expectation.

Drawing on earlier ideas presented by Sabatier (1988) who pointed to the importance of advocacy coalitions for policy change, recent work on lobbying in the United States has furthermore identified the size of lobbying coalitions as an important issue-related variable affecting interest group influence (Leech et al. 2007; Baumgartner et al. 2009). Lobbying coalitions are defined as sets of actors who share the same policy goal (Baumgartner et al. 2009, 6). Accordingly, several scholars have studied interest group coalitions (Salisbury et al. 1987; Hojnacki 1997, 1998; Gray and Lowery 1998; Pijnenburg 1998; Hula 1999; Mahoney 2007*b*). These works, however, focus mainly on explaining the formation of coalitions and do not analyze the effect of coalition building on interest group influence. Baumgartner et al. (2009) were the first to point out the importance of lobbying coalitions for interest group influence. They demonstrated that not only individual interest group properties, but also characteristics of lobbying coalitions have to be taken into account to understand interest group influence in the United States. Similarly, Klüver (2011) shows that lobbying coalitions play a crucial role for lobbying success in the European Union. She, however, only focuses on the mere size of lobbying coalitions without taking into account further characteristics of lobbying coalitions such as their information supply or their resources. The lack of empirical evidence on issue-related factors is a more general problem of the literature. Since most of the few studies on interest group influence in the European Union concentrate on one or just a few policy issues, the effect of issue characteristics could not be tested empirically since the issue context is held constant (for exceptions, see Mahoney 2007*a*, 2008; Klüver 2011).

The third group of factors that have been identified in the literature are interest group characteristics. Several hypotheses link the properties of individual interest groups to influence over policy outputs. These properties can be distinguished into permanent and non-permanent characteristics. Permanent characteristics refer to interest group properties which are constant across different issues whereas non-permanent features vary from issue to issue.

In terms of permanent characteristics, actor type and resources have been identified as important explanatory variables. A prominent hypothesis concerning actor type is that interest groups which defend diffuse interests are less successful in influencing policy-making than interest groups representing concentrated interests. On the one hand, diffuse interests should find it more difficult to get organized than concentrated interests (Olson 1965). On the other hand, once organized, diffuse interests should also find it more difficult to mobilize resources from their members and they are therefore disadvantaged when it comes to influencing European policy-making (Dür and De Bièvre 2007*a*). However, the empirical findings concerning this hypothesis are contradictory: Whereas Schneider and Baltz (2003) and Dür and De Bièvre (2007*a*) confirm the hypothesis that diffuse interests are less influential than concentrated interests, other authors contend that diffuse interests were in fact capable of exerting a considerable amount of influence on European policy-making (e.g. Pollack 1997*b*; Warleigh 2000).

The positive impact of resources on interest group influence is another very prominent hypothesis in interest group research that has gained a lot of attention (e.g. Gerber 1999; Hall and Deardorff 2006; Mahoney 2007*a*, 2008; Baumgartner et al. 2009; Eising 2009). Most notably, American interest group scholars have investigated the impact of resources on voting behavior in Congress by studying the effect of campaign contributions to members of Congress (for a review, see Smith 1995). Since the European Union is largely isolated from political campaigns, EU scholars have instead focused on the positive effect of resources on the ability to effectively organize and lobby the European institutions which presumably increases their chance to influence policy-making. Accordingly, Coen and Dannreuther (2003), Eising (2007*b*, 2009), and Klüver (2010) demonstrated that resource endowment has a positive effect on interest group access to the European institutions. Recent empirical evidence, however, questions the seemingly simple story. Mahoney (2007*a*, 2008) and Baumgartner et al. (2009) did not find any clear relationship between resources and lobbying success. The contradictory effect of resources can partly be due to the unclear usage of the concept "resources." Resources mentioned in the literature include money, legitimacy, political support, and knowledge and sometimes also information is subsumed under the term "resources" (Dür 2008*b*, 1213–1215). Conceptual clarifications are therefore necessary when investigating the effect of interest group resources on their ability to influence policy-making in the European Union. In addition, the contradictory effect can also be a result of measuring different concepts since "access" does not necessarily translate into "influence" and the results of access studies can therefore not be directly linked to interest group influence (Dür and De Bièvre 2007*a*).

Concerning non-permanent features of interest groups, lobbying strategies and information supply have been highlighted in the literature. When lobbying on a policy issue, interest groups can choose between inside strategies, by establishing direct contacts with decision-makers and exchanging information, and outside strategies, which refer to demonstrations or protests to pressure decision-makers by increasing the awareness of the general public (Kollman 1998; Beyers 2004). Mahoney (2007a, 2008) hypothesized that the use of outside lobbying should increase the chance of interest groups to influence policy-making. However, her empirical results showed the contrary. Making use of outside lobbying tactics has instead a negative effect on interest group influence in the European Union. By contrast, Beyers (2004) found that outside strategies are positively correlated with access to the European institutions. The empirical results concerning the impact of lobbying strategies on interest group influence are therefore inconclusive. The contradictory effects can again be a result of measuring different concepts since Beyers (2004) examined "access" and Mahoney (2007a, 2008) investigated "success."

The importance of information supply for interest group influence has been discussed extensively in the literature (e.g. Potters and van Winden 1990, 1992; Austen-Smith 1993; Lohmann 1995, 1998; Grossman and Helpman 2001; Crombez 2002; Broscheid and Coen 2003; Bernhagen and Bräuninger 2005; Bernhagen 2007). It is generally argued that decision-makers need external information and that interest group influence increases with the amount of information they can supply. Whereas the literature is characterized by a wide variety of theoretical models on how information supply affects interest group influence, empirical tests are scarce (for exceptions, see Austen-Smith and Wright 1994; Broscheid and Coen 2003; Bouwen 2004a; Bernhagen and Bräuninger 2005; Bernhagen 2007; Eising 2007b). Austen-Smith and Wright (1994) test their theoretical argument based on data provided by interest groups on their lobbying efforts in the confirmation battle over the nomination of Robert Bork to the US Supreme Court. Bouwen (2004a) tested his exchange model based on interviews with public officials in the European institutions. However, he limited his analysis to interest group access in the financial sector and he did not directly measure information supply, but a priori assumed that different types of actors (companies, national associations, and European associations) provide different types of information to a varying degree. This constitutes an oversimplifcation since differences among actor types are not taken into account. Eising (2007b) analyzed the effect of information supply on interest group access by asking interest groups about their frequency of information provision. Even though his analysis is based on a broad empirical basis, he does not account for issue-specific differences, but simply measures information supply on the aggregate level. Bernhagen and Bräuninger (2005) empirically test their signaling model based on two case studies which makes it difficult to draw general conclusions for the entire population of interest groups. Hence, whereas the empirical evidence on the effect of lobbying strategies on interest group influence is characterized by contradictory findings, empirical evidence on the hypothesized effect of information supply is still lacking.

In conclusion, whereas each of the cited studies has great merits in pointing out possible determinants of interest group influence in the European Union, a multitude of hypotheses has been suggested and empirical evidence is still scarce. For instance, even though the effect of information supply on interest group influence has been discussed extensively in the theoretical literature on lobbying, there is hardly any empirical evidence on this topic. In addition, even though the importance of the issue context for interest groups has recently been highlighted, most of the few studies on interest group influence in the European Union did not take into account the characteristics of policy issues. What is more, the few existing empirical studies are characterized by contradictory findings. For instance, whereas Dür and De Bièvre (2007*a*) and Schneider and Baltz (2003) found that diffuse interests are less influential than concentrated interests, Pollack (1997*b*) and Warleigh (2000) came to the conclusion that diffuse interests are very well able to influence European policy-making. Similarly, Eising (2007*b*) and Klüver (2010) demonstrated that resource endowment has a positive effect on interest group access to European institutions, which has often been considered to be a good proxy for influence, whereas Mahoney (2007*a*, 2008) did not find any clear relationship between resources and lobbying success in the European Union. More generally, one can assert that the findings concerning the effect of interest group characteristics are mostly contradictory, whereas empirical evidence on issue-related characteristics is largely missing. Contradictory results are mainly due to the fact that the few existing studies typically focus on one particular group type and/or one or just a few policy issues. It is therefore difficult to draw general conclusions for the entire population of interest groups and policy issues. The lack of large-N empirical studies on interest group influence across different group types and across different policy issues which allow for testing the effects of issue characteristics is largely due to methodological difficulties in operationalizing interest group influence. This book therefore provides three important contributions to the literature on lobbying and interest groups.

First, it presents a coherent theoretical model of interest group influence on policy-making in the European Union which systematically combines explanatory variables that have so far largely been treated in isolation from each other. Based on deductive reasoning, lobbying is conceptualized as an exchange relationship between interdependent actors in which the European institutions trade influence for information, citizen support, and economic power. The ability of interest groups to influence policy-making is therefore hypothesized to vary with the capacity to provide these goods to the European institutions. Taking into account the contextual nature of lobbying, I moreover argue that it is not sufficient to look at individual interest groups. By contrast, lobbying has to be conceptualized as a complex collective process in which the aggregated information supply, citizen support, and economic power of entire lobbying coalitions are decisive for explaining interest group influence.

Second, this book introduces and tests a new measurement approach of interest group influence which enables interest group scholars to study interest group influence on a large empirical scale. The scarce and contradictory empirical evidence on interest group influence in the European Union is primarily caused by methodological difficulties to operationalize influence (Dür 2008c). So far, three different approaches to the measurement of interest group influence can be identified: process-tracing, assessing attributed influence, and gauging the degree of preference attainment (Dür 2008c).[6] Process-tracing is the most frequently applied approach to the study of interest group influence (e.g. Cowles 1995; Warleigh 2000; Michalowitz 2004, 2007; Woll 2007, 2008). Although process-tracing provides high internal validity and is well-suited for checking rival theories and for generating new hypotheses, the analysis is usually limited to a specific group type and to one or just a few policy issues. It is therefore difficult to draw general conclusions for the entire population of interest groups and policy issues. The attributed influence method draws either on the self-evaluation of interest groups or on the assessment of experts and can be applied to a large number of cases (e.g. Pappi and Henning 1999; Dür and De Bièvre 2007a). However, it measures "perceived" rather than "actual" influence. The preference attainment approach compares the policy preferences of interest groups with the policy output in order to draw conclusions about the winners and losers of the decision-making process (e.g. Mahoney 2007a, 2008; Schneider and Wagemann 2007; Baumgartner et al. 2009). This approach is promising since it provides an objective measurement, covers all channels of influence and can be applied to a large number of cases. However, one of the major problems associated with the preference attainment technique is how to measure policy preferences. This book therefore proposes a new methodological approach to measure policy preferences, thus paving the way for the large-scale measurement of interest group influence.

Third, using this proposed measurement approach this book empirically tests the theoretical expectations across a wide variety of policy issues and group types. I constructed a large new dataset that combines the measurement of interest group influence with explanatory variables identified in the theoretical model. These explanatory variables were measured by coding interest group websites, by conducting a survey of interest groups, and by retrieving issue-related information from the European Union databases *PreLex* and *EurLex*. I therefore present a unique empirical analysis of interest

---

[6] For a thorough discussion of these approaches, see chapter 3.

group influence on policy-making in the European Union. Based on this large-scale analysis, general conclusions concerning the determinants of interest group influence on European policy-making can be drawn.

1.3 THE ARGUMENT: LOBBYING IN COALITIONS

To remedy the shortcomings of the literature, this book presents a coherent theoretical model that explains interest group influence on policy-making in the European Union. The development of the theoretical model proceeds in two major steps: I first elaborate an exchange model of lobbying that conceptualizes the relationship between interest groups and the European institutions as an exchange relationship between interdependent actors (Pfeffer and Salancik 1978; Pappi and Henning 1999; Bouwen 2002). I then embed this exchange model into a broader theoretical model that takes into account the contextual nature of lobbying. The theoretical model is illustrated in figure 1.2.

The starting point for the exchange model are theoretical assumptions about the logic of action and the objectives of interest groups, the European Commission, the Council, and the European Parliament. By taking the institutional context into account in which the European institutions and interest groups interact, I derive propositions about the strategies that interest groups and the European institutions employ in order to advance their objectives. I assume that interest groups and the European institutions are

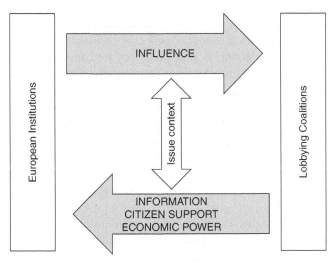

Fig. 1.2 Theoretical model

rational, goal-oriented, and purposeful actors that aim at maximizing the attainment of their preferences. I furthermore assume that interest groups are driven by the desire to exert influence on policy-making, that the Commission aims at proposing policy proposals that successfully pass the legislative process, and that national governments in the Council and Members of the European Parliament (MEPs) strive for reelection.

Based on their preferences and the institutional context in which interest groups and the European institutions are embedded, I conceptualize EU lobbying as an exchange relationship between interdependent actors. Interest groups demand influence on policy-making from the European Commission, the Council, and the European Parliament. In exchange, the European institutions demand three goods from interest groups in order to pursue their individual objectives: policy-relevant information, citizen support, and economic power. The ability of interest groups to influence policy-making is therefore hypothesized to vary with the capacity to provide these goods to the European institutions. Interest groups which can provide a lot of information, citizen support, and economic power have a very good chance to shape the outcome of a legislative debate whereas interest groups that supply little information, citizen support, and economic power have a very low chance to influence policy-making in the European Union.

Whereas the exchange model identifies the provision of information, citizen support, and economic power as crucial determinants of interest group influence, it is not sufficient to focus only on the exchange between individual interest groups and the European institutions to explain variation in interest group influence. It is misleading to simply look at the amount of goods that are provided by individual interest groups to draw conclusions about their influence on policy-making. Policy issues raise the attention of multiple interest groups at the same time. Lobbying is therefore not an individual endeavor, but a complex collective process of multiple interest groups simultaneously trying to shift the policy outcome towards their ideal point. In order to understand why some interest groups win and others lose on a policy issue, it is therefore important to examine how interest groups align in the policy space on any given policy issue. More precisely, the grouping of interest groups into lobbying coalitions is crucial in order to understand lobbying success. A lobbying coalition is defined as a group of actors who share the same policy goal (Baumgartner et al. 2009, 6). These lobbying coalitions are by definition issue-specific since the policy preferences of interest groups concerning specific policy issues determine whether they pull decision-makers in the same direction.

I therefore embed the exchange relationship into a broader theoretical model that takes the context into account in which interest groups and the European institutions interact. Rather than focusing on individual interest group properties or permanent networks, I expect that the issue-specific grouping of interest groups into lobbying coalitions is the decisive point in understanding lobbying success. Since interest groups that belong to the same lobbying coalition push the European institutions in the same direction of the policy space, the likelihood that interest groups are able to influence the policy-making process increases with the aggregated amount of information, citizen support, and economic power provided by their lobbying coalitions. I therefore argue that the aggregated information supply, citizen support, and economic power of lobbying coalitions explains the variation in interest group influence.

In addition, I expect that the issue context affects the intensity of the exchange relationship between interest groups and the European institutions with regard to information supply. Every policy issue is distinct as policy issues differ extensively in terms of complexity. Some issues are highly technical whereas the complexity of other issues is rather low. The characteristics of the policy issue at hand therefore considerably affect the ability of interest groups to succeed in their lobbying attempts. If a policy issue is highly complex, the European institutions need a high amount of information from interest groups. Hence, interest groups which can supply the information needed by the Commission, the Council, and the European Parliament should be in a good position to influence the policy-making process. However, if a policy issue is hardly complex at all, the European institutions barely need any information. Interest groups which rely mainly on providing information to European decision-makers should thus find it very difficult to have an impact on the legislative debate. I therefore expect that the positive effect of information supply on interest group influence is moderated by the complexity of the policy issue.

1.4 THE METHOD: MEASURING INTEREST GROUP INFLUENCE USING QUANTITATIVE TEXT ANALYSIS

Even though the question of influence is central to the study of interest groups and public policy, interest group scholars have largely avoided studying influence as discussed earlier in this chapter. The major problem that has prevented interest group scholars from analyzing influence is the difficulty in operationalizing influence. This book therefore introduces a new approach to the measurement of interest group influence drawing on recently developed quantitative text analysis techniques to analyze policy-related consultations conducted by the European Commission. Using this methodological innovation, the theoretical model presented in chapter 2 is tested across 56 policy issues and 2,696 interest groups.

Following the influence conceptualization discussed earlier in this chapter (see section 1.1.2), I measure interest group influence drawing on the preference attainment approach by comparing the policy preferences of interest groups with the legislative output of the policy-making process in order to draw conclusions about the winners and the losers of European policy-making. The preference attainment approach has several advantages over other approaches to influence measurement (Dür 2008c). First, comparing the policy preferences of interest groups with the policy output allows objective assessments of who was successful in lobbying political decision-makers. Second, the preference attainment approach captures interest group influence which has been exercised through various channels since influence should by definition be observed in the convergence of the policy outcome with an interest group's ideal point. Finally, the preference attainment method can be applied to a large number of cases which makes it possible to draw general conclusions about the determinants of interest group influence (for an extensive discussion, see chapter 3).

In order to provide a profound understanding of the influence process, the hypotheses derived from the theoretical model are tested separately for the policy formulation and the decision-making stage (see figure 1.3). The policy formulation stage begins with the preliminary draft proposal on which basis the European Commission launches a public consultation. This stage ends with the adoption of the official legislative proposal which at the same time marks the beginning of the decision-making stage. During this stage, the Council, the European Parliament, and the European Commission negotiate the design of the final legislative act. I therefore compare the policy preferences of interest groups with the preliminary draft proposal, the official policy proposal issued by the European Commission, as well as the final legislative act adopted by the Council and the European Parliament.

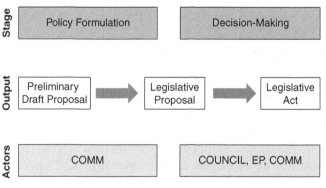

Fig. 1.3 EU policy-making process

It has been a long-standing problem of the preference attainment approach to measure policy positions of interest groups and the legislative output. In order to overcome this problem, this book introduces quantitative text analysis to the study of interest group preferences. More specifically, I draw on the recently developed quantitative text analysis technique *Wordfish* that allows estimating the policy positions of texts solely based on the relative frequencies of words they contain (Slapin and Proksch 2008). Policy preferences of interest groups were extracted from their submissions to Commission consultations. Based on a preliminary draft proposal, interest groups can submit comments before the European Commission adopts its final policy proposal. These consultations provide a rich new data source for interest group research that has so far been overlooked for the study of interest group preferences and influence. The policy positions of the European institutions are extracted from official summaries of the preliminary draft proposal, the legislative proposal, and the final legislative act.

Drawing on the proposed measurement approach to interest group influence, I constructed a large new dataset on lobbying in the European Union. I first selected 56 policy proposals and then gathered the submissions of 2,696 associations and companies which participated in the consultations preceding the adoption of these policy proposals. This dataset was enriched by information gathered by coding interest group websites, by a survey of the interest groups which participated in the consultations, as well as by information retrieved from the European Union databases *PreLex* and *EurLex*. Due to the two-stage selection process, interest groups are clustered into policy issues and I therefore use multilevel modeling to analyze the data. Testing the hypothesized effects across such a large number of policy issues and interest groups allows for drawing general conclusions about the determinants of interest group influence on policy-making in the European Union.

1.5 OVERVIEW OF THE BOOK

Chapter 2 presents the theoretical model. The chapter starts by specifying theoretical assumptions concerning the logic of action and the preferences of interest groups and the European institutions. Taking into account the institutional context, propositions about goods that are exchanged between interest groups and the European institutions are then deduced. It is reasoned that the European institutions trade influence for information supply, citizen support, and economic power that are provided by entire coalitions of interest groups pursuing the same policy objective. In addition, it is expected that the issue context affects the intensity of the exchange relationship between interest groups and the European institutions. The chapter concludes with the specification of the hypotheses derived from the theoretical model that guides the empirical analysis presented in the book.

Chapter 3 presents a case study that introduces and tests a new measurement approach to interest group influence. The chapter starts by explaining the underlying conceptual approach which draws on the comparison of interest group preferences and policy outputs. The chapter then presents a new measurement approach to policy positions of interest groups which uses quantitative text analysis to analyze consultations of the European Commission. Since this is a novel approach and text analysis has not been used in interest group research so far, the validity of this measurement approach is demonstrated by presenting a case study in which the results obtained by computerized text analysis are compared with traditional hand-coding. In the light of the findings of the case study, conclusions for the applicability of text analysis in interest group influence research in general and for measuring interest group influence in this book in particular are drawn.

Chapter 4 explains how the dataset for this book was constructed. The chapter starts by illustrating the practical implementation of the proposed influence measurement approach across a large number of interest groups and policy issues. The chapter provides a step-by-step guide of the document selection, the document preparation, and the actual text analysis. Next, the chapter discusses how the policy issues and interest groups were selected for this study. Afterwards, the operationalization of the explanatory and control variables is laid out and summary statistics of all the variables used in this book are presented. Finally, the specification of the statistical model is discussed on which basis the hypotheses are tested in chapter 6 and chapter 7.

Chapter 5 provides an overview of the policy debates studied in this book. This chapter first investigates the characteristics of the policy issues on which interest groups lobby the European institutions. The chapter sheds light on which types of issues are typically discussed, how salient and complex these issues are, and how much conflict they generate among interest groups. Afterwards the population of interest groups that mobilized in the selected policy debates is closely examined by investigating which types of interest groups mobilize, where they come from, and what resources they have at their disposal. Finally, this chapter provides a thorough analysis of the structure of conflict underlying the policy debates and the lobbying coalition patterns that have emerged on these issues. The chapter concludes with a summary of the most important features of policy debates in the European Union.

Chapter 6 tests the hypotheses derived from the theoretical model for the policy formulation stage in which the European Commission drafts the legislative proposal. This chapter first gives a short overview of the policy formulation stage in the European Union. Afterwards, the hypotheses are tested step-by-step using multilevel regression analysis. All analyses are accompanied by a thorough illustration and interpretation of the results and examples from the policy debates studied in this book are presented. Finally, the nature of the coalition effects is analyzed by investigating whether interest groups can free-ride on powerful groups that share the same policy preferences. The chapter concludes with a summary of the findings.

Chapter 7 shifts the focus from the policy formulation to the decision-making stage of the European policy-making process in which the Council, the European Parliament, and the European Commission bargain about the design of the final legislative act. The chapter first briefly summarizes the decision-making process in the European Union. Afterwards, multilevel regression analyses are presented on which basis the effects of information supply, citizen support, and economic power of lobbying coalitions are tested for the decision-making stage. All analyses are enriched by examples taken from the 56 policy debates studied in this book to illustrate the effects of information supply, citizen support, and economic power based on real-world policy debates. Finally, it is investigated whether lobbying coalitions enable free-riding before the chapter concludes with a summary of the results.

Chapter 8 summarizes the main argument and the empirical results of the study. Based on the large-scale analysis of interest group influence across a wide variety of policy issues and interest groups, general conclusions concerning the determinants of interest group influence on European policy-making are drawn. In the light of the findings of this study, the contribution of this book to the literature on European politics and interest groups is highlighted by pointing out the implications for our understanding of the EU policy-making process, the democratic legitimacy of the European Union, and the study of interest groups more generally. Finally, open questions and directions for further research are discussed.

2

Lobbying in Coalitions

In this chapter, I develop a theoretical model that explains why some interest groups are able to influence policy-making in the European Union while others are not. The development of the theoretical model proceeds in two major steps: I first elaborate an exchange model of lobbying that conceptualizes the relationship between interest groups and the European institutions as an exchange relationship between interdependent actors (Pfeffer and Salancik 1978; Pappi and Henning 1999; Bouwen 2002). I then embed this exchange model into a broader theoretical framework that takes into account the contextual nature of lobbying.

The starting point for the exchange model are theoretical assumptions about the logic of action and the objectives of interest groups and the European institutions. I develop a hierarchically ordered set of preferences that specifies the objectives of interest groups and the Commission, the Council, and the European Parliament in the context of European policy-making. These are axioms from which I then derive propositions about the goods that are exchanged between interest groups and the European institutions. I expect that interest groups demand influence from the European institutions whereas the European Commission, the Council, and the European Parliament demand policy-relevant information, citizen support, and economic power from interest groups. The ability of interest groups to influence policy-making is hypothesized to vary with the capacity to provide these goods to the European institutions.

However, since lobbying takes place in a complex environment, it is not sufficient to focus only on the exchange between individual interest groups and the European institutions to explain variation in interest group influence. I therefore embed this exchange relationship into a broader theoretical model that takes into account the context in which interest groups and the European institutions interact. To fully understand why some interest groups win while others lose, it is necessary to acknowledge that lobbying is a collective process in which decision-makers are confronted with multiple interest groups at the same time. I therefore argue that the aggregated information supply, citizen support, and economic power of entire coalitions of interest groups which fight for the same policy objective are decisive. In addition, I expect that the issue context affects the intensity of the exchange relationship between interest groups and the European institutions with regard to information supply.

The chapter proceeds as follows: I first theorize about the supply side of lobbying by illustrating the theoretical assumptions concerning the logic of action and the preferences of interest groups. I then proceed by discussing the demand side of lobbying by specifying the underlying logic of action and the preferences of the European Commission, the European Parliament, and the Council from which I deduce propositions about the goods they demand from interest groups which I will explain in detail in the next section. Afterwards, the chapter discusses the role of lobbying coalitions and brings together the propositions about the demands of interest groups and the European institutions in specifying hypotheses concerning the determinants of interest group influence on policy-making in the European Union. Finally, I highlight the importance of the issue context and derive hypotheses on how it affects the ability of interest groups to shape policy-making outcomes. The chapter concludes with a summary of the theoretical model (see also figure 1.2 for an overview).[1]

2.1 THE SUPPLY SIDE OF LOBBYING: OBJECTIVES OF INTEREST GROUPS

In order to understand the role of interest groups in European policy-making, I first conceptualize the nature and the goals of interest groups. This is important since a theoretical model of interest group influence must depart from a proper theoretical understanding of what interest groups are trying to achieve (Goldstein 1999, 128). As discussed in section 1.1.1, interest groups are actors who have a political interest, who are organized, and who do not strive for public office or are subject to the state. Drawing on rational choice theory, I assume that interest groups are rational, goal-oriented, and purposeful (collective) actors that follow a fixed set of ordered goals (Downs 1957; Coleman 1990). I distinguish four types of objectives (Woll 2008, 33–35): "basic interests," "role-specific interests," "means preferences," and "policy preferences." Basic interests are the general or universal interests of organizations. Role-specific interests apply the basic interest to the specific situation of the actor in question. Means preferences are strategies

---

[1] This chapter partly draws on ideas developed in "Lobbying as a Collective Enterprise: Winners and Losers of Policy Formulation in the European Union." *Journal of European Public Policy*, 20(1) 2013.

organizations can employ in order to achieve their role-specific and ultimately their basic interests. Policy preferences finally constitute the policy positions interest groups adopt concerning concrete policy issues that accommodate their role-specific interests.

The basic interest of interest groups is survival, the most fundamental objective of organizations (e.g. Gray and Lowery 1996; Lowery 2007). All other goals of interest groups are secondary since survival is the precondition for achieving any of the other objectives. Survival is the basic interest of both associations and companies. As specified in section 1.1.1, the key difference between associations and companies is membership. Whereas associations are membership organizations that have individuals, companies, public institutions, or other associations as members, companies are corporate actors that do not have any members. Associations and companies therefore have different internal structures and different functions so that the pathway to survival is different (see table 2.1).

Associations are membership organizations whose primary function is to represent their members before government (Berry 1997, 6–7). Since members are their main resource providers, associations are competing for members to extract adequate resources from them to ensure their survival (McCarthy and Zald 1977; Schmitter and Streeck 1999). Members can be individual citizens or other organizations such as companies, public authorities, or other associations. Members control the flow of resources to associations and are therefore essential for their survival. The type of members does not really make a difference for associations. They strive to increase the number of active members as well as "cheque-book members" (Grant 1997; Maloney 1999). Even though cheque-book members do not actively participate in associations, they provide financial resources that are important for the functioning and the survival of associations. The role-specific interest of associations is therefore the acquisition and maintenance of members.

Individuals or organizations become members of associations for two reasons: First, individual or collective members delegate the representation

Table 2.1 Objectives of interest groups

Type of objective	Associations	Companies
1. Basic interest	Survival	Survival
2. Role-specific interest	Acquisition of members	Maximizing profitability
3. Means preference	1. Maximizing political influence 2. Provision of services	1. Acquisition of customers 2. Reducing costs 3. Maximizing political influence
4. Policy preference	Policy position concerning concrete policy initiative	Policy position concerning concrete policy initiative

of their interests to associations which will lobby political institutions in order to realize their political interests (Marsh 1976; Moe 1980, 30–35). Members therefore expect that their associations will influence legislators so that the policy outcome is as close as possible to their policy preferences. For instance, individuals become members of an environmental group since the protection of the environment is important to them. They provide resources such as financial contributions or labor to the environmental group and expect in exchange that it lobbies legislators in order to improve environmental protection. Second, individual or collective actors join associations due to special services they provide to their members (Olson 1965).[2] For example, workers might enter trade unions due to the financial support they provide during strikes or due to the professional training they offer. Car drivers might join automobile associations due to the repair and pick-up service they offer in case of car breakdown. The satisfaction of these demands is important for keeping a large member basis and thereby ensuring the flow of resources and ultimately the survival of associations. Accordingly, the means preferences of associations are maximizing their influence on the political decision-making process and the provision of services to their members.

The fourth type of goals are policy preferences which constitute the ideal points of actors concerning the policy outcome. The formation of policy preferences of associations can be conceptualized as a two-stage process: At the first stage, the policy preferences of associations are internally determined by their constituencies; at this stage policy preferences develop endogenously. At the second stage, associations represent these internally determined policy preferences towards the external environment; here policy preferences are exogenously given.

Thus, to put it in a nutshell: Associations want to ensure their survival. In order to do so, they strive for members since these are the main resource providers. In order to attract and retain members, they provide special services to them and try to maximize their political influence on legislators so that the policy outcome is as close as possible to the policy preference determined by their members.

Companies are by contrast non-membership organizations whose function is the production of goods and services which they offer on the marketplace in order to make profits. The main resource providers for companies are customers who buy their goods and services. Companies therefore compete for customers and strive for high profits which ensure their survival (Knoke and

---

[2] Olson (1965) specified coercion as a third reason for joining associations. However, coercion hardly applies to any associations that are active at the European level. Obligatory membership usually only applies to chambers, such as the German chambers of skilled crafts in which all craftsmen are members by law. Chambers represent, however, only 1.7 percent of all interest groups which actively lobby the European Union and coercion can therefore be neglected (Wonka et al. 2010).

Prensky 1984, 4–6). Companies are only able to survive if the money they make is higher than the costs they are facing. Since high profits guarantee the survival of companies, the role-specific interest of companies is the maximization of their profitability.

The profitability of companies depends on three factors: the acquisition of customers, the costs of providing goods and services, and their influence on legislation. Companies can increase their profitability if they are able to increase the number of customers who are buying their products. There are various opportunities to increase sales, for instance reducing prices, introducing a new innovative product, or entering an entirely new market (e.g. Porter 1980; Grant 1991). In addition, companies can augment their profitability by reducing their costs. They can for example reduce the number of employees, outsource production to countries with lower labor costs, or form alliances with other companies in order to share costs for a common task (e.g. airline alliances) (e.g. Lewis 1990; Kraft 1991; Görg and Hanley 2004). The profitability of companies, however, not only depends on their own characteristics and strategies, it is also affected by the political environment. For instance, companies have to pay taxes and customs, their products have to comply with regulatory standards, and the expenses for staff strongly depend on the labor market and social welfare legislation. Companies can therefore attempt to maximize their profitability by influencing the political decisions to their advantage (Stigler 1971; Peltzman 1985; Coen 1997, 1998; Woll 2007, 2008). The means preferences of companies are therefore threefold: Companies can acquire new customers, reduce costs internal to their production process, or influence policy-making in order to generate a more favorable environment for their business. In order to influence political decisions, companies can draw on three different lobbying strategies: delegation, insurance, and sophistication (Coen, Grant, and Wilson 2010*b*). Companies can pursue a delegation strategy by forming an association with other companies in order to pool resources and to speak with one voice. Companies can also pursue an insurance strategy by acting individually to gain privileged access to decision-makers. Finally, companies can also choose a sophistication strategy by combining individual lobbying efforts with delegation to trade associations.

Policy preferences constitute policy positions of companies concerning a concrete legislative proposal that accommodate their role-specific and basic interest. For instance, automobile manufacturers lobbied against stricter limits of CO_2 emissions from cars since these would result in additional costs and would therefore decrease their profitability (see chapter 3).

To sum up, the basic interest of companies is survival. In order to ensure their survival, companies aim at maximizing their profitability which constitutes their role-specific interest. Companies can enhance their profitability by employing three different strategies (means preferences): acquiring new customers, reducing costs, or influencing the policy-making process in their interest. Policy preferences constitute the policy positions that companies adopt concerning a concrete policy issue.

In conclusion, associations and companies share the same basic interest: They both want to ensure their survival. In order to do so, associations have to attract members which control the flow of resources and companies have to maximize their profitability. Associations can draw on two strategies to attract and retain members: They can maximize their political influence and they can provide services to members. Companies can choose from a set of three different strategies: They can acquire new customers, they can reduce costs which are internal to their production process, or they can influence policy-making in order to bring about a more favorable regulatory environment. Hence, maximizing political influence is an important strategy for associations as well as companies. Interest groups therefore lobby the European institutions in order to influence the policy-making process. This is a common aim of both types of interest groups, associations, and companies. Accordingly, the following proposition can be derived:

Propositon 1: *Interest groups demand influence from the European institutions.*

2.2 THE DEMAND SIDE OF LOBBYING: OBJECTIVES OF THE EUROPEAN INSTITUTIONS

I conceptualize lobbying as an exchange relationship between interest groups and the European institutions in which goods are exchanged. In order to understand variation in interest group influence on policy-making in the European Union, it is necessary to understand what goods the European institutions require from interest groups. To comprehend why the European institutions engage in an exchange relationship with interest groups, it is therefore crucial to thoroughly analyze the institutional role, the objectives, and the demands of the European Commission, the European Parliament, and the Council. In the ensuing sections, I will therefore carefully analyze the role of the European Commission, the European Parliament, and the Council in the institutional setting of the European Union on which basis I then make assumptions about their preferences and their incentives to engage in an exchange relationship with interest groups.

For the sake of analytical parsimony, I treat the European Commission as a unitary actor while I theorize about the objectives of the European Parliament and the Council on the level of individual MEPs and national governments respectively. I assume that the role-specific interest of the European Commission is the presentation of policy proposals that successfully pass the legislative process while the role-specific interest of MEPs and national governments is reelection. I choose this approach in order to gain general insights into the incentives of the European institutions to engage in an exchange relationship with interest groups that allows for drawing general conclusions concerning the determinants of interest group influence on European policy-making. It is unquestionably correct that the European Commission, the Council, and the European Parliament are collective actors that are composed of a number of different bureaucratic subunits and thousands of individuals who have their own preferences. However, what matters is whether we can attribute shared organizational preferences to an institutional actor that account for a coherent and predictable behavior (March and Olsen 1984, 738–739). Thus, the question for the purpose of this book is not whether the European Commission is a genuinely unitary actor or whether MEPs and national governments have indeed uniform preferences, but rather whether these actors behave with sufficient coherence vis-à-vis interest groups and other actors so that we can, for the purpose of the analysis, make assumptions about shared preferences that guide their behavior (Pollack 2003, 36).

2.2.1 The European Commission

Drawing on rational choice theory, I assume that the European Commission is a rational, goal-oriented, and purposeful (collective) actor that follows a fixed set of ordered goals (Downs 1957; Coleman 1990). In order to comprehend the behavior and the preferences of the European Commission, it is important to understand its emergence and its role in the EU policy-making process. Moravcsik (1993, 1998) argues that member states have delegated competences to supranational institutions including the European Commission for two reasons: First, supranational institutions increase the efficiency of interstate bargaining by providing a permanent negotiation forum and by monitoring compliance of other member states. Second, supranational institutions strengthen autonomy vis-à-vis the domestic arena by augmenting the legitimacy and credibility of policies and insulating the decision-making process from domestic opponents. Pollack (1997a, 2003) similarly argues that member states delegate competences to the European Commission in order to reduce the transaction costs of EU policy-making and to credibly commit themselves to their agreements. Thus, from a functionalist perspective of institutional choice, member states granted powers to the European Commission in order to acquire policy-relevant expertise and to maintain the credibility of their own commitments since non-compliance, time inconsistency of preferences, and ill-defined property rights might endanger common agreements (see also Majone 2001).

In order to fulfill these functions, member states delegated important oversight, policy implementation, and agenda-setting competences to the European Commission. First, the European Commission was assigned important monitoring and enforcement power so that it functions as a "guardian of the treaties." In the case of non-compliance by a member state, the European Commission can warn this member state by issuing a reasoned opinion and launching an infringement proceeding before the European Court of Justice. If this member state still does not comply with Community legislation, the Commission can ultimately ask the Court to issue a fine against this member state. Second, member states delegated policy implementation competences to the European Commission. The Commission is responsible for adopting implementing regulations for secondary legislation, it is in charge of EU spending programs in certain areas and the Commission directly applies Community law in specific policy domains, e.g. competition policy. Third, and analytically most important for the goal of this study, member states delegated the sole right of legislative initiative to the European Commission so that the legislative process always starts with a policy proposal from the Commission.[3] The European Commission therefore plays a central role for policy formulation in the European Union.

Principals, however, face the problem of agency-shirking which occurs when agents behave opportunistically by pursuing their own interests (Moe 1990, 121; Kiewiet and McCubbins 1991, 5). Member states have therefore installed several oversight mechanisms to control the behavior of the European Commission, such as the appointment process of Commissioners, the comitology procedure, the possibility of judicial review by the European Court of Justice, and the requirement that the Council has to approve any proposal of the European Commission before it can enter into force (Pollack 1997a, 2003). The College of Commissioners is appointed by member states with the consent of the European Parliament. Member states can therefore appoint Commissioners with congruent preferences (Döring 2007; Wonka 2007). The Commission's implementation powers are controlled by comitology committees. These committees oversee the implementation activity of the Commission, and their power ranges from mere "assistance" to "supervision" of the Commission (for a detailed discussion of the comitology control mechanism, see Pollack 2003, 114–145). The European Court of Justice can finally control the behavior of the European Commission by annulling legislative acts which have been adopted illegally (e.g. despite a lack of EC competence) and by examining complaints concerning the failure of the European Commission to act upon a requirement set out in the treaties or in secondary legislation. The monopoly of legislative initiative of the European

[3] This applies to the first pillar of the European Union which is arguably the most important and therefore the focus of this study.

Table 2.2 Objectives of the European Commission

Type of objective	Objective of the European Commission
1. Basic interest	Survival
2. Role-specific interest	Presenting successful policy proposals
3. Means preference	1. Acquisition of policy-relevant information 2. Obtaining citizen support 3. Gaining support of actors with economic power
4. Policy preference	Policy position concerning concrete policy initiative

Commission is restricted by the requirement that the Council and under Codecision also the European Parliament have to give their consent to policy proposals of the European Commission.[4] All Commission proposals therefore need to be approved by the member states.

After having laid out the reasons for delegating powers to the European Commission, the competences of the Commission, and the control mechanisms member states have installed to oversee Commission behavior, the next question is what motives drive the European Commission. In order to understand how interest groups can influence the European Commission and thus policy formulation, it is necessary to understand its motivation. Following Woll (2008, 33–35), I distinguish again between "basic interests," "role-specific interests," "means preferences," and "policy preferences" (see table 2.2).

I assume that the basic interest of the European Commission is survival which is a common assumption in organizational theory (e.g. Buckley 1967; Hannan and Freeman 1977). Accordingly, Majone (1996*a*, 73) states that supranational institutions "have interests of their own, including survival." For the European Commission, survival means that it retains its competences that were delegated by member states. In order to avoid member states cutting its competences and therefore threatening its survival, the European Commission has to successfully carry out the functions delegated by the member states. Concerning policy-making, which is of analytical interest in this study, the role-specific interest of the European Commission is therefore to present policy proposals that successfully pass the legislative process and at best even extend its competences (Niskanen 1971; Niskanen 1975; Majone 1996*a*, 61–79; Tallberg 2002, 34). However, as outlined before, member states have established several control mechanisms to monitor the Commission and confine autonomous behavior. The ability of the European Commission

---

[4] The Treaty of Lisbon renamed the Codecision procedure the "ordinary legislative procedure." However, as the analysis is limited to proposals that have been adopted before the Treaty of Lisbon entered into force, I use the term "Codecision procedure" throughout this book.

to initiate legislation is limited by the requirement that member states in the Council (and the European Parliament under Codecision) have to give their consent to every proposal before it can enter into force. Hence, the European Commission wants to make sure that its policy proposal will gain the approval of national governments and if applicable the European Parliament. In order to secure their consent, the European Commission is in need of policy-relevant information, citizen support, and the backing of economically powerful actors. In order to introduce policy proposals that gain the consent of the Council and the EP, the European Commission needs technical expertise and information about the demands of important stakeholders. In addition, the European Commission needs to rally the support of interest groups with a large membership base and with a high degree of economic power in order to get the approval of the Council and the European Parliament for its policy initiatives. Obtaining information, citizen support, and economic power therefore constitutes the means preference of the European Commission in order to achieve its role-specific and basic interests. Whether interest groups can influence the decisions of the European Commission depends on their ability to provide these goods to the Commission. At a later stage in this chapter, I will therefore illustrate the demand for these goods in greater detail. The policy preference is the policy position that the European Commission adopts on a specific policy issue that advances its role-specific and ultimately its basic interest.

2.2.2 The European Parliament

The European Parliament is the only directly elected institution of the European Union. Whereas functionalist approaches to institutional choice provide powerful explanations for the delegation of competences to the European Commission, they are not able to account for the empowerment of the European Parliament (Rittberger 2003, 2005). From a functionalist point of view, delegation of powers to supranational institutions results from the principals' desire to enhance decision-making efficiency and to credibly commit themselves to long-term policy goals since non-compliance, time inconsistency of preferences, and ill-defined property rights might endanger common agreements (Majone 2001; Pollack 2003). The functionalist approach, however, fails to explain the decision of member states to empower the European Parliament. Whereas the European Commission is a non-majoritarian institution whose legitimacy is based on enhancing the problem-solving capacity of supranational policy-making, the European Parliament is a majoritarian institution that is directly accountable to voters (Majone 1996b). The delegation of powers to the European Parliament is therefore surprising as it displays all the problems that national governments wanted to overcome by delegating powers to non-majoritarian institutions in the first place (Rittberger 2005, 205).

Rittberger (2003, 2005) suggests an alternative approach that explains delegation of powers to the European Parliament in terms of the desire to overcome the democratic deficit of the European Union. The increasing transfer of competences to non-majoritarian institutions at the European level has resulted in an asymmetry between consequentialist and procedural legitimacy. While non-majoritarian institutions increase the problem-solving capacity of supranational policy-making, they are not directly accountable to citizens and therefore lack procedural legitimacy. In order not to be blamed for violating key principles of democratic governance, national governments have empowered the European Parliament in order to overcome the legitimacy deficit of the European Union. The function delegated to the European Parliament is therefore very different to the function of the European Commission: Whereas the European Commission is designed to increase the efficiency of supranational policy-making, the European Parliament is designed to assure the democratic accountability of the European polity. Members of the European Parliament are therefore accountable to voters and subject to electoral scrutiny.

In order to ensure the democratic accountability of supranational governance, member states delegated three major competences to the European Parliament: supervisory powers over other EU institutions, budgetary powers, and legislative powers. First, the European Parliament has the right to censure the European Commission and its consent is necessary for the appointment of the Commission president and the entire College of Commissioners. In addition, the European Parliament has a number of further instruments at its disposal to monitor and control the behavior of the other EU institutions, such as the right to table written and oral questions, the right to set up a committee of inquiry that investigates alleged cases of misconduct of other EU institutions, or the right of recourse before the European Court of Justice to ask for an annulment of a legislative act or to complain if the Commission and the Council fail to fulfill their institutional obligations. Second, the European Parliament has important budgetary powers. Together with the Council, it is responsible for the adoption of the annual budget of the European Union. The Council cannot approve the annual budget against the veto of the European Parliament. Third, and most important for the objective of this book are the legislative powers of the European Parliament. On the basis of a legislative proposal elaborated by the European Commission, the Council and the European Parliament are responsible for the adoption of Community legislation. Whereas the European Parliament has only limited powers under the Consultation and the Cooperation procedure, its consent is required for the adoption of proposals under the Codecision procedure. The Treaty of Lisbon renamed the Codecision procedure the "ordinary legislative procedure" and almost doubled its reach by extending its scope from 44 policy areas under Nice to 85 policy areas (European Parliament 2009, 5).

In terms of control mechanisms, the European Parliament also considerably differs from the European Commission. Whereas the European Commission is subject to various oversight mechanisms installed by member states, national governments retain relatively few controls over the European Parliament (see also Pollack 2003, 253–255). The Members of the European Parliament are not appointed by member state governments, but are selected by national parties and elected by national voters. Moreover, member states cannot remove Members of the European Parliament. Similarly, the European Parliament is not subject to active member state oversight as the European Commission in its executive role. However, member states retain some informal control through national parties and they formally oversee the legislative behavior of the European Parliament since their consent is required for adopting legislation. Member state governments are able to exercise some control over individual MEPs belonging to the same national parties as these are responsible for the nomination and selection of candidates (Hix 2002). In addition, even though the legislative powers of the European Parliament have increased considerably over time, it still requires the consent of the member states in the Council for the adoption of legislative acts. Under Codecision, both legislative bodies—the European Parliament and the Council—have to approve a legislative proposal before it can enter into force. What is more, under Cooperation and Consultation, it is ultimately the Council which decides about the adoption of a legislative initiative.

I have so far discussed the emergence of the European Parliament, its institutional role, and its relation with member states. In order to understand the ability of interest groups to influence the behavior of the European Parliament, it is necessary to understand its motivation. When discussing the preferences of the European Commission, it was treated as a unitary actor even though it is composed of a number of different bureaucratic subunits and thousands of individuals (Nugent 2001). Even though it is unquestionably correct that all these actors have their own preferences, we can attribute shared organizational preferences that account for a coherent and predictable behavior of the European Commission (March and Olsen 1984, 738–739). The European Commission is subject to "collective responsibility" which obliges Commissioners to follow the line of the majority in the public no matter whether they supported or rejected a proposal in the College of Commissioners (Hix and Høyland 2011, 35). Most of the time the College of Commissioners decides by consensus and if a vote is actually taken, the results are confidential and the Commissioners have to publicly follow the preference of the majority. In addition, the Commission draws upon an extensive permanent bureaucracy which ensures institutional stability. By contrast, the European Parliament is composed of individual MEPs from all 27 member countries of the European

Table 2.3 Objectives of Members of the European Parliament

Type of objective	Objective of MEPs
1. Basic interest	Survival
2. Role-specific interest	Reelection
3. Means preference	1. Obtaining citizen support
	2. Gaining support of actors with economic power
	3. Acquisition of policy-relevant information
4. Policy preference	Policy position concerning concrete policy initiative

Union. Every five years, the MEPs are elected by European citizens to whom they are accountable. In contrast to the College of Commissioners, MEPs can only draw on a small permanent bureaucracy which is mainly responsible for procedural issues and MEPs are not bound by collective responsibility. If they have a preference that differs from that of the majority, they can vote accordingly and they are not expected to publicly support the majority opinion. Due to the different make-up of the European Commission and the European Parliament, I treat the European Commission as a unitary actor whose preferences are theorized on the institutional level whereas I analyze the European Parliament on the individual MEP level.

What motivates Members of the European Parliament? Drawing on the classical rational choice literature, I assume that MEPs are rational, goal-oriented, and purposeful political actors that aim at achieving a hierarchically ordered set of objectives (Downs 1957; Coleman 1990). I assume that MEPs are office-seeking actors whose basic interest is to ensure their survival as parliamentary deputies (Downs 1957; Riker 1962) (see table 2.3). More specifically, they want to keep their seat in the European Parliament. In order to ensure their parliamentary survival, Members of the European Parliament strive first and foremost for reelection. In order to achieve this role-specific objective, MEPs have to satisfy the demands of national voters who constitute their ultimate principals that delegate the representation of their political interests on the European level to MEPs.[5] In order to satisfy the demands of voters and to thereby maintain their seat in the Parliament, MEPs are in need of citizen support, policy-relevant information, and the support of economically powerful actors. The ability of interest groups to influence the behavior of the European Parliament thus depends on their ability to supply these goods to MEPs. I will therefore explain the demand for these three goods in further detail at a later stage in this chapter. Policy preferences constitute the

[5] Hix (2002) additionally considers national parties and the party groups in the European Parliament as principals whose interests individual MEPs have to take into account. However, national parties and European party groups are also driven by the desire to maximize votes and therefore also seek to satisfy the demands of voters (Downs 1957). For the sake of analytical parsimony, I therefore only consider voters as ultimate principals of MEPs.

positions that MEPs adopt concerning specific policy initiatives. MEPs choose their policy preferences in such a way that they advance their role-specific and basic interests.

2.2.3 The Council

The member state governments have delegated important competences to supranational institutions, most notably to the European Commission and the European Parliament. The rationale for granting powers to these two institutions, however, differs as discussed in the previous sections. Whereas member states allocated powers to the European Commission in order to reduce transaction costs and to enhance the problem-solving capacity of supranational policy-making, they empowered the European Parliament in order to decrease the democratic deficit of the European Union. At the same time, member states have established several oversight mechanisms to monitor and control the behavior of the European Commission and the European Parliament. Above all, the member state governments have assigned to themselves the dominant role in the supranational polity as members of the European Council and the Council of the European Union to retain control over and to actively shape European policy-making (Pollack 2003, 3).

The European Council was established in 1974 as an informal coordination forum for the heads of state. It only obtained a formal status in the Treaty of Maastricht; the Treaty of Lisbon finally turned the European Council into one of the seven official EU institutions. The European Council provides general political guidelines and impetus for the activities of the European Union. In addition, it has an important appointment function: It proposes a candidate for the post of President of the European Commission and in accordance with the designated president, it suggests a list of candidates for the College of Commissioners including the High Representative for Foreign Affairs and Security Policy who is at the same time the Vice-President of the European Commission. As the European Council, however, does not have any legislative responsibilities that are of analytical interest in this study, I focus in the following on the Council of the European Union.

The origin of the Council of the European Union dates back to the foundation of the European Coal and Steel Community in 1951. In order to control the behavior of the High Authority which later developed into the European Commission, the member states established the (Special) Council of Ministers (Hayes-Renshaw 2006, 61). As member states have shifted ever more competences to the European level and have therefore extended the powers of the European Commission and the European Parliament, the competences of the Council have simultaneously been increased in order to effectively control supranational governance (Hayes-Renshaw 2006, 62). The Council of the European Union is composed of national ministers and comes together in ten different formations depending on the subject under discussion. For instance, the agricultural ministers come together in the Council of Agriculture and Fisheries whereas the environment ministers assemble in the Council of Environment.

The Council of the European Union exercises important executive, budgetary, and legislative functions. In executive terms, the Council is responsible for coordinating broad economic goals among member states, it concludes international agreements, it coordinates the Common Foreign and Security Policy, and it organizes police and judicial cooperation. In budgetary terms, the Council adopts the annual EU budget together with the European Parliament. Finally, in legislative terms the Council is responsible for adopting legislation. Under the Consultation procedure, the Council can decide autonomously about a legislative proposal after consulting the European Parliament whose opinion is not binding on the Council. Under the Cooperation procedure, the Council can only override an objection by the European Parliament if it decides unanimously. Finally, under Codecision the Council cannot adopt a legislative act without the consent of the European Parliament. Even though the legislative competences of the European Parliament have been considerably increased over time, no legislative act can enter into force without the approval of the Council of the European Union. This requirement is a very powerful oversight mechanism which allows member states to ultimately control the legislative activities of the European Commission and the European Parliament. Due to its extensive legislative responsibilities, the Council is a promising lobbying target for interest groups (Hayes-Renshaw 2009, 80; Saurugger 2009, 105). Particularly domestic interest groups lobby their national governments in an effort to influence European policy-making through the Council (Eising 2004; Schneider and Baltz 2004; Schneider, Finke, and Baltz 2007; Klüver 2010).

In order to explain why interest groups are able to influence policy decisions taken by the Council, it is important to understand its motivation and its preferences. In contrast to the European Commission and the European Parliament, the members of the Council of the European Union are not elected or appointed on the supranational level, but membership depends on governmental responsibility at home. Its composition is therefore not fixed by a supranational legislative term, but it is altered whenever elections in one of the 27 member states take place that lead to changes in the configuration of domestic governments. The central actors within the Council of the European Union are national governments and their ministers respectively who are bound to represent the interests of their home countries. Unlike the European Commission, I therefore do not consider the Council as a unitary actor, but I analyze the Council at the level of the national government and therefore

Table 2.4 Objectives of national governments in the Council

Type of objective	Objective of national governments in the Council
1. Basic interest	Survival
2. Role-specific interest	Reelection
3. Means preference	1. Obtaining citizen support
	2. Gaining support of actors with economic power
	3. Acquisition of policy-relevant information
4. Policy preference	Policy position concerning concrete policy initiative

follow the tradition of the Council voting behavior literature that investigates decision-making processes in the Council of the European Union (e.g. Mattila 2004; Zimmer, Schneider, and Dobbins 2005; Hagemann and Høyland 2008).

What motivates national governments in the Council of the European Union? Drawing on classical rational choice theories, I assume that national governments are rational, goal-oriented, and purposeful collective actors that aim at achieving a set of hierarchically ordered objectives (Downs 1957; Coleman 1990). The basic interest of national governments is survival (Downs 1957; Riker 1962) (see table 2.4). More specifically, I assume that they are office-seeking actors who aim at maintaining their mandate. Accordingly, Moravcsik (1993, 483) states "the primary interest of governments is to maintain themselves in office." As member state governments have to compete in regular national elections that decide about the composition of domestic governments, their role-specific interest is therefore reelection. In order to secure their reelection, national governments have to obtain three goods: policy-relevant information, citizen support, and economic power. National governments need technical expertise in order to adopt legislation that constitutes a technically appropriate solution to a given policy problem. They furthermore need citizen support as they aim at finding political solutions that are favored by a majority of their electorate. Finally, national governments also require the backing of economically powerful actors as their behavior has an important impact on the economy. Economic crisis can lead to major opposition of domestic voters and national governments therefore accommodate the demands raised by important economic players. Interest groups which are able to supply national governments with the required goods are in a good position to influence European policy-making through the Council. I will therefore explain the need for policy-relevant information, citizen support, and economic power in further detail below. Policy preferences are the policy positions that national governments adopt with regard to a concrete policy initiative that advance their role-specific and basic interests.

2.3 EXCHANGE GOODS

In the previous sections, I have thoroughly analyzed the institutional role of the European Commission, the European Parliament, and the Council. Based on assumptions about the underlying logic of action and the institutional constraints in which the European institutions are embedded, I have deduced a set of hierarchically ordered preferences that guide their behavior. I have argued that the basic interest of the European Commission, the Members of the European Parliament, and the governments in the Council is survival. This common survival objective translates into different role-specific interests depending on the institutional role of the European institutions. In order to ensure its survival, the European Commission aims at presenting policy proposals that successfully pass the legislative process by gaining the approval of the Council and the European Parliament. In order to ensure their survival as deputies in the European Parliament, Members of the European Parliament strive for reelection. Similarly, the survival interest of national governments translates in the role-specific interest to gain reelection in their home country. In order to achieve their role-specific and ultimately their basic interests, the European Commission, the MEPs, and national governments in the Council need three goods: policy-relevant information, citizen support, and economic power. The ability of interest groups to influence policy-making in the European Union depends on their capacity to provide these goods to the European institutions. In the ensuing sections, I therefore discuss the institutional demands for these goods in further detail.

2.3.1 The need for information

In order to pursue their objectives, I have argued that the European Commission, the Members of the European Parliament, and the national governments in the Council are in need of policy-relevant information. The importance of information supply for policy-making in general has been highlighted by an extensive body of formal theoretical literature (e.g. Potters and van Winden 1990, 1992; Austen-Smith 1993; Lohmann 1995, 1998; Grossman and Helpman 2001; Crombez 2002). I will explain the need for information in greater detail in this section.

The European Commission enjoys the monopoly of legislative initiative and is therefore solely responsible for drafting new proposals. Drafting legislation is a highly complex and challenging process. The European Commission therefore needs to gather expertise in order to elaborate a policy proposal that provides a technically appropriate solution to the policy problem at hand. In addition, the Commission has to acquire information about the policy positions of the member state governments and in case of Codecision also of the European Parliament since the success of its legislative proposals depends on their consent. However, despite the increasing competences of the European Union and the high complexity of European policy-making, the European Commission is notoriously understaffed (McLaughlin, Jordan, and Maloney 1993, 201; Marks and McAdam 1999, 105; Bouwen 2009, 20). In 2000, the European Commission employed only 16,409 people which merely corresponds to the size of a larger city administration (Nugent 2001, 163). The administrative staff of the European Commission is for instance much smaller than the administrative staff of the local government of the city of Rotterdam (Bouwen 2009, 20). In order to gather policy-relevant information, the European Commission therefore widely consults among interest groups (Majone 1996a, 72–74). The Commission is eager to interact with interest groups since it needs their information in order to fulfill its institutional role (Bouwen 2009, 22). Hence, the European Commission demands information from private actors and by supplying this information, interest groups are able to influence the content of the policy proposal (Aspinwall and Greenwood 1998, 7).

Once the European Commission adopts its legislative proposal, it is forwarded to the Council and the European Parliament. In order to assess the often very detailed and highly technical proposal, MEPs need information that allows them to asses the legislative initiative (Kohler-Koch 1997; Bouwen 2002; Kluger Rasmussen 2011). To understand the consequences that a proposal has for their constituents, MEPs need information in order to evaluate the impact of the proposed legislative framework. The parliamentarians are, however, not well-staffed and they have an extremely busy agenda. They travel between Brussels, Strasbourg, and their electoral district at home and usually rely on one or two policy advisers, a secretary, and an intern to deal with the flood of legislative proposals. Interest groups are therefore a welcome source of information for MEPs (Kohler-Koch 1997, 6). Accordingly, a policy adviser stated:

> We cannot do our work without the information from interest groups. They send us amendments and voting lists prior to the committee and plenary vote. Sometimes it is very tempting to copy and paste their amendments and voting lists. I mean we are all so busy in Parliament. (Kluger Rasmussen 2011, 8)

Whereas the European Commission takes a couple of years to prepare a legislative initiative, the rapporteur who issues a report on the Commission proposal on which basis the EP takes its decision only has a few months to draft his report (Kluger Rasmussen 2011, 8). In order to fulfill their institutional role and present a thorough and well-prepared report, particularly rapporteurs rely on information provided by interest groups. Accordingly, a representative from BUSINESSEUROPE, which is the general European umbrella association of business interests, explained "the Parliament's lack of in-house expertise leaves a huge space for interest group influence. Especially the rapporteurs are starving for our advice" (Kluger Rasmussen 2011, 8). In conclusion, MEPs and particularly rapporteurs require external information in order to assess the impact of legislative proposals tabled by the European Commission. Interest groups are therefore welcome guests who facilitate their parliamentary work in providing the desperately required information.

National governments in the Council also need policy-relevant information in order to decide about policy proposals presented by the European Commission. Accordingly, Saurugger (2009, 122) notes "member state governments call upon national interest groups for information and expertise." They require information in order to evaluate the technical quality and to foresee the impact of a legislative initiative on their constituents. In contrast to the European Commission and MEPs, national governments can draw on national ministries as an important source of technical expertise (Franchino 2007, 21). However, national ministries also rely to a large extent on information provided by external actors in particular when it comes to the position of major stakeholders who are affected by legislative proposals (Pappi and Henning 1999, 279). An important channel through which interest groups can influence the policy positions of their national governments in the Council are therefore national ministries which regularly consult domestic interest groups (Saurugger 2009, 106–112). The most important access points for lobbying the Council on the European level are the permanent representations and the sophisticated system of preparatory bodies (Coen and Richardson 2009a, 10; Saurugger 2009, 112–118). Permanent representations coordinate and organize the activities of their member states on the European level. Council meetings are furthermore prepared by working groups and committees to facilitate the work of the national ministers. These bodies are composed of national officials from each member state and representatives from the European Commission. Coreper, the most senior preparatory body that is composed of the heads or deputy heads of the permanent representations, filters the Council agenda in A and B points of which the former have already been settled by the preparatory bodies while the latter could not be resolved and therefore need to be discussed and negotiated by national ministers. Hayes-Renshaw (2006, 50) reports that insiders estimate that the preparatory bodies have already reached an agreement for about 85 percent of all the Council decisions so that the national ministers are largely only approving decisions that already have been taken by working groups or Coreper. Even though members of the preparatory bodies are generally well-informed, they also rely on the expertise provided by interest groups (Saurugger 2009, 120). Interest groups can therefore transmit information to the Council at the domestic level through national ministries or at the European level by lobbying permanent representations or members of the preparatory bodies.

I expect that the European institutions demand two different types of information (see also Broscheid and Coen 2003, 170): First, the European institutions require policy expertise and second, they are in need of information on the preferences of major stakeholders.[6] First, every policy initiative starts with a policy problem defined as a need for legislation. In order to be able to develop a policy proposal that addresses the problem, the Commission requires expertise to provide an appropriate solution to the policy problem at hand (Buholzer 1998; Pappi and Henning 1999; Radaelli 1999; Bouwen 2002). Similarly, in order to be able to assess a legislative proposal tabled by the Commission, MEPs and national governments require information about the technical details of the legislative initiative. When the European institutions for instance deal with a legislative initiative on financial services, they need information on how the market is functioning, who are the players, what is the latest technological development, and so forth. Hence, in order to produce legislation, the European institutions require expertise provided by external actors (Mazey and Richardson 1992; Balme and Chabanet 2002; Saurugger 2002, 2003).

Interest groups by contrast are specialists that are only concerned with very specific issues and are in close contact with the market or their members who are directly affected by policies. They therefore dispose of specialized issue-relevant expertise and enjoy informational advantages vis-à-vis policy-makers (Hall and Deardorff 2006, 73). For instance, the European Lamp Companies Federation is only concerned with policy issues affecting lamp manufacturers and is very well informed about the functioning and the developments of the lamp market. The Coalition Clean Baltic by contrast only works on policies which affect the Baltic Sea and is therefore a specialist on its environmental conditions and natural resources. The European institutions are, however, dealing with multiple issues at the same time and lack resources to gather sufficient expert knowledge. Accordingly, the European Commission declared in a discussion paper on the partnership with civil society organizations that interest groups can provide important expertise for EU policy-making

> through their links at local, regional, national and European level. ... In particular, they can provide feedback on the success or otherwise of specific policies thereby contributing to the Commission's task of defining and implementing policies by fully taking into account its overall public policy responsibility. (European Commission 2000, 5)

In this vein, Sandholtz (1992, 16) demonstrated in an analysis of the emergence of the ESPRIT program that member states settled on the Commission

---

[6] Similarly, Hall and Deardorff (2006, 74) distinguish between policy expertise and legislative intelligence.

proposal since they lacked information about policy alternatives.[7] He argues that the European Commission was successful in gaining member states' approval because by widely consulting among industry groups "it had 'done its homework' and understood in detail the condition of the IT industries and their future prospects" (Sandholtz 1992, 5). Thus, when preparing a policy proposal the European institutions consult interest groups to benefit from their highly specialized policy expertise in order to develop policy proposals of high technical quality.

The European institutions, however, not only require policy expertise, but also need information about the preferences of major stakeholders and constituents. Even though the European Commission has the sole right of initiative, all proposals require the consent of the Council and for proposals subject to Codecision also the approval of the European Parliament. Hence, the European Commission needs to take into account their policy positions when preparing a legislative initiative. Policy-making is, however, a lengthy process and the Council and the European Parliament have often not arrived on a clear policy position concerning a Commission initiative during the policy formulation stage. National governments and Members of the European Parliament in turn aim at adopting policy proposals which are preferred by a majority of their voters (Lohmann 1993, 320). Hence, they try to find policy solutions that have a low negative impact on their electorate. However, decision-makers operate in highly uncertain environments (Hansen 1991, 5): They have a broad idea about the policy preferences of their electorates, but they are not entirely sure. Opinion polls are only of minor use since they only cover very general trends and do not supply information about preferences of voters on specific policy issues. Interest groups, however, offer help by providing information about their constituents' preferences on specific policy decisions. Correspondingly, Bouwen (2002, 381) argues that

> MEPs need information about their national electorate. This access good
> provides them with information about the needs and preferences of their voters.
> Furthermore, the MEPs are eager to deal with interest groups that provide this
> good because they might also be able to mobilize their constituents.

The European Commission can therefore use interest groups as an indicator for the policy positions of the European Parliament and the Council. Accordingly, Butt Philip (1985, 42) already noted in 1985 that the European Commission "both wants and needs contact with the many interest groups in Europe. It too needs information about the variety of positions and aspirations of Euro-groups and national pressure groups." Similarly, Richardson and Coen (2009, 339) point out, "it would be very odd indeed (and certainly foolish) for any policy-maker to plough ahead with a proposal in total ignorance

---

[7] ESPRIT stands for European Strategic Programme for Research and Development in Information Technologies.

of how the affected interests might react or of whether there might be some practical/technical difficulties which could make the desired policy unworkable." Hence, since the support of interest groups is important for their reelection, national governments and Members of the European Parliament have to take their demands into account when making policy decisions. Since the European Commission requires the consent of the Council and the European Parliament, it therefore anticipates their policy positions by relying on interest group information. In this vein, McCubbins, Noll, and Weingast (1987, 173–175) argue that the consultation of interest groups which are politically relevant to the principals enables agents to define politically safe ground and to thereby avoid costly sanctions from the principals.

In conclusion, the European institutions aim at presenting a technically appropriate solution to a given policy problem, but also want to make sure that they avoid the opposition of major societal interests. Hence, the European institutions require technical expertise as well as information about the policy positions of major stakeholders. The following proposition can be derived:

Propositon 2: *The European institutions demand information from interest groups.*

2.3.2 The need for citizen support

In order to advance their individual objectives, the European Commission, the Council, and the European Parliament not only need information, but they also require citizen support. Citizen support is needed for two reasons: First, the European institutions require electoral support and second, citizen support enhances the legitimacy of European policy initiatives.

The importance of electoral support for influencing public policy has been discussed extensively in the public choice literature (e.g. Stigler 1971; Kau and Rubin 1979; Plotnick 1986; Grossman and Helpman 2001). National governments as well as Members of the European Parliament are subject to electoral scrutiny. As discussed previously, I assume that they are office-seeking actors who strive for reelection and therefore aim at maximizing votes (Downs 1957; Riker 1962; Mayhew 1974). If a large majority of citizens supports a policy proposal which decision-makers do not approve, they could pay for it in the next election (Mayhew 1974). Decision-makers therefore attempt to adopt policy proposals which are supported by a majority of their electorate to avoid electoral punishment (Lohmann 1993, 320). As Peltzman, Levine, and Noll (1989, 6–7) put it, citizens that are affected by a political decision "will be moved to vote for or against the representative politician. Because his ultimate goal is securing and enhancing his power, the politician prefers decisions that directly elicit favorable votes."

In order to gain reelection, national governments in the Council as well as Members of the European Parliament therefore seek to adopt policy proposals that are favored by their electorate. Accordingly, Moravcsik (1993, 483, 1997, 531) argued that national governments are responsive to the demands of voters and interest groups which represent their voters in order to gain their support for staying in office. National governments carefully examine the consequences of legislative initiatives for their constituencies and aim to adopt proposals that have a low negative impact on their domestic voters (Hix and Høyland 2011, 61–62). Similarly, Members of the European Parliament have to compete in elections every five years to secure their seat in the Parliament. In order to gain enough electoral support from citizens, MEPs are responsive to the concerns of national voters when evaluating legislative proposals. MEPs and national governments therefore particularly take into account demands raised by interest groups with a large membership base since they represent a large number of voters (Kohler-Koch 1997, 11). For instance, the likelihood that national governments and MEPs take into account the preferences of a trade union rises with the number of its members. The higher the number of members of an interest group, the more relevant is this group to elected officials since it can mobilize a large number of voters. Thus, national governments and Members of the European Parliament are therefore particularly attentive to requests voiced by large associations which is reflected in their voting behavior on policy proposals tabled by the European Commission.

The European Commission can exploit the electoral dependence of MEPs and national governments. In order to make sure that the Council and the European Parliament approve a new legislative initiative, it can strategically rally the support of interest groups with a broad membership base. If interest groups represent a big share of their electorate, national governments and MEPs are eager to accommodate their interests as these groups are able to mobilize a large number of voters. In order to avoid electoral punishment induced by interest groups whose demands were ignored, the Council and the European Parliament therefore approve Commission proposals that enjoy the support of interest groups that speak for a large number of citizens.

Citizen support is also important to add legitimacy to European policy initiatives. Following Schimmelfennig (2001, 2003), I expect that the European institutions engage in "rhetorical action" by strategically using citizen support as a source of legitimacy and by employing legitimacy-based arguments instrumentally to promote favored proposals. I assume that the European Commission, Members of the European Parliament, and member state governments are rational actors who pursue their own personal interests, but who belong to a political community whose constitutive values and norms they share (Schimmelfennig 2001, 62). They have institutionalized a standard of political legitimacy which is based on the norms and values of the community (Schimmelfennig 2001, 62). This standard of legitimacy defines which political actions are desirable and permissible. These community norms, however, do not determine the preferences of the European institutions, but they constitute an institutional constraint which the institutions have to take into account when pursuing their own interests (Schimmelfennig 2001, 63). They have to justify their actions on the ground of common norms and values.

I argue that the most fundamental value of the political community that structures political action is democratic governance. Since all EU member states are liberal democracies, the European institutions are committed to democratically organized political institutions that are accountable to citizens (Rittberger 2005, 62–63). The delegation of competences to the European institutions has, however, resulted in an asymmetry between "consequentialist" and "procedural" legitimacy which represents the legitimacy deficit (Rittberger 2003, 2005).[8] Whereas consequentialist legitimacy is based on the efficiency of institutions in producing policy outputs, procedural legitimacy is based on the acceptance of rules and procedures whereby political decisions are taken. The European institutions are well aware of this legitimacy deficit: Ever since the Maastricht treaty was signed, the media and academics have devoted considerable attention to the lack of legitimacy of the European polity (Rittberger 2005, 28–34). The democratic deficit of the European Union is therefore a particularly salient problem that attracts wide attention and so facilitates the use of rhetorical action (Rittberger and Schimmelfennig 2006; Schimmelfennig et al. 2006). Since the vibrant debate on the democratic deficit of the European Union threatens the stance of the European institutions, they strategically use interest group inclusion as a means to increase their procedural legitimacy, thereby strengthening their position in the light of the perceived democratic deficit. Bouwen (2009, 22–23) reasons accordingly that "through wide consultation of private interests with a particular emphasis on consulting representative interests with broad constituencies, the Commission aims at enhancing its legitimacy and securing support for its proposals during the later stages of the legislative process."

Why should the consultation and inclusion of interest groups have an effect on the behavior of the European institutions? Following Schimmelfennig (2001, 2003), I argue that shaming plays a fundamental role in binding political actors to the norms and values of the political community. Member state governments, MEPs, and the European Commission have committed themselves to the principles of democratic governance according to which political institutions represent the interests of citizens to which they are accountable. If they choose to deviate from these values, other actors of the community can publicly blame them for not adhering to their commitments. Thus, if MEPs and national governments resist giving their consent to a

---

[8] Similarly, Scharpf (1970, 1999) distinguishes between "input legitimacy" and "output legitimacy."

policy proposal that is supported by a large number of citizens, the European Commission can publicly blame them for not conforming with the principle of democratic governance.

As deliberations in the European Parliament are open to the public and as more and more voting records of MEPs and national ministers in the Council are publicly available, the publicity of the EU legislative process facilitates the use of rhetorical action (Rittberger and Schimmelfennig 2006; Schimmelfennig et al. 2006). For instance, a public website called "Votewatch.eu" monitors MEPs and national ministers and makes information about their legislative behavior easily accessible to citizens.[9] Hence, by not behaving in accordance with the common norms and values, political actors risk their standing, their reputation, and their credibility in the political community. As Schimmelfennig (2001, 65) points out, the community values even constrain members that have only used the standard of legitimacy strategically to pursue their self-interest since "they can become entrapped by their arguments and obliged to behave as if they had taken them seriously." In order to avoid being publicly blamed for not representing citizen demands and not being reelected due to deviation from the standard of legitimacy, national governments and Members of the European Parliament therefore give their consent to policy initiatives that are supported by a large number of citizens.

However, despite the increasing transparency of EU decision-making, shaming only works for policy issues that are highly salient such as the Services Directive which has raised considerable public attention. While citizen attention to policy issues dealt with at the European level is usually fairly low, other political actors such as interest groups or the European Commission can strategically increase the salience of an issue to mobilize public opinion for their cause. An interest group which is supported by a large number of citizens can therefore strategically mobilize its constituents to pressure the European institutions.

Since the European Commission strives to present policy proposals that successfully pass the legislative process and since the Council and the European Parliament have committed themselves to represent the interests of their citizens, the European Commission attempts to introduce policy proposals that enjoy wide support among the public. The European Commission is therefore more responsive to demands raised by interest groups which represent a large number of citizens (see also Bouwen 2002). With the backing of these groups, the European Commission can signal broad citizen support for its policy initiative and thereby appeal to the principle of democracy and accountability which constrains the behavior of the Council and the European Parliament.

---

[9] This website can be accessed on http://www.votewatch.eu.

In conclusion, the European Commission, the Council, and the European Parliament need citizen support to pursue their individual objectives. In order to guarantee the success of its policy proposals, the European Commission strategically uses citizen support in order to signal electoral support to the Members of the European Parliament and national governments. They in turn aim at adopting policy proposals that are supported by a majority of their voters to secure their reelection. Citizen support is also a means for the European institutions to add legitimacy to policy initiatives as they are constrained by the principles of democratic governance and want to avoid being publicly blamed for adopting policies without the support of European citizens. In conclusion, the following proposition can be derived:

Propositon 3: *The European institutions demand citizen support from interest groups.*

2.3.3 The need for economic power

I have theorized that the primary goal of national governments and Members of the European Parliament is reelection. In order to attain this goal, they need policy-relevant information and citizen support to adopt legislation that is technically appropriate and that is supported by a majority of their electorate. To obtain the support of voters, national governments and MEPs have to accommodate their interests. Drawing on models of economic voting, I furthermore assume that vote choices of citizens are primarily driven by economic motives. As a consequence, national governments and MEPs have to secure the support of economically powerful actors as their behavior crucially affects economic performance. It is therefore argued in this section that the European institutions demand economic power from interest groups in the sense that they are more responsive to concerns raised by interest groups that control an important economic sector than to interest groups that do not have an impact on business investment or employment.[10]

Economic power is defined as the ability of an actor to control business investment and job creation. It describes the economic weight of an actor in terms of generating growth and controlling jobs. Following the structural power argument put forward by Lindblom (1977) and Przeworski and Wallerstein (1988), it is argued that economic actors enjoy a structurally powerful position that enables them to achieve favored policy outcomes without even having to lobby for their cause. The structural power of business

---

[10] It is not the case that interest groups directly provide economic resources such as assets in European companies to the European institutions. What is decisive is that the European institutions can draw on the political support of economic actors that control business investments and job creation in the European Union when drafting and implementing legislation.

is based on its central role for the functioning of the economy. The behavior and performance of firms has a major impact on politics and society. It affects economic growth, the number of jobs, and the economic security of employees. Policies that have a negative effect on the profits of companies may therefore result in disincentives for investment, a slowdown of economic growth, increasing unemployment, and decreasing tax revenues (Przeworski and Wallerstein 1988, 12).

A loss of jobs, inflation, or other economic distress can lead to major opposition from citizens who might punish decision-makers at the next election. Accordingly, Przeworski and Wallerstein (1988, 12) state that reelection-seeking politicians must anticipate the impact of their policies on business decisions as these affect inflation, employment, and the personal income of voters. One can accordingly observe that fighting unemployment and avoiding inflation are major issues in electoral campaigns. The importance of economic performance for the popularity and electoral success of politicians has been famously acknowledged by Bill Clinton's strategic adviser, James Carville, who placed a sign in the Little Rock headquarters of the 1992 presidential campaign displaying the famous phrase (Safire 1993, 376): "It's the economy, Stupid!" In a similar vein, Duch and Stevenson (2005b, 1) describe the importance of the economy for the outcome of elections as follows:

> It is virtually a universal belief among politicians, political commentators, and even voters that elections are referenda on the economy. Politicians fill their speeches with economic rhetoric; political commentators generate endless streams of economic analysis, and high-paid consultants base their statistical predictions on little else.

Accordingly, an entire strand of the voting behavior literature explains the vote choice of citizens with "economic voting" (e.g. Lewis-Beck and Stegmaier 2000; Duch and Stevenson 2005a,b). Models of economic voting consider voters as primarily driven by economic motives. Voters are conceptualized as principals who delegate competences to policy-makers (agents) to provide future economic benefits. In order to prevent politicians from shirking, they provide disincentives via electoral punishments (Duch and Stevenson 2005a, 389). As voters cannot directly observe the behavior of their agents, they condition their vote choice on the overall macroeconomic performance (Duch and Stevenson 2005a, 389). Empirical research across a wide variety of established democracies has confirmed the expectations of the economic voting model: Economic indicators such as unemployment, income, inflation, and gross national product can account for much of the variation in government support (Lewis-Beck and Stegmaier 2000). The importance of the economy for the reelection of politicians is summarized by Lewis-Beck and Stegmaier (2000, 211) as follows:

The powerful relationship between the economy and the electorate in democracies the world over comes from the economic responsiveness of the electors, the individual voters. Among the issues on the typical voter's agenda, none is more consistently present, nor generally has a stronger impact, than the economy. Citizen dissatisfaction with economic performance substantially increases the probability of a vote against the incumbent.

Similarly, Bernhagen (2007, 44) reasons that "economic voting is the mechanism through which the structural power of business unfolds." Thus, national governments and MEPs accommodate the interests of important economic actors as they have a major impact on the economy and can therefore ultimately affect the vote choice of citizens. Interest groups representing important economic actors can therefore yield influence on decision-makers simply because of the impact that business decisions can have on whether or not to invest in a specific area (Bernhagen and Bräuninger 2005; Bernhagen 2007). For instance, the likelihood that national governments and MEPs give their consent to a policy proposal which is supported by the European Automobile Manufacturer's Association is extremely high since it represents one of the most important industries if not *the* most important industry in Europe. A prominent example of the effect of economic power on governmental decision-making is the recent crisis of General Motors in which the affected national governments were trying to accommodate the demands of General Motors to keep as many jobs as possible in their country. Hence, when policy issues are much contested and many interest groups try to influence the decision-making process, it is likely that those interest groups that dispose of the highest economic power will prevail. Moravcsik (1998, 18) similarly states that "European integration can best be explained as a series of rational choices made by national leaders. These choices responded to constraints and opportunities stemming from the economic interests of powerful domestic constituents."

The European Commission is well aware of the dependence of national governments and MEPs on economically powerful actors. If a Commission proposal has the backing of major companies and entire industries as in the case of the Single Market Program, national governments and Members of the European Parliament will most likely approve the Commission's initiative. In order to promote its policy proposals and to ensure the consent of the Council and the European Parliament, the European Commission therefore strategically forms alliances with private business actors who lobby member state governments and MEPs to accept its initiatives (Coen 1997, 96, 1998, 79).

Several studies have documented the impact of industry groups on European policy: Sandholtz (1992, 16) has demonstrated in an analysis of the emergence of the ESPRIT program that the key to winning the approval of the national governments was the alliance that the European Commission formed with industry. Similarly, Peterson (1991) analyzed the emergence of technology policy at the European level and came to the conclusion that the support of important industry groups was essential for the success of the Commission initiatives in this field. Finally, Sandholtz and Zysman (1989) and Cowles (1995) investigated the creation of the 1992 Single Market Program and argued that the European Commission formed an alliance with powerful industry groups in order to promote its initiative. Shortly after the newly installed Commission president, Jacques Delors, announced the new Commission's intention to create a fully unified single market by 1992 in January 1985, leading CEOs (chief executive officers) of multinational firms declared on the front page of the *Financial Times* that they would take their companies overseas if member state governments did not follow the Commission's proposal for a united Europe (Cowles 1995, 515–516). The CEO of Philips furthermore threatened the national governments in a public speech by saying "if Europe is neither able nor willing to develop its economic structure, then the consequences of that must be drawn" (Cowles 1995, 516). In order to pressure national governments to quickly realize the common market, the European Round Table of Industrialists furthermore published the following press release in January 1986:

> If progress towards the implementation of the European market is as slow as at present, it is unavoidable that European industries might have to reconsider their long-term strategies in order to stay competitive, with the possibility of redirecting investments to other parts of the world outside Europe. This could lead to a serious setback in Europe's industrial development with grave consequences for economic activity, employment and general welfare in Europe. (European Round Table of Industrialists 1987, cited in Cowles 1995, 519)

To sum up, the primary concern of national governments in the Council and Members of the European Parliament is reelection. In order to win their voters' approval, national governments and MEPs need to take into account their preferences. Drawing on models of economic voting, I have argued that voters are primarily driven by economic considerations when making their vote choice. In order to guarantee a smooth functioning of the economy, national governments and MEPs therefore have to accommodate the interests of economically powerful actors as their behavior crucially determines economic performance. National governments and MEPs therefore listen to the demands raised by interest groups with a high degree of economic power to avoid opposition from major economic players. The European Commission strategically exploits this dependence: In order to acquire the consent of the Council and the European Parliament for its policy proposals, the European Commission attempts to build alliances with economically powerful actors. Hence, the following proposition can be derived:

Propositon 4: *The European institutions demand economic power from interest groups.*

2.4 LOBBYING COALITIONS

In the preceding sections, I have developed an exchange model that conceptualizes lobbying as an exchange relationship between interest groups and the European Commission, the Council, and the European Parliament. Drawing on theoretical assumptions about the logic of action and the preferences of interest groups and the European institutions, I have derived propositions about goods that are exchanged. I theorized that interest groups demand influence from the European institutions and that these in turn demand three goods from interest groups to pursue their individual objectives: policy-relevant information, citizen support, and economic power. The ability of interest groups to influence policy-making in the European Union thus depends on their capacity to supply these goods to the European institutions.

However, it is misleading to simply look at the amount of goods that are provided by *individual* interest groups to draw conclusions about their influence on European policy-making. Policy issues raise the attention of multiple interest groups at the same time. Lobbying is therefore not an individual endeavor, but a complex collective process of multiple interest groups simultaneously trying to shift the policy outcome towards their ideal point. Hence, interest groups are not lobbying individually, they are lobbying together (Hula 1999). Correspondingly, Baumgartner et al. (2009, 22) assert

> in spite of journalistic accounts suggesting that much lobbying involves a single corporation attempting to get a single favor or contract with no broader implications for others, such "lone ranger" lobbying is far from the norm.

It is therefore necessary to take into account how interest groups come together in lobbying coalitions on any given policy issue in order to understand what makes an interest group a winner or a loser (Sabatier 1988).

Accordingly, several scholars have studied interest group coalitions (Salisbury et al. 1987; Hojnacki 1997, 1998; Gray and Lowery 1998; Pijnenburg 1998; Hula 1999; Mahoney 2007*b*). These studies, however, focused mainly on explaining the establishment of formal, long-term coalitions and did not analyze the effect of issue-specific lobbying coalitions on interest group influence. I argue instead that issue-specific lobbying coalitions play a major role in understanding interest group influence and policy change (see also Sabatier 1988; Leech et al. 2007; Baumgartner et al. 2009). Moreover, I go beyond earlier studies on lobbying coalitions by not focusing solely on formal

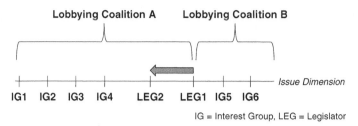

Fig. 2.1 Lobbying coalitions

coalitions which interest groups officially join. By contrast, I expect that the alignment of interest groups in the policy space is the decisive point in understanding the importance of lobbying coalitions for policy-making. Following Baumgartner et al. (2009, 6), I therefore define a lobbying coalition as a "set of actors who share the same policy goal." Thus, interest groups which are located on the same side of the policy space on a given issue form one lobbying coalition.[11]

It has to be noted that the term lobbying coalition employed in this book differs from the use of the term "coalition" in the literature on coalition governments (e.g. Müller and Strøm 2000; Martin and Vanberg 2011). Coalition government scholars use the coalition term to denote alliances that political parties deliberately form for the purpose of governing together. In order to effectively pursue a common government agenda, coalition parties coordinate their activities and exchange information. By contrast, lobbying coalitions as defined in this book are solely based on the idea that interest groups pursue the same policy objective. There is no need for officially joining an alliance or coordinating lobbying strategies. As long as interest groups fight for the same policy goal, they pull decision-makers in the same direction and therefore form a common lobbying team. From a policy-maker's perspective it is not important whether interest groups formally cooperate or not. As long as they share the same policy objective and lobby for their cause, they are part of the same camp.

The role of lobbying coalitions is demonstrated in figure 2.1. A legislator at two different time points and six interest groups are indicated in a unidimensional policy space. In order to determine issue-specific lobbying coalitions, the decisive reference is the location of the legislator in the policy space (LEG1). Interest groups which are positioned on the same side of the

---

[11] A lobbying coalition shares some similarities with an issue network defined as "a shared-knowledge group having to do with some aspect... of public policy" (Heclo 1978, 103). Lobbying coalitions revolve around specific policy issues just like issue networks. However, issue networks are not based on agreement, they only define a group of actors that are knowledgeable and concerned about a certain policy issue. Issue networks may therefore be divided into several lobbying coalitions of interest groups sharing knowledge and interest in a particular issue, but pursing different policy objectives.

initial legislator ideal point form a joint lobbying coalition as they share the same policy preference. For instance, IG1, IG2, IG3, and IG4 all share a common policy objective in the sense that they collectively pull the legislator towards the left side of the policy space. They therefore constitute lobbying coalition A. Similarly, IG5 and IG6 also pursue the same policy goal as they simultaneously pull the decision-maker towards the right side of the policy space and as a result form lobbying coalition B.

These lobbying coalitions are by definition issue-specific since the policy preferences of interest groups on specific policy issues determine whether they pull decision-makers in the same direction. I therefore do not focus on permanent, formal coalitions which interest groups deliberately decide to join. Instead, I argue that the location of interest groups in the issue-specific policy space determines the grouping of interest groups into lobbying coalitions. It is not necessary that interest groups formally cooperate or exchange information. As long as they share the same policy objective, they push the European institutions in the same direction and therefore form a lobbying coalition.

The composition of lobbying coalitions varies extensively across policy issues as different actors are involved and interest groups that work together on one issue can be opposed on another issue. Many lobbying coalitions extend beyond a small circle of friends since policy issues can cut across a wide variety of groups and policy domains. Consequently, Baumgartner et al. (2009) found that lobbying coalitions (or "lobbying sides" as they call them) are rarely homogeneous since policy issues are highly complex and raise the attention of a wide variety of actors. Even interest groups that might otherwise oppose each other can work together on a specific policy issue (see also Beyers 2008, 1206–1207). For instance, Aguilar Fernández (1997, 105) pointed out that German car manufacturers strongly rejected the introduction of speed limits and thus opposed environmental groups on this issue whereas German manufacturers supported environmental NGOs in demanding the mandatory imposition of catalytic converters throughout Europe in which they had invested in order to export to the US.

Baumgartner et al. (2009) have made an important contribution by pointing out the role of issue-specific lobbying coalitions. However, they have limited their focus to examining the composition of lobbying coalitions and to analyzing the effect of aggregated coalition resources on lobbying success without systematically embedding coalitions into an exchange framework in order to identify the goods demanded by decision-makers. Baumgartner et al. (2009) have only looked at several resource indicators such as lobbying expenditures or campaign contributions, but not at the three goods identified here, namely information, citizen support, and economic power. Drawing on the propositions that were developed in the previous sections and going beyond Baumgartner et al. (2009), I argue that it is necessary to take into account the aggregated information supply, citizen support, and economic power of entire lobbying coalitions in order to understand lobbying success. The European institutions are confronted with a wide variety of interest groups which seek to shape the outcome of the legislative process. One individual interest group is not very likely to determine the policy outcome. By contrast, what matters is the strength of a coalition of interest groups that share the same policy goal. The European institutions most likely take into account the policy preferences of those interest groups which are members of the strongest coalition since this lobbying team can supply them with a higher amount of information, citizen support, and economic power than its opposing coalition.

I therefore argue that information supply, citizen support, and economic power have to be taken into account at the lobbying coalition level (see also Baumgartner et al. 2009). To illustrate this point, imagine the following example: IG1, IG2, IG3, IG4 individually supply only a medium amount of information, citizen support, and economic power to the European institutions while IG5 supplies a large amount and IG6 provides a small amount of these goods to the European Commission, the Council, and the European Parliament. Looking solely at individual interest groups would lead to the expectation that IG5 should be able to influence European policy-making as it provides the largest amount of exchange goods to the European institutions. However, taking into account the issue-specific grouping of interest groups into lobbying coalitions changes the picture. On the aggregate level, IG1, IG2, IG3, and IG4 provide more information, citizen support, and economic power to the European institutions than their opposing groups IG5 and IG6. Consequently, the former are together able to pull the legislator towards their ideal point while the latter fail in their lobbying attempts. Thus, when trying to understand why some interest groups successfully shape European policy-making while others do not, it is important to take into account the aggregated characteristics of issue-specific lobbying coalitions rather than focusing on individual interest group properties.

Hence, when trying to understand why some interest groups successfully shape policy-making in the European Union while others do not, the aggregated information supply, citizen support, and economic power of issue-specific lobbying coalitions are decisive. What matters, however, are not the values of absolute coalition characteristics, but information supply, citizen support, and economic power of a lobbying coalition in relation to its opposing coalition. To illustrate this point, imagine the following scenario: There are two policy issues and on each issue, two lobbying coalitions are trying to influence policy-making. On issue 1, lobbying coalition *A* might represent 20,000 citizens and lobbying coalition *B* might represent 60,000 citizens. On issue 2, lobbying coalition *C* might only represent 8,000 citizens and lobbying coalition *D* 2,000 citizens. A comparison of the absolute values of citizen support would lead to the conclusion that lobbying coalition

A and lobbying coalition *B* are stronger than lobbying coalition *C* and *D*. This is, however, misleading since the relative citizen support as compared to the opposing coalition on the same issue is decisive. According to this measurement, lobbying coalition *A* supplies 25 percent, coalition *B* supplies 75 percent, coalition *C* provides 80 percent, and coalition *D* provides 20 percent of the overall citizen support to the European institutions. Hence, one would conclude that lobbying coalition *B* and *C* should have higher chances to influence policy-making.

In conclusion, bringing the propositions about the exchange goods together with the lobbying coalition as the decisive level of analysis, the following hypotheses can be formulated:

Hypothesis 1: *The higher the relative information supply by a lobbying coalition, the higher the probability that an interest group belonging to this lobbying coalition influences policy-making in the European Union.*

Hypothesis 2: *The higher the relative citizen support of a lobbying coalition, the higher the probability that an interest group belonging to this lobbying coalition influences policy-making in the European Union.*

Hypothesis 3: *The higher the relative economic power of a lobbying coalition, the higher the probability that an interest group belonging to this lobbying coalition influences policy-making in the European Union.*

2.5 ISSUE CONTEXT

I have so far argued that lobbying can be conceptualized as an exchange relationship between the European institutions and lobbying coalitions in which the Commission, the Council, and the European Parliament trade influence for information supply, citizen support, and economic power. The intensity of the exchange relationship, however, varies across policy issues as the demand for information changes with the issue context. Every policy issue is distinct as policy issues differ extensively in a variety of characteristics. Some issues might be highly technical whereas the complexity of other issues might be rather low. Hence, lobbying does not take place in a vacuum, rather interest groups are embedded in an issue environment with which they have to interact. The characteristics of the policy issue at hand therefore considerably affect their ability to succeed in their lobbying attempts. Thus, the issue context defines the environment in which interest groups are competing for influence and it can facilitate or hamper their ability to influence European policy-making.

More specifically, I hypothesize that the effect of information supply varies with the complexity of the policy issue (Smith 2000; Dür and De Bièvre 2007*b*;

Woll 2007; Dür 2008*b*). Complexity denotes the degree to which a given policy problem is difficult to analyze, understand, or solve. Policy-making is a very challenging task and decision-makers are increasingly lacking sufficient information about the impact of specific policy measures. The European Commission, the European Parliament, and the Council are therefore gathering external information by widely consulting among interest groups to compensate for their lack of information (Majone 1996*a*, 72–74; Bouwen 2009, 22). Hence, decision-makers demand information from private actors and by supplying this information, interest groups are able to influence the outcome of policy-making processes. Correspondingly, Austen-Smith (1993, 799–800) points out that

> decision-makers are frequently choosing policies without complete information on their consequences, in which case, information becomes valuable, and those who possess it are accordingly in a position to influence policy.

However, the need for external expertise varies from policy proposal to policy proposal: Some proposals may concern the entire internal market and may be highly technical whereas other proposals may only affect a very small sector and merely constitute a small modification to existing legislation. If policy proposals are highly complex, the need for external expert knowledge is very high and the European institutions are particularly open for an exchange with interest groups. However, if a policy issue is very simple in nature, the demand for information should be very low and interest groups should find it more difficult to influence European policy-making through information transmission.

I therefore expect that there is an interaction effect between the complexity of policy issues and information supply by interest groups. If a policy issue is highly complex, the European institutions need a high amount of information from interest groups. Hence, interest groups which can supply the information needed by the Commission, the Council and the European Parliament should be in a good position to influence the policy-making process. However, if a policy issue is hardly complex at all, the European institutions barely need any information. Interest groups which rely mainly on providing information to European decision-makers should thus find it very difficult to have an impact on the legislative debate. I therefore expect that the positive effect of information supply on interest group influence is moderated by the complexity of the policy issue. The effect should be strong on highly complex issues and it should be weak on issues of low complexity. Hence, the following conditional hypothesis can be derived:

Hypothesis 4: *The higher the complexity of a policy issue, the stronger the positive effect of relative information supply by lobbying coalitions on interest group influence on policy-making in the European Union.*

2.6 CONCLUSION

This chapter laid out the theoretical model guiding this study. It has been argued that lobbying is an exchange relationship in which the European institutions demand policy-relevant information, citizen support, and economic power from interest groups. The ability of interest groups to supply these goods to the Commission, the Council, and the European Parliament explains why some interest groups are able to succeed in their lobbying activities while others fail to shape the policy process. It has furthermore been argued that lobbying is a collective enterprise. Policy issues mobilize numerous interest groups which simultaneously lobby the European institutions. Interest groups pursuing the same policy goal pull the decision-makers in the same direction and therefore form a lobbying coalition. What is decisive is therefore not the supply of exchange goods by individual interest groups, but the aggregated provision of information, citizen support, and economic power by entire lobbying coalitions. Finally, it has been theorized that the information needs of the European institutions vary with the complexity of policy issues. As a result, the effect of information supply should increase with the complexity of policy proposals. The next chapter turns to the empirical part of the book by laying the foundation for testing the specified hypotheses.

3

How to Measure Interest Group Influence

Analyzing interest group influence should be of central concern to scholars of European policy-making.[1] However, only few researchers have in fact studied interest group influence, mainly owing to methodological difficulties in operationalizing influence. This chapter therefore presents and tests a new methodological approach to measure interest group influence that draws on quantitative text analysis to analyze consultations of the European Commission. By extracting policy positions from interest group consultation submissions and comparing them with the Commission's preliminary consultation draft, the Commission's final policy proposal, and the final legislative act adopted by the Council and the European Parliament, I am able to draw conclusions about the winners and the losers of the policy-making process in the European Union. Since this is a novel approach and text analysis has not been used before in interest group research, I demonstrate the validity of this measurement approach by presenting a case study in which I compare the results obtained by computerized text analysis with traditional hand-coding. The results correlate highly and quantitative text analysis proves to be a powerful tool to measure interest groups' policy positions thus paving the way for the large-scale analysis of interest group influence conducted in this book.

The chapter proceeds as follows: I first present a review of methodological approaches that have been suggested for the measurement of interest group influence. I thoroughly discuss the advantages and disadvantages of each approach and point out their shortcomings. I then propose a new approach to influence measurement that draws on quantitative text analysis and enables researchers to study interest group influence across a wide variety of policy issues and interest groups. I present this new approach by first discussing several text analysis techniques that could potentially be used for the study of interest group influence and then comparing these approaches in a case study in which I test the applicability of these techniques in interest group

[1] This chapter constitutes a revised and much extended version of "Measuring Interest Group Influence Using Quantitative Text Analysis" which was published in *European Union Politics* (10, 4) in 2009.

research. Based on the results of the case study, I finally draw conclusions for the applicability of text analysis in interest group influence research in general and for the measurement of interest group influence in this study in particular.

3.1 OVERVIEW OF APPROACHES TO INFLUENCE MEASUREMENT

The lack of empirical studies on interest group influence is largely due to methodological difficulties in operationalizing interest group influence. So far, three different approaches to the empirical measurement of interest group influence can be identified: process-tracing, assessing attributed influence, and gauging the degree of preference attainment (Dür 2008*c*).

Process-tracing is the most frequently applied methodological approach to interest group influence measurement (e.g. Cowles 1995; Long 1995; Michalowitz 2007; Princen 2007). Process-tracing offers major strengths (Dür 2008*c*): Due to the small number of cases, scholars have a profound knowledge of the examined cases and are able to include nearly all explanatory factors in the analysis. These studies therefore provide high internal validity and are well-suited for checking rival theories and for generating new hypotheses. However, process-tracing also suffers from several shortcomings (Dür 2008*c*): Case studies typically focus on one particular issue so that it is not possible to examine the effect of the issue context since contextual variables are held constant. Moreover, the concentration on one or just a few cases limits the external validity, that is, the generalizability of the results. In addition, process-tracing mostly relies on observable actions and since lobbying often takes place behind closed doors or structural power is at work, important channels of influence might not be covered.

The second methodological approach is the attributed influence method which draws either on the self-evaluation of interest groups or on the assessment of experts (e.g. Egdell and Thomson 1999; Pappi and Henning 1999; Dür and De Bièvre 2007*a*). This method has several advantages (Dür 2008*c*): It is relatively simple, it can be applied to a large number of cases, and it captures all channels of influence. However, it is certainly debatable (Dür 2008*c*): Self-evaluation rests on the subjective assessment of the interest group leaders and is subject to misleading incentives (e.g. Whiteley and Winyard 1987). On the one hand, groups might exaggerate their influence in order to signal success to their members (Dür and De Bièvre 2007*a*). On the other hand, groups might understate their influence in order to drive public authorities to grant them more access and to avoid the creation of counterlobbies. Expert assessment may be shaped by prominent cases or findings of other academic studies. A more general problem of the attributed influence method is the fact that it measures *perceived* rather than *actual* influence (Polsby 1960).

The third methodological approach is assessing the degree of preference attainment (see e.g. Schneider and Baltz 2003; Bailer 2004; Selck and Steunenberg 2004; Schneider, Finke, and Baltz 2007; Dür 2008*a*; Bernhagen 2012). Political controversies are modeled spatially and each actor involved can be placed on a point of a policy scale to represent the position that it favors. By comparing the policy outcome with the policy preferences of interest groups, one can draw conclusions about the winners and losers of the decision-making process. This approach offers several advantages (Dür 2008*c*): It provides an objective measurement of influence, it covers all channels of influence, and it can be applied to a large number of cases.

First, in contrast to the attributed influence approach which relies on the subjective evaluation of experts or interest groups themselves to assess the degree of interest group influence, the preference attainment approach provides an influence measurement which is not biased by subjective perception. Comparing the policy preferences of interest groups with the Commission's preliminary draft proposal, the Commission's final proposal, and the final legislative act adopted by the Council and the European Parliament allows one to objectively assess who was successful in shifting the policy output over the course of the legislative process towards their ideal points.

Second, the preference attainment approach captures interest group influence which has been exercised through various channels. One can distinguish four major ways in which interest groups can influence policy-making: Interest groups can influence policies by employing an "inside lobbying" strategy, that is, directly exchanging policy-relevant information with decision-makers through formal or informal contacts (e.g. Hansen 1991; Bouwen 2004*b*; Eising 2007*a*; Coen 2009). Interest groups can also employ an "outside lobbying" strategy by conducting protests or demonstrations to exert pressure on policy-makers via the public arena (e.g. Lipsky 1968; Kollman 1998; Imig and Tarrow 2000; Imig 2002). In addition, interest groups can shape policy-making by influencing the selection of decision-makers (e.g. Austen-Smith 1987; Fordham and McKeown 2003; Maniadis 2009). Finally, interest groups can affect policy-making through structural power, that is, interest groups simply have an impact on policy decisions since they control business investments and job creation (e.g. Lindblom 1977; Bernhagen and Bräuninger 2005). No matter through which of these channels interest group influence is in fact exerted, the preference attainment method is able to capture it since influence should by definition be observed in the policy outcome (see section 1.1.2).

Third, in contrast to process-tracing, the preference attainment method can be applied to a large number of cases which allows for generalizations of the findings. In addition, analyzing a large number of interest groups and policy issues implies that errors made in the evaluation of an actor's influence in specific cases should cancel out across the entire analysis (see also Dür 2008c, 567).

The preference attainment approach, however, also suffers from several problems, namely the black-boxing of the processes through which influence is exercised, alternative explanatory factors accounting for the coincidence between policy output and preferences, and the measurement of policy positions (Dür 2008c).

While it is an advantage of the preference attainment approach that it covers all paths to influence, it is not clear through which of these processes influence is in fact exerted. However, the black-boxing of the processes through which influence is exerted is not very problematic for this study since the goal of this book is only to explain variation in influence, but not to account for different channels or strategies. The objective is to explain why some interest groups are more influential than others, but since the theoretical model does not consider lobbying strategies or channels as important explanatory variables, the black-boxing is not a severe problem for this study.

The problem of controlling for alternative explanatory factors refers to the fact that if the policy output reflects the policy preference of an interest group, it does not necessarily mean that the policy output can be attributed to the lobbying activities of this particular group. The objectives of interest groups and the policy preferences of decision-makers could, for instance, just coincide in which case an interest group was just lucky (Barry 1980a,b). To empirically disentangle influence and luck, I draw on the observable implications illustrated in figure 1.1. The crucial point that distinguishes influence from pure luck is a causal link between the policy preference of the actor and the output of the policy-making process (Nagel 1975, 29). If an interest group is able to influence a political decision, there must be a causal connection between the attributes of this interest group and the political decision. Hence, there should be a systematic association between actor properties and the policy output. If an actor has indeed been able to influence political decisions which brought about the policy output, one can observe a systematic, that is, statistically significant effect of actor properties.

The third problem of the preference attainment approach is the measurement of policy preferences. So far, two approaches can be distinguished: Some researchers just assumed certain policy preferences a priori (e.g. Frieden 2002; Dür 2008a). This approach is associated with the following limitations: First, it is only applicable to a very general left–right dimension such as business, as opposed to environmental groups or to importers versus exporters. Second, it cannot take into account differences within a certain type of group, such as differences among various environmental associations. Thus, policy preferences have to be measured empirically for each interest group and each issue under analysis. So far, this has only been done by asking interest groups themselves about their policy positions (e.g. Mahoney 2007*a*, 2008; Baumgartner et al. 2009). However, preferences may change over time and thus policy positions cannot be measured at a precise time point (Laver and Garry 2000, 622). Similarly, interviewees may have trouble recollecting their positions and activities on issues that occurred a long time ago and as a result, interviews can only be used to gather information about interest group preferences on recent issues. What is needed is a more objective measurement of interest groups' policy preferences at a precise point in time that allows measurement of issue-specific policy positions of interest groups across a large number of cases and without any time limitations.

To sum up, the preference attainment approach to interest group influence is the most promising since it provides an objective measurement, covers all channels of influence, and can be applied to a large number of cases. I therefore draw on the preference attainment technique to measure interest group influence in this book. However, as illustrated above, one of the major problems associated with this approach is the measurement of policy positions. In order to overcome this problem, I looked into other subfields of political science and found that research on political parties has long been dealing with the measurement of policy positions. Party scholars have developed new promising research methods for extracting policy positions from party manifestos by drawing on text analysis (Laver and Garry 2000; Budge et al. 2001; Laver, Benoit, and Garry 2003; Klingemann et al. 2006; Klemmensen, Hobolt, and Hansen 2007; Slapin and Proksch 2008).[2] Combined with the increasing electronic availability of interest group documents, I expect that interest group researchers can benefit enormously from crossing the borders to party research and learn from its experiences. In particular, I argue that text analysis can be a very helpful tool for measuring interest group influence since it allows the large-scale measurement of policy positions as required by the

[2] Two further techniques to measure policy positions are roll-call analysis (e.g. Clinton, Jackman, and Rivers 2004; Poole 2005) and expert surveys (e.g. Huber and Inglehart 1995; Benoit and Laver 2006; Marks et al. 2006). Whereas roll-call analysis could in principle be applied to standardized consultations that consist of closed questions and answers in order to locate interest groups in the policy space, the measurement of the position of the European institutions is problematic since they do not complete questionnaires. The usefulness of expert surveys is equally limited since these typically measure the general positioning of actors in the policy space, such as a placement on the left–right dimension. Since the relative positioning of interest groups in the policy space can, however, vary considerably across issues, an approach is needed that measures the policy preferences of political actors regarding a specific policy proposal. As a result, roll-call analysis and general expert surveys cannot be applied in this particular study.

preference attainment approach to influence measurement. Since quantitative text analysis is a fairly recent technique which has not been applied to the study of interest groups so far, I test the applicability of text analysis to interest group research in the following sections. After a short summary of the development of text analysis, I present an overview of three widely used and promising text analysis techniques for the measurement of policy positions. I then conduct a case study in which I test the applicability of these three approaches to interest group research for one policy issue.

3.2 OVERVIEW OF TEXT ANALYSIS TECHNIQUES

Textual data are arguably the most widely available source of evidence on political processes. Content analysis was developed to make systematic use of this rich data source. It is a "research technique for making replicable and valid inferences from texts . . . to the context of their use" (Krippendorff 2004, 19). Berelson and Lazarsfeld (1948) were probably the most important pioneers of systematic content analysis. They analyzed German media broadcasts during World War II for the American government in order to understand and predict events in Nazi Germany. After World War II and probably as a result of their work, content analysis has spread to numerous disciplines. Content analysis has been used for various purposes, such as analyzing media coverage, propaganda analysis, or authorship studies (e.g. Mosteller and Wallace 1964). As the development of computers progressed, so did the use of computer-aided quantitative text analysis (Alexa and Züll 2000; Roberts 2000; Lowe 2003).

Political documents have a great potential to reveal information about the policy positions of their authors: Texts can be analyzed as many times as one wishes and they provide information about policy positions at a specific point in time. By 1979, political scientists had therefore begun to use content analysis for the measurement of policy positions of political parties. Ian Budge and David Robertson initiated the Comparative Manifesto Project (CMP) which analyzed party manifestos in Eastern Europe, the European Union, and the OECD from 1945 until today by means of manual hand-coding. Since the manual analysis of party manifestos is extremely time-consuming and cost-intensive, computer-based text analysis approaches for the measurement of policy positions have been developed in recent years (Laver and Garry 2000; Budge et al. 2001; Laver, Benoit, and Garry 2003; Klingemann et al. 2006; Klemmensen, Hobolt, and Hansen 2007; Slapin and Proksch 2008). The most important advances for extracting policy positions from texts are *Wordscores* (Laver, Benoit, and Garry 2003) and *Wordfish* (Proksch and Slapin 2008; Slapin and Proksch 2008). Whereas the CMP draws on quasi-sentences as the unit of analysis, *Wordscores* and *Wordfish* employ the so-called "bag of words" approach by using single words as the unit of analysis. Even though single word usage ignores the contextual nature of language, Benoit and Laver (2003*b*) have demonstrated that the results based on single words do not differ much from the results obtained drawing on word pairs and triplets which capture the close context of words.

The quality of a content analysis is evaluated according to its validity and its reliability. Validity is "the extent to which a measuring procedure represents the intended, and only the intended concept" (Neuendorf 2002, 112). Reliability is "the extent to which a measuring procedure yields the same results on repeated trials" (Neuendorf 2002, 112). Hand-coding is usually associated with a high degree of validity but only low reliability. By contrast, the great advantage of *Wordscores* and *Wordfish* is a high degree of reliability, but these are often criticized for a lack of validity. Hence, in the ensuing sections, the validity of *Wordscores* and *Wordfish* is tested by comparing them with hand-coding. In the following sections, I illustrate the CMP as well as the *Wordscores* and *Wordfish* approaches in more detail before turning to the actual comparison of the three approaches.

3.2.1 Hand-coding

Manual hand-coding is probably the most widespread approach in text analysis. A hand-coded content analysis involves the following steps: First, the researcher develops a categorization scheme based either on theoretical assumptions or on inductive reasoning. Second, the texts are divided into smaller units of analysis, such as paragraphs, sentences, or words depending on the research design. Third, the text units are assigned to the categories of the coding scheme based on human judgment. The manual hand-coding analysis results in a dataset which contains the number of text units per category of the coding scheme. The Comparative Manifesto Project (Budge et al. 2001; Klingemann et al. 2006) has probably produced the most well-known and widely used dataset for party positions by manually coding party manifestos (for applications, see e.g. Adams et al. 2006; Marks et al. 2007; Knill, Debus, and Heichel 2010). The CMP has used trained human coders to analyze 3,018 party manifestos of 780 different parties in 54 countries over the postwar era (Volkens 2005). The CMP developed a classification scheme with 56 categories grouped into seven policy domains. Where possible, directly opposing pro and contra categories were specified. However, in addition to bipolar issues which are clearly positional (such as "social services expansion" positive or negative), also unipolar issues were defined as "left" or "right" such as "nationalization," which is classified as a left-wing issue, or "law and order," which is considered to be an issue on the "right." In total thirteen categories were defined as left and thirteen categories were defined as right.

The unit of analysis is a quasi-sentence, defined as "an argument or phrase which is the verbal expression of one idea or meaning" (Klingemann et al. 2006, xxiii). Human coders divided the party manifestos into quasi-sentences and allocated them to one of the specified categories. In the end, the number of quasi-sentences per category was obtained for every manifesto. The construction of the left–right scale is based on saliency theory which assumes that policy positions are revealed by the number of statements devoted to an issue. The central idea is that parties compete with each other by emphasizing different policy priorities rather than by directly opposing each other on the same issues (Budge and Bara 2001, 6–7). The left–right scale is constructed in the following way:[3] First, the percentages of left and right categories of the total number of coded quasi-sentences are computed. Then, the percentage of left sentences is subtracted from the percentage of right sentences. Negative scores represent left positions and positive scores represent right positions. At the extreme, a party devoting its entire program to left-wing issues would score −100; similarly a totally right-winged program would receive a score of +100. An example: Imagine a party manifesto contained 200 quasi-sentences, out of which 100 (50 percent) are allocated to left categories and 40 (20 percent) are allocated to right categories. This manifesto would receive a score of −30 (i.e. 20−50).

The CMP developed the most comprehensive dataset on policy positions of political parties across countries over time and it is accordingly widely used among political scientists. While hand-coding claims validity as its central advantage over computerized text analysis, the content analysis approach of the CMP has been severely criticized for a number of reasons. The validity of the CMP policy position estimates is questioned due to its theoretical foundation. Scholars argue that parties do not compete by placing emphasis on different issues as assumed by salience theory, but that they seek direct confrontation on the same issues (Riker 1996; Laver and Garry 2000). Furthermore, the manifestos have been coded only once so that there is no measure of uncertainty for the policy position estimates based on the CMP (Bakker, Edwards, and de Vries 2006; Mikhaylov, Laver, and Benoit 2012). Even though Benoit, Laver, and Mikhaylov (2009) have developed a technique to measure the uncertainty of CMP policy position estimates, the lack of reliability is still a severe problem of manual hand-coding in general. In addition, hand-coding is very time- and labor-intensive which makes it difficult to analyze large amounts of texts.

---

[3] This is the so-called *rile* scale procedure suggested by the CMP researchers. In addition, several other scholars have suggested alternative ways to compute policy positions based on the CMP dataset (see for instance Gabel and Huber 2000; Linhart and Shikano 2007; Lowe et al. 2011).

3.2.2 *Wordscores*

Due to the lack of reliability and the amount of labor associated with manual hand-coding, computer-based text analysis approaches have been developed in recent years. A major step forward was undertaken by Laver, Benoit, and Garry (2003): They developed a fully automated text analysis program for measuring policy positions of texts (for applications, see e.g. Benoit and Laver 2003*a*; Benoit et al. 2005; Hug and Schulz 2007). Instead of relying on dictionaries as done earlier, this method uses reference texts and reference values in order to predict policy positions.[4] The basic idea is that one can estimate policy positions by comparing two sets of texts: "Reference texts" and "virgin texts."

"Reference texts" are documents whose policy positions are known to the researcher (e.g. by relying on expert surveys). "Virgin texts" by contrast are documents about which one does not know anything apart from the words they contain. By comparing the relative frequencies of words in the reference texts with the relative frequencies in the virgin texts one can calculate the probability P_{wr} that one is reading a particular reference text r given a specific word w. So it is assumed that each word provides a little piece of information about which of the reference texts the virgin text most closely resembles. Thus, the more words a document contains, the more confident one is in judging which reference text is closest to the virgin text. Since the policy positions of the reference texts, A_{rd}, are known, one can use the probabilities, P_{wr}, together with the reference values, A_{rd}, to produce a score, S_{wd}, for each word w on dimension d. This is the expected policy position on dimension d of any text given a word w. Then the relative frequency of each virgin text word as a proportion of the total number of words in the text, F_{wv}, is computed. The policy position raw score, S_{vd}, of any virgin text is then the mean dimension score S_{wd} of all the scored words that it contains, weighted by the frequency of the scored words, F_{wv}. In order to compare the scores of the virgin texts directly with those of the reference texts, these raw scores are finally transformed into S^*_{vd} (for further details, see Laver, Benoit, and Garry 2003). Confidence intervals are obtained by estimating the variance, V_{vd}, of the individual word scores around the text's mean score.

Wordscores is based on a number of assumptions: First, it assumes that policy positions are reflected in the relative frequency of words used within and across texts. Second, it is assumed that word meaning remains stable over time. Time-series analysis of policy positions can therefore be problematic since

[4] In an earlier article, Laver and Garry (2000) constructed a word-based dictionary drawing on the categories defined by the CMP. They identified key words for predefined policy positions and then ran a computer program to count the number of times each key word is mentioned in a text. Even though this method decreases the problem of reliability of coding the texts, it is still severely vulnerable to human error: As Laver, Benoit, and Garry (2003, 312) state, it relies on heavy human input in order to develop and test coding dictionaries. Thus, even though it enables reliable coding of texts, the creation of dictionaries imports the weaknesses of traditional hand-coding.

new themes and accordingly also new words come up so that the vocabulary changes over time. Third, *Wordscores* assigns all words the same weight in the estimation process. Hence, words that occur frequently in all texts, such as conjunctions and articles, are equally contributing to the policy position estimates as words with high political connotation. Thus, frequent words that occur in all texts without carrying substantial meaning pull the document scores towards the center of the policy space which makes them incomparable to the policy position values of the reference texts. In order to overcome this problem, Laver, Benoit, and Garry (2003) standardize the raw scores by stretching the variance of the virgin text scores to equal the variance of the reference text scores.[5] Fourth, *Wordscores* requires that all words of interest are contained in the reference texts.

In practical terms, the following steps are necessary to conduct a *Wordscores* analysis: First, one has to define the policy dimension to be investigated. Second, one then has to choose a set of reference texts with known policy position estimates. Choosing the reference texts is a crucial step and the following guidelines should be followed: The reference texts should use the same vocabulary as the virgin texts. For instance, one cannot compare speeches with laws as the latter contain a very specialized legal terminology that is very different from the words used in speeches. Furthermore, the texts should at best reflect the extreme positions on the policy scale. Finally, the reference texts should contain as many different words as possible. The requirement to choose reference texts is the biggest disadvantage of *Wordscores* since one has to draw on an independent source for the policy position estimates. Whereas this is a rather easy task in party research due to the Comparative Manifesto Project and several expert surveys, it might be very difficult to find reference values for other fields of investigation. The last step in applying *Wordscores* is to run the computer program which performs the above explained estimation procedure.

3.2.3 *Wordfish*

The most recent innovation in quantitative content analysis is *Wordfish* (Proksch and Slapin 2008; Slapin and Proksch 2008). It is a statistical scaling model that allows one to estimate policy positions of texts on a predefined policy dimension simply by drawing on relative word frequencies in texts (for applications, see Schmitt 2008; Pappi and Seher 2009; Proksch and Slapin 2010). Hence, in contrast to *Wordscores*, *Wordfish* does not require reference documents and reference values. The model is based on the assumption that

---

[5] Throughout this study, the standardization procedure suggested by Laver, Benoit, and Garry (2003) is used. This standardization procedure, however, raised some criticism. Martin and Vanberg (2008) for instance suggested another way of standardizing the raw scores. See Lowe (2008) for a thorough discussion of *Wordscores* and its problems.

words are distributed according to a Poisson distribution. This distribution was selected since it resembles the highly skewed distribution of word usage in natural language and since it is simpler than alternative distributions such as the negative binomial distribution. The Poisson distribution has only one parameter, λ, which is at the same time the mean and the variance. The model underlying the estimation of policy positions is the following:

$$y_{ij} \sim Poisson(\lambda_{ij})$$

$$\lambda_{ij} = exp(\alpha_i + \psi_j + \beta_j * \omega_i)$$

y_{ij} is the count of word j in text i. α is a set of text effects that control for the length of the documents. ψ is a set of word fixed effects that control for the fact that some words, such as articles or prepositions, are generally used more frequently than other words. β is an estimate of a word specific weight capturing the importance of word j in discriminating between policy positions and ω is the estimate of actor i's policy position. The entire right-hand side of the equation is estimated by an expectation maximization (EM) algorithm (for further details see Slapin and Proksch 2008). In order to identify the model, the first text effect α_1 and the mean of all policy positions of actors are set to zero and the standard deviation is set to one. Confidence intervals for the policy position estimates are obtained drawing on a parametric bootstrap. The use of a parametric bootstrap implies that the confidence intervals shrink as the number of unique words increases since this model treats each unique word as an independent observation. Thus, the higher the number of unique words, the more data are available for estimating the policy positions and thus the higher the confidence in the obtained policy position estimates.

Wordfish is based on a number of assumptions: First, it is assumed that policy positions are reflected in the relative frequency of words used within and across texts. Second, it is assumed that word meaning remains stable over time. Third, the algorithm estimates the policy positions on a single dimension. Thus, it is assumed that the documents used for the analysis are encyclopedic statements of the actors' policy positions. If one wants to calculate the policy position on a specific issue that is only discussed in a particular section of a document, only this particular section should be used for the analysis. For instance, if the policy positions of political parties on environmental issues are to be extracted from party manifestos, all text passages not directly referring to environmental policy need to be removed from the document.

In practical terms, *Wordfish* requires the following steps. First, one has to define the policy dimension that should be studied and select documents that deal with this policy dimension and that use a comparable pool of words. Second, one then has to remove all text passages that do not refer to the policy dimension in question. Third, Proksch and Slapin (2009*a*,*b*) in addition recommend various preprocessing steps, such as removing stopwords, eliminating words that have only been mentioned very rarely, and stemming, that is, reducing words to their roots. Fourth, one has to produce a word frequency matrix, which contains words in rows and texts in columns indicating the number of occurrences of words in the different texts, which serves as input for the *Wordfish* program.

3.3 RESEARCH DESIGN OF THE CASE STUDY

In order to examine the applicability of the three previously discussed text analysis approaches to the study of interest group influence, a case study is presented that compares hand-coding, *Wordscores*, and *Wordfish*. In the ensuing sections, I proceed as follows: I first illustrate the research design of the case study by explaining in detail which policy issue I selected for the case study and what texts I used to measure the policy positions of interest groups and the European institutions. I then compare the results obtained by hand-coding, *Wordscores*, and *Wordfish* before drawing conclusions for the applicability of quantitative text analysis to the study of interest group influence.

In order to test the different quantitative content analysis approaches, I selected the policy proposal concerning the reduction of CO_2 emissions from cars. On 7 February 2007, the European Commission published a communication in which it proposed a legislative framework to reduce CO_2 emissions from cars to 120g/km in 2012. The Commission called for improvements in vehicle technology that should account for an emission reduction to 130g/km, while efficiency improvements for tires and air conditioning systems as well as a greater use of biofuels should contribute to further emissions cuts of 10g/km. Furthermore, the Commission suggested fiscal measures, improved consumer information, and a code of good practice on car marketing to decrease the popularity of cars with high CO_2 emissions. The Commission then launched a public online consultation which ran from 7 February until 15 July 2007 and was open to anyone interested in this issue. The Commission adopted its legislative proposal in December 2007 and forwarded it to the Council and the European Parliament, for legislative discussion under the Codecision procedure. The Council and the European Parliament approved the final legislative act after the first reading in April 2009. In order to study interest group influence during the policy formulation stage in which the Commission develops its final policy proposal based on the communication, I will compare the policy preferences of interest groups with the position of the Commission before the consultation as reflected in the communication and after the consultation as reflected in the final policy proposal. In order to evaluate interest group influence during the decision-making stage in which the Council, the European Parliament, and the European Commission negotiate the design of the final legislative act based on the proposal issued by the European Commission, I will compare the policy preferences of the interest groups with the final legislative act while taking into account the Commission position expressed in the communication and the proposal.

The policy positions of the European institutions and the interest groups are measured on a single "pro environmental control" and "anti environmental control" policy dimension. Being located at the "pro environmental control" end of the policy scale implies that interest groups support the framework suggested by the Commission and might even go beyond the proposed measures. Interest groups located at the "anti environmental control" end of the policy scale are against the measures proposed by the Commission.

This policy issue was selected for various reasons. First, a wide variety of actors took part in this consultation and one can therefore assume a broad range of policy positions (see table 3.1). I classified the actors into five groups: traditional automobile industry groups (n = 9); alternative industry groups (n = 6), which promote the use of biofuels or electric vehicles; environmental groups (n = 7); national authorities (n = 3); and other groups (n = 9). Second, the number of submissions is not too high, so that a hand-coded content analysis could be conducted. In total, 45 comments were submitted by interest groups and national authorities. Ten submissions were not written in English and were excluded since *Wordscores* and *Wordfish* can only be applied to texts in the same language. One further submission was excluded since it only consists of a PowerPoint presentation. Hence, 34 submissions remain for the analysis.

In order to measure policy positions of interest groups, their submissions to the public consultation preceding the adoption of the policy proposal were analyzed. The European Commission introduced the online consultation instrument in 2000. Interest groups are consulted on a preliminary proposal before the final policy proposal is decided upon by the College of Commissioners and passed on to the Council and the European Parliament. Consultation submissions are usually published on the website of the European Commission and thus provide researchers with a fruitful new data source.

The communication and a summary of the policy proposal issued by the European Parliament will be used to measure the Commission position before and after the consultation. The location of the final legislative act will be extracted from a summary of the legislative act issued by the European Parliament. In theory, one could also use the communication, the proposal, and the regulation directly. This is, however, associated with a problem of comparability: Whereas the communication is written as a continuous political text, the proposal and the final legislative act consist of the explanatory memorandum, the preamble, and the actual regulation and therefore use very specific legal terminology. Thus, these texts employ a very different vocabulary and cannot be compared directly using computer-based content

Table 3.1 Further information about actors and texts

Abbreviation	Name of actor	Words
ACEA	European Automobile Manufacturers' Association	2817
ADTS	Associação per la Divulgação de les Tecnologies Sostenibles	403
AEGPL	European Liquefied Petroleum Gas Association	2946
AVELE	Spanish Association for the Promotion of Electric and Non-Contaminant Vehicles	402
AVERE	European Association for Battery, Hybrid and Fuel Cell Electric Vehicles	466
BEUC	European Consumer Organization	1570
BVRLA	British Vehicle Rental and Leasing Association	1225
COMM 1	Commission 1 (Communication February 2007)	3995
COMM 2	Commission 2 (Proposal December 2007)	658
DE	Germany	3367
EBB	European Biodiesel Board	2397
ENGVA	European Natural Gas Vehicles Association	4966
EP, COU, COMM	EP, Council and Commission (Regulation April 2009)	943
ETRMA	European Tire and Rubber Manufacturers' Association	653
ETSC	European Transport Safety Council	290
ETUC	European Trade Union Confederation	1016
FAEP	European Federation of Magazine Publishers	626
FANC	Finnish Association of Nature Conservation	611
FOEIT	Friends of the Earth Italy	2799
FOEUK	Friends of the Earth UK	1258
GM	General Motors	5321
GREENPEACE	Greenpeace	550
JAMA	Japan Automobile Manufacturers' Association	1214
KAMA	Korea Automobile Manufacturers' Association	1016
LTI	LTI Vehicles	671
MICHELIN	Michelin	1431
NL	Netherlands	664
RAI	RAI Vereniging – Rijwel and Automobiel Industrie	466
RSPB	Royal Society for the Protection of Birds	1017
SHECCO	Shecco	769
SMMT	Society of Motor Manufacturers and Traders	2264
T&E	Transport and Environment	6791
UK	United Kingdom	1249
UKAA	UK Advertising Association	759
VDA	Verband der Automobilindustrie	7272
VW	Volkswagen	7233
WWF	World Wide Fund for Nature	2009

analysis (Laver, Benoit, and Garry 2003, 315). In order to test the validity of the preference measurement based on the communication and the summaries of the proposal and the final act, press releases accompanying the launch of the consultation and the adoption of the policy proposal as well as the preamble of the policy proposal and the final legislative act were also hand-coded. On a pro/anti environmental control scale ranging from −100 (pro) to +100 (anti), the Commission communication receives a score of −61.33 whereas the press release accompanying this communication receives a score of −58.70. The EP summary of the final policy proposal receives a score of −30.43 whereas the press release accompanying the proposal receives a score of −27.66 and the preamble of the proposal itself scored −28.99. The policy position of the final legislative act obtained by coding its EP summary is −31.48 whereas coding the preamble of the final act lead to a policy position estimate of −28.05. Hence, one can conclude that the different documents deliver nearly identical results and hence the validity of the preference measurement based on the communication and the EP summaries of the policy proposal and the final legislative act has been demonstrated.

3.4 ANALYSIS

In this section, I present the analysis of the case study. More specifically, I illustrate the policy position estimates obtained by hand-coding, *Wordscores*, and *Wordfish*. I test the quality of these policy position estimates by systematically comparing the results obtained by the three techniques and by conducting several reliability and validity checks. I start with the hand-coding analysis and then proceed to *Wordfish* and *Wordscores*. In the light of the findings of the case study, I finally draw conclusions about the applicability of text analysis to the study of interest group influence.

3.4.1 Hand-coding

First, a hand-coded analysis largely based on the design of the CMP was performed. I developed a coding scheme to systematically capture the content of the texts. This coding scheme was developed inductively on the basis of in-depth reading of the interest group submissions and the policy documents of the European institutions. At first, I read all EU institution documents and made a list of all issues that were discussed in these texts. Afterwards, I carefully read all interest group submissions and added issues to the list that were mentioned by interest groups while not being discussed by the European institutions. I arrived at 20 different policy issues. In order to not only focus on the varying emphasis of interest groups to these different issues, but to also capture the direct confrontation of actors on the same issues, I developed bipolar categories. All statements that could not be allocated to one of these categories were grouped into an "others" category. The final coding scheme therefore consists of 41 categories of which 20 categories were classified as "pro environmental control" and 20 as "anti environmental control" (see table 3.2).

Table 3.2 Hand-coding classification scheme

Overall category	Environmental control	
	Pro	Anti
Reduction target	positive	negative
Appropriateness of measure	positive	negative
Inclusion of vans	positive	negative
Code of good practice on car advertising	positive	negative
Improved labeling to promote the purchase of fuel-efficient cars	positive	negative
Fiscal measures to promote the purchase of fuel-efficient cars	positive	negative
Penalties to enforce CO_2 reductions	positive	negative
Efficiency improvements of tires	positive	negative
Efficiency improvements of air conditioning	positive	negative
Greater use of alternative fuels or automotive technology	positive	negative
Long-term reduction strategy	positive	negative
Averaging	negative	positive
Pooling	negative	positive
Banking	negative	positive
Individual targets for small-scale manufacturers	negative	positive
Exceptions for special-purpose vehicles	negative	positive
Weight as a parameter for calculating reduction targets	negative	positive
Inclusion of CO_2 reduction from cars in general Emissions Trading Regime	negative	positive
Monitoring	positive	negative
Crediting	negative	positive
Other	–	–

The units of analysis are natural sentences separated by full stops, semicolons, or colons. Natural sentences were selected as units of analysis as they provide equally valid content estimates as quasi-sentences while at the same time performing better with regard to reliability (Däubler et al. 2012). Each sentence was allocated to at least one of the specified categories. In the end, for each coded document, the number of sentences per category has been obtained. The pro/anti environmental control scale was produced according to the CMP procedure. First, the percentages of pro and anti environmental control categories of the total number of coded statements per text were calculated. Then, the pro percentage was subtracted from the anti percentage. Negative scores represent pro environmental control positions and positive scores represent anti environmental control positions.

Figure 3.1 plots the policy position estimates obtained using this classification scheme. In order to guarantee comparability with the other content analysis approaches, the estimates were transformed so that they are measured on the same scale as the *Wordfish* and *Wordscores* estimates. All traditional industry actors are located closer to the "anti environmental control" end of the policy scale than the Commission's communication (COMM 1), the Commission's legislative proposal (COMM 2), and the final

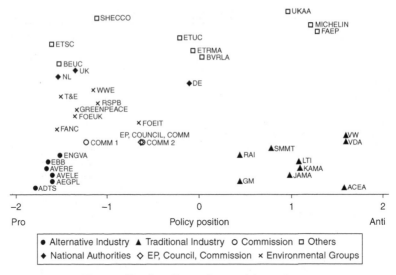

Fig. 3.1 Hand-coding policy position estimates

legislative act (EP, COUNCIL, COMM). All alternative industry actors are located closer to the "pro environmental control" side of the policy scale than the European institutions. Four of the environmental groups (FANC, T&E, FOEUK, GREENPEACE) are located closer to the "pro environmental control" side of the policy scale than all European institution positions and three (WWF, RSPB, FOEIT) are located in between the Commission's communication on the one hand and the legislative proposal and the final legislative act on the other hand. The Netherlands and the UK are located closer to the "pro environmental control" side of the policy scale than the European institutions whereas Germany is located closer to the "anti environmental control" end of the policy spectrum. Two of the remaining actors, BEUC, which is a European consumer association, and ETSC, which is an interest group promoting transport security, are located closer to the "pro environmental control" spectrum of all three European institution positions whereas SHECCO, which is a consultancy specialized in climate friendly products, is located in between the Commission's communication on the one hand and the Commission's proposal and the final legislative act adopted by the Council and the European Parliament on the other hand. The rest of the other actors (ETUC, ETRMA, BVRLA, UKAA, MICHELIN, FAEP) are located closer to the "anti environmental control" end of the policy scale than the European institutions. The Commission moved from a policy position of –1.23 to a policy position of −0.61, so it clearly moved towards Germany and the traditional automobile industry. The Council and the European Parliament then adopted the final legislative act which received a score of −0.63 and therefore hardly differs from the proposal presented by the European Commission. Hence, drawing on hand-coding one would conclude that Germany and the traditional automobile industry were successful in shifting the European Commission during the policy formulation stage towards their ideal points and were largely able to maintain this shift during the decision-making stage in which the Council, the European Parliament, and the European Commission negotiated the final legislative act. The alternative industry associations, the environmental groups, as well as the Netherlands and the UK could not influence the policy formulation process and were hardly able to influence the Council and the European Parliament during the decision-making stage as the final legislative act closely resembles the proposal.

As explained before, one major problem of manual hand-coding is the low degree of reliability. I therefore conducted a reliability test to check the robustness of the content analysis across different coders (see table 3.3). Students of an undergraduate political science class recoded the first three pages of 27 documents.[6] Thus, for 27 of the 37 texts in the analysis, two codings exist: one performed by myself and one conducted by a student. Due to time constraints, students could not be trained before and the texts were already divided into units of analysis in advance. The reliability measures were computed in two different ways: According to the first procedure, the calculation of reliability estimates was based on the entire 41 categories. Hence, I tested whether the students allocated sentences to the exact same categories out of the 41 possible options. Secondly, I based the calculation of reliability measures on the difference between "pro," "anti," and "neutral" categories since this distinction is decisive for the computation of policy position estimates. Hence, I tested whether the students coded sentences as "pro," "anti," or "neutral," no matter whether they picked exactly the same category out of the 41 possible options. Thus, according to the first procedure, there are 41 possible coding options and according to the second procedure, there are only three coding options.

At first, the percent agreement between the students' and my codings was calculated for all 27 documents based on the coding of sentences to all 41 categories. Then, all coders whose mean percent agreement with my own codings was less than 50 percent were excluded from the reliability analysis. The remaining 16 codings were used to produce the final reliability estimates. Overall reliability estimates were obtained by using the mean reliability estimates across the 16 codings. Concerning the allocation of every single

[6] The reliability check was conducted for the earlier version of this chapter as published in *European Union Politics* (Klüver 2009). For this analysis, I only focused on 27 documents and therefore reliability estimates are only available for these 27 texts. Since I used Commission press releases to extract policy positions of the Commission in this earlier version of the chapter, reliability estimates for the Commission texts refer to the press releases and not to the communication and the EP summary.

Table 3.3 Hand-coding reliability test

Coefficients	All categories			Pro, Anti, Neutral		
	Mean	Min	Max	Mean	Min	Max
Percent agreement	64.16%	50.00%	82.09%	78.75%	56.25%	100%
Cohen's kappa	0.47	0.06	0.71	0.53	0.14	1.00
Krippendorf's alpha	0.47	0.04	0.72	0.53	0.10	1.00
Correlation of policy estimates			0.97, $p \leq 0.001$			

sentence to one of the 41 possible categories, the average percent agreement between the students' and my codings is 64.16 percent. If one only considers whether a sentence was allocated to a pro, anti, or the neutral category, the average percent agreement amounts to 78.75 percent.

Furthermore, two reliability coefficients (Cohen's kappa and Krippendorf's alpha) were estimated which take into account that coder agreement can just be due to chance. Both reliability measures range from 0.00 to 1.00 whereby 0.00 indicates agreement at chance level and 1.00 indicates perfect agreement. A value of less than 0.00 indicates agreement less than chance. Cohen's kappa and Krippendorf's alpha are 0.47 for the allocation to all 41 possible categories. If one only looks at the allocation of sentences to a pro, anti, or the neutral category, Cohen's kappa and Krippendorf's alpha are 0.53. According to Landis and Koch (1977), an agreement above 0.41 constitutes a fair to good agreement beyond chance. The reliability coefficients therefore indicate a reasonable agreement across coders.

Since the most important result of the hand-coding is the estimation of policy positions, it is necessary to also compare these estimates. The policy position estimates based on the students' coding and my coding correlate at 0.97. The reliability test has therefore demonstrated the robustness of the policy position estimates across different coders. Despite differences in the coding of single sentences, the general policy positions of the documents remain stable across coders. Hence, one can conclude that even though there is no perfect coding agreement for every single sentence, the very high correlation between the policy position estimates indicates that my codings are by and large confirmed by the students' codings.

In order to check the validity of the results obtained by hand-coding, the content of the communication, the proposal, and the final legislative act were compared with the documents of the interest groups which are located on the extremes of the policy scale. Table 3.4 summarizes the content of the five texts based on the categorization scheme developed for the hand-coding analysis. The content of the two Commission documents before (communication) and after the consultation (proposal) differs considerably: Whereas the communication contains "pro environmental control" sentences

Table 3.4 Hand-coding validity check

Overall Category	Commission 1		Commission 2		EP, Council, Commission		ADTS		VDA	
	Pro	Anti	Pro	Anti	Pro	Anti	Pro	Anti	Pro	Anti
Reduction target	7.3		17.4		18.52	11.11	5.3		0.3	10.9
Appropriateness of measure	28.0	2.0	26.1	8.7	11.11		5.3		0.3	55.8
Inclusion of vans	0.7			4.4						0.3
Code of good practice on car advertising	2.0									
Improved labeling to promote the purchase of fuel-efficient cars	3.3								0.3	
Fiscal measures to promote the purchase of fuel-efficient cars	10.0						5.3		0.3	0.3
Penalties to enforce CO$_2$ reductions	0.7		13.04		11.11				0.3	3.3
Efficiency improvements of tires	1.3				1.85					
Efficiency improvements of air conditioning	0.7				1.85					
Greater use of alternative fuels or automotive technology	2.7				11.11		73.7			
Long-term reduction strategy	5.3				5.56					
Averaging				4.4		16.67				2.6
Pooling				8.7						
Banking										2.0
Exceptions for small-scale manufacturers						1.85				
Exceptions for special purpose vehicles										
Weight as a parameter for calculating reduction targets				4.4						6.9
Inclusion of CO$_2$ reduction from cars in general Emissions Trading Regime	2.0	0.7	4.4						1.6	1.3
Monitoring									0.7	
Crediting										
Other	33.3		8.7		33.3		10.5		12.8	
Total no. of sentences (unit of analysis)	150		23		54		19		305	
Percentage of pro and anti sentences	64.0	2.7	60.9	30.4	61.11	29.63	89.5	0	3.9	83.3

on the inclusion of vans, a code of good practice on car advertising, improved labeling and fiscal measures to promote the purchase of fuel-efficient cars, efficiency improvement of tires and air conditionings, greater use of alternative fuels or technologies, and a long-term reduction strategy, the EP summary of the policy proposal does not contain any of these statements. By contrast, whereas the communication contains no "anti environmental control" sentences on the inclusion of vans, averaging, pooling and weight as a parameter for calculating reductions, the summary of the policy proposal contains statements in all of these categories. In total, whereas only 2.7 percent of the sentences in the communication were classified into "anti-environmental control" categories, 30.4 percent of the sentences in the EP summary of the policy proposal fall into the "anti environmental control" categories. Thus, just by looking at the allocation of sentences to the categories, one can conclude that the Commission moved towards the traditional automobile industry on the "anti environmental control" end of the policy scale during the policy formulation stage.

In terms of specific policy categories, the final legislative act somewhat differs from the proposal. Whereas the proposal contains no "pro" sentences on efficiency improvements for tires or air conditioning, on a greater use of alternative fuels and technologies, and on a long-term reduction target, these categories are all present in the final legislative act. By contrast, whereas the proposal contains no "anti" sentences on the reduction target, 11.11 percent of the sentences of the final act belong to this category. Similarly, only the proposal contains supporting statements for pooling whereas only the final act contains statements in favor of exceptions for small-scale manufacturers. When it comes to the overall share of "pro" and "anti" sentences, the final legislative act, however, closely resembles the policy proposal. While the proposal contains 60.9 percent "pro" sentences and 30.4 percent "anti" sentences, the final legislative act comprises 61.11 percent "pro" and 29.63 percent "anti" sentences. Thus, even though the emphasis of specific issues slightly changed over the course of bargaining process between the Council, the European Parliament, and the European Commission, the overall location of the final act in the policy space does not vary considerably from the location of the proposal. The demands of the traditional industry groups were taken up in terms of the timing of the reduction targets, but at the same time long-term reduction targets, penalties for exceeding CO_2 consumption, and efficiency improvements for tires and air conditioning were taken up in the final proposal as demanded by environmental groups and the alternative automobile industry.

The most "pro" text by ADTS strongly emphasizes the superiority of electric vehicles and, thus, devotes 73.7 percent of all sentences to the "pro" category on greater use of alternative fuels and engine technologies. If the Commission had taken into account the position of ADTS, one should observe a stronger emphasis of this topic in the final policy proposal. However, the share of sentences devoted to this category decreased from 2.7 percent in February to 0 percent in December. Hence, one can conclude that the Commission did not move towards the ideal point of ADTS. However, during the decision-making stage, the European institutions picked up this demand since 11.11 percent of the sentences in the final legislative act are devoted to this issue.

The German Automotive Manufacturers' Association, VDA, was successfully lobbying the European Commission during the policy formulation stage in various aspects: The VDA promotes averaging, calls for using weight as a parameter for calculating the reduction targets, and opts against the inclusion of vans. All of these demands were taken up by the Commission: Whereas the communication does not include any sentences on these topics, all categories are represented in the EP summary of the policy proposal. Moreover, the Commission not only changed the substance, but also its rhetoric: It devoted more than four times as many sentences to the "anti environmental control" category on the appropriateness of the suggested measures and, thereby, responded to the argumentation of the VDA which devoted 55.8 percent of all sentences to that category. During the decision-making stage, some of the demands by the VDA were dropped such as the inclusion of vans, but at the same time, the final legislative act introduces a transition period to meet the reduction targets as advocated by the VDA. In addition, it devotes about four times more sentences to the opportunity of averaging the reduction targets across the entire car fleet of a manufacturer as demanded by the VDA. In conclusion, one can ascertain that the policy proposal and the final legislative act are clearly closer to the ideal point of the VDA than the Commission communication and, thus, the policy position estimates obtained by hand-coding are confirmed by this validity check.

The manual hand-coding analysis leads to the following conclusions: Interest groups representing the traditional automobile industry are located on the "anti" environmental control side of the policy space and therefore oppose the Commission's initiative to reduce CO_2 emissions from cars. By contrast, alternative industry associations as well as environmental groups are located on the opposite end of the policy spectrum. They support the Commission proposal and even demand further measures to reduce CO_2 emissions from cars. During the policy formulation stage, the European Commission moved from the "pro" end to the "anti" end of the policy scale and thus towards the traditional automobile industry. The Council, the European Parliament, and the European Commission largely maintained this shift as the regulation closely resembles the policy proposal. In terms of influence, one can therefore conclude that whereas the traditional automobile industry was successful in lobbying the European institutions, the alternative industry associations as well as the environmental groups did not manage to pull the policy outcome towards their ideal points. Reliability and validity checks confirmed the policy position estimates.

3.4.2 *Wordfish*

In a second step, I analyzed the documents using *Wordfish*. In order to employ *Wordfish*, all the texts were preprocessed. The interest group and European institution documents were all in portable document format (*pdf*) and were first transformed into *txt* files which are the basis for the quantitative text analysis. I then removed symbols, unified British and American spelling, and transformed all words to lowercase. Since the documents used for the analysis need to be encyclopedic statements of the actors' policy positions, all text passages not directly referring to the policy issue in question were removed from the documents. Accordingly, contact details or self-descriptions of interest groups were eliminated manually from the texts. Then, interest group names were removed from each submission and spelling errors were corrected. As *Wordfish* requires a word frequency matrix as input for the analysis, the program *jfreq* (Lowe 2009a) was used to produce such a matrix. Using *jfreq*, stop words, numbers, and currencies were removed from the documents and the words were stemmed (reduced to their root). At last, following the recommendation of Proksch and Slapin (2009a,b), all stems that were only mentioned in 15 percent or less of the texts per policy issue were removed from the word matrix so that 675 unique stems remain for the analysis. Figure 3.2 plots the policy position estimates obtained by *Wordfish* together with a 95 percent confidence interval indicating the uncertainty of the estimates.

All traditional automobile industry groups are located closer to the "anti environmental control" end of the policy scale than the communication (COMM 1) issued by the European Commission. Four of the traditional automobile industry actors (ACEA, JAMA, VDA, VW) are also positioned closer to the "anti environmental control" end of the scale than the proposal (COMM 2) and the final legislative act (EP, COUNCIL, COMM). The remaining five traditional automobile industry actors (RAI, SMMT, GM, LTI, KAMA) are located between the communication on the one hand and the proposal and the final regulation on the other hand. By contrast, all alternative industry actors are located closer to the "pro environmental side" of the policy scale than the European institution positions. Germany is located closer to the "anti environmental control" side of the policy spectrum than the communication, the proposal, and the final act. By contrast, the UK and the Netherlands as well as the majority of the environmental groups are located closer to the "pro environmental control" side of the policy spectrum than

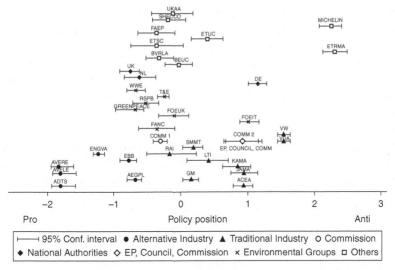

Fig. 3.2 *Wordfish* policy position estimates

the European institution positions. During the policy formulation stage, the Commission moved from a policy position of −0.30 (communication) to a policy position of 0.93 (proposal) towards Germany and the traditional automobile industry at the "anti environmental control" end of the policy scale. This shift is statistically significant since there is no overlap of confidence intervals. During the decision-making stage, the European institutions only marginally amended the proposal so that the final legislative act largely resembles the proposal in terms of its location in the policy space (0.92). This is confirmed by the overlap of confidence intervals of the proposal and the final act which indicates that there is no statistically significant difference between them. Thus, using *Wordfish* I also come to the conclusion that Germany and the traditional automobile industry were successful in pulling the European Commission towards their ideal point during the policy formulation stage and in maintaining this shift during the decision-making stage. By contrast, alternative industry associations, environmental groups, as well as the Netherlands and the UK could neither exert any influence during the policy formulation nor during the decision-making stage.

In order to check the validity of the *Wordfish* results, I examined the word parameters as recommended by Proksch and Slapin (2009*a,b*). As illustrated before, *Wordfish* estimates policy positions drawing on relative frequencies of single words. More specifically, *Wordfish* discriminates between policy positions of texts drawing on words weights (parameter β in the model). The higher the word weight, the more a word is responsible for the estimation of the text's policy position. Word fixed effects, by contrast, capture the fact that some words are used very often in general such as articles or conjunctions (parameter ψ in the model). Words with a high fixed effect should, thus, not discriminate between policy positions since all actors use them very frequently. By contrast, words which are mentioned very infrequently should carry more politically relevant meaning. These words should, thus, have very low word fixed effects and high positive or negative word weights. This expectation is confirmed by Figure 3.3 which plots the estimated word fixed effects against the word weights. The so-called "Eiffel Tower of Words" (Slapin and Proksch 2008) is approximately centered around a word weight of zero. Hence, words with high word fixed effects have very low word weights. Examples for such frequent stems with very high word fixed effects and low word weights are "vehicle," "car," and "CO_2" which are used very often in all 37 texts. Stems with high political connotation, by contrast, have very low word fixed effects and high positive or negative word weights. On the "pro environmental control" side of the policy scale, stems such as "zero-emiss," "batteri," or "warm" have very high negative word weights. On the "anti environmental control" side of the policy scale, stems such as "tire" and "resist" and "disadvantage" have very high positive word weights.

Using the keyword-in-context-function of the text analysis program *Yoshikoder* (Lowe 2009*b*), I examined the context in which words with high word weights are used (see table 3.5). The stem "zero-emiss" is employed by alternative industry associations and environmental groups to emphasize that hybrid vehicles and electric cars are much more environment-friendly than traditional cars. Similarly, the stem "urban" is used to illustrate the

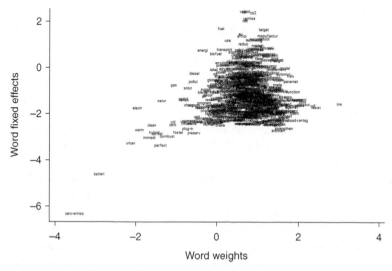

Fig. 3.3 Word weights vs. word fixed effects

Table 3.5 Top ten word weights and word fixed effects

Top ten word weights: Pro	Top ten word weights: Anti	Top ten word fixed effects
zero-emiss	tire	vehicl
batteri	resist	car
urban	roll	co2
electr	polit	emiss
warm	pressur	by
immedi	evalu	not
clean	segment	fuel
hybrid	basic	target
so-cal	disadvantag	eu
perfect	differenti	manufactur

advantages of electric vehicles over petrol-based cars in urban areas in terms of CO_2 efficiency. "Warm" is mainly used by environmental groups in the sense of "global warming" in order to point out the negative consequences of CO_2 emissions. "Electr" and "hybrid" are used mainly by alternative industry actors to emphasize the superiority of electric vehicles in terms of energy efficiency and CO_2 emissions. These stems therefore clearly capture that alternative industry associations and environmental groups support stricter environmental emission regulation on the European level.

By contrast, "tire" was used almost exclusively by automobile and tire manufactures when arguing against efficiency requirements for tires. Especially tire manufactures point out that tires are already very energy efficient and that only the mishandling of consumers causes higher energy use related to tires. "Disadvantag" was used by automobile manufactures to underline the negative repercussions of strict emission standards for the competitiveness of the European automobile industry on the world market. "Differenti" was used by ACEA as well as the VDA in order to argue for flexible reduction targets. The VDA, for instance, calls for a "differentiated approach that does justice to different vehicle classes." Thus, stems with a high word weight on the "anti" side of the environmental control scale clearly capture the intention of the automobile industry to promote more flexible reduction targets, thus allowing bigger cars to emit more CO_2 than smaller cars. In conclusion, words with high political connotation according to the estimated word weights clearly indicate distinct ideological positions.

The top ten words with high fixed effects, thus hardly discriminating between policy positions, also make sense substantially: The terms "vehicle," "car," "co2," and "emiss" clearly need to be employed by all actors, no matter whether they support or oppose the legislative initiative on CO_2 emission reduction. In conclusion, word weights are highest for words with strong political connotation and lowest for words with high word fixed effects. In

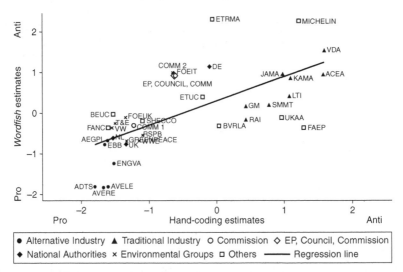

Fig. 3.4 Comparison of *Wordfish* and hand-coding policy position estimates

addition, stems with high word weights clearly indicate distinct ideological positions. Thus, the analysis of word weights and word fixed effects has demonstrated that *Wordfish* is correctly capturing the policy space.

In order to further check the validity of the *Wordfish* estimates, I cross-checked them with the policy position estimates obtained by hand-coding. Figure 3.4 plots the estimates together with a fitted regression line.[7] The estimates correlate highly ($r = 0.68$, $p \leq 0.001$) and therefore largely cross-validate each other. However, whereas both methods predict a clear move towards the "anti environmental control" end of the policy scale, hand-coding sees the communication, the legislative proposal, and the final regulation closer to the "pro" end of the policy scale. This difference could be due to the dichotomous categorization: A sentence is allocated either to a "pro" or to an "anti" environmental control category. This leads to a certain loss of information since ordinal differences cannot be captured. In theory, one could also use a more fine-grained categorization scheme. This would, however, increase the complexity and, thus, lead to lower reliability and higher coding costs.

In conclusion, the *Wordfish* policy position estimates provide a similar picture to the hand-coding analysis. Alternative industry associations as well as environmental groups are located on the "pro" side of the policy scale. By contrast, traditional industry associations are opponents of stricter

---

[7] The results of the ordinary least squares (OLS) regression are: $N = 37$, $R^2 = 0.47$, coefficient $= 0.79$, $p \leq 0.001$, standard error $= 0.14$.

environmental regulation which are located on the "anti" end of the policy space. This general pattern confirms the findings of the hand-coding analysis and the *Wordfish* and hand-coding estimates accordingly also correlate highly. It can therefore be concluded that hand-coding and *Wordfish* indeed arrive at essentially the same results even though hand-coding draws on human judgment to manually analyze documents whereas *Wordfish* estimates the policy positions based on relative word frequencies in texts.

3.4.3 *Wordscores*

As illustrated earlier, *Wordscores* requires the choice of reference texts as well as reference values that denote the policy positions of these texts. Whereas this is a rather easy task for party researchers since the CMP and numerous expert surveys provide independent measures that could be used, interest group research so far lacks empirical estimates of policy positions. There are no large empirical datasets that could be used for reference values of interest groups' policy positions. Even if there were estimates, it is questionable whether these would be useful: Interest groups usually represent very specific interests. However, even though one would assume stable preferences, the policy positioning of interest groups relative to others may vary from issue to issue. For instance, as discussed in section 2.4, Aguilar Fernández (1997, 105) found that German car manufacturers strongly rejected the introduction of speed limits and thus opposed environmental groups on this issue. On another issue, German manufacturers were, however, fighting for the mandatory imposition of catalytic converters together with environmental groups. Hence, if one wants to determine the degree of influence of an interest group, one has to estimate the policy positions for every single issue under consideration. One can thus already conclude that currently *Wordscores* constitutes no methodological tool to measure policy positions of interest groups across a large number of policy issues and interest groups.

However, what one can do using *Wordscores* is to cross-check the policy positions estimated by other approaches. In order to check the hand-coding and *Wordfish* estimates presented above, I used the documents with the most extreme policy positions at the "pro" and "anti" environmental control ends of the policy scale according to the hand-coding analysis as reference texts and their policy position estimates produced by hand-coding and *Wordfish* as reference values. However, the most "pro" environmental control document from ADTS comprises only 403 words. Since reference texts should contain as many words as possible (Laver, Benoit, and Garry 2003, 315), I collapsed the five most "pro" documents (ADTS, AVERE, EBB, AEGPL, AVELE) into a single document (6,614 words) and assigned the mean of their hand-coding

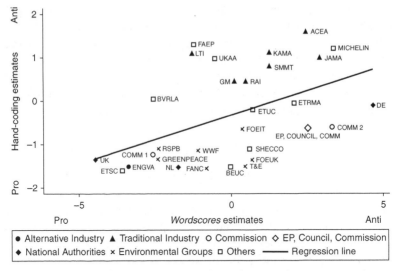

Fig. 3.5 Comparison of hand-coding and *Wordscores* policy position estimates

estimates weighted by the number of words of each text as its reference value. The most "anti" environmental control text, by VDA, comprises 7,272 words.[8]

In a first step, *Wordscores* was used to test the policy position estimates obtained by hand-coding. Figure 3.5 plots the policy position estimates derived from both methods together with a fitted regression line.[9] The majority of the traditional automobile industry organizations is again located on the "anti" environmental control side of the policy scale. Most of the environmental groups as well as the alternative industry associations are located on the "pro" environmental control end of the policy space. The Netherlands and the UK are also positioned closer to the "pro" environmental control than to the "anti" environmental control side of the policy scale. By contrast, Germany is located at the opposite side of the policy scale. Finally, as in the case of the preceding hand-coding and *Wordfish* analysis, the Commission moves from the "pro" end of the policy spectrum (COMM 1) to the "anti" side of the policy scale (COMM 2). Similarly, the position of the final regulation (EP, COUNCIL, COMM) that was adopted by the Council and the European Parliament is very close to the proposal, indicating that the traditional automobile industry was largely successful in maintaining their lobbying success during the decision-making stage. The location of the major actors thus confirms the results obtained by hand-coding and *Wordfish*. Accordingly, the policy

---

[8] Since VDA and VW submitted identical comments to the consultation, I did not include the VW text in the analysis because it would have received an extreme score.

[9] The OLS regression produced the following results: N = 30, $R^2 = 0.23$, coefficient = 0.22, $p \leq 0.01$, standard error = 0.08.

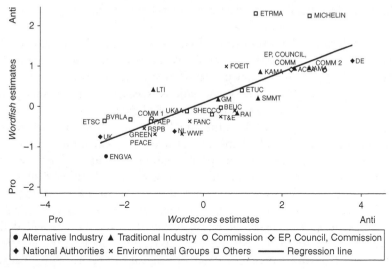

Fig. 3.6 Comparison of *Wordfish* and *Wordscores* policy position estimates

position estimates obtained by hand-coding and *Wordscores* correlate to a moderately high degree (r = 0.47, p ≤ 0.01). However, there is a lot of random noise: Only 23 percent of the variance of the hand-coding estimates can be explained by the *Wordscores* estimates.

In a second step, the policy position estimates derived by *Wordfish* were checked using *Wordscores*. The *Wordscores* estimates highly correlate with the *Wordfish* estimates (r = 0.78, p ≤ 0.001). To illustrate the comparison, figure 3.6 plots the policy position estimates generated by both methods together with a fitted regression line.[10] If we look closer at the location of the different actors, the *Wordfish* results are also largely confirmed by the *Wordscores* analysis: Most of the traditional automobile industry actors are located on the "anti" environmental control side of the policy scale. By contrast, most of the environmental groups as well as the alternative industry associations are positioned at the "pro" side of the policy space. The Netherlands and the UK are also placed closer to the "pro" side whereas Germany can be found at the "anti" side of the policy spectrum. During the policy formulation stage, the European Commission moved from the "pro" side of the policy scale towards the "anti" side of the scale. Thus, one can again clearly observe a move towards the "anti" end of the policy scale. Similarly, the final legislative act largely resembles the policy proposal which is indicated by the proximity of their locations in the policy space. Hence, it can be

---

[10] The OLS regression produced the following results: N = 30, R^2 = 0.61, coefficient = 1.61, p ≤ 0.001, standard error = 0.24.

concluded that the *Wordfish* results are largely validated by the *Wordscores* estimates.

In conclusion, the *Wordscores* analysis confirms the results of the hand-coding and the *Wordfish* analysis. Whereas the traditional automobile industry actors are located on the "anti" environmental control side of the policy space, alternative industry associations as well as environmental groups are located on the "pro" environmental control side. Similarly, whereas the Netherlands and the UK support the initiative of the European Commission, Germany opposes the enforcement of stricter CO_2 emissions. During the policy formulation stage, the European Commission moved from the "pro" environmental control side of the policy scale towards the "anti" environmental control side. This shift was maintained during the decision-making stage since the regulation adopted by the Council and the European Parliament largely resembles the policy proposal. It can therefore be concluded that the traditional automobile industry was successfully lobbying the European institutions. However, whereas the *Wordscores* results correlate to a high degree with the *Wordfish* results, they only correlate to a medium degree with the policy position estimates obtained by hand-coding.

3.5 CONCLUSION

The aim of this chapter was to introduce and test a new measurement approach to interest group influence. I have started by discussing existing approaches to interest group influence measurement of which the preference attainment technique has turned out to be most promising for the large-scale empirical analysis of interest group influence on European policy-making. The preference attainment approach compares policy preferences of interest groups with the policy output in order to draw conclusions about the winners and the losers of the decision-making process.

The measurement of policy preferences, however, still constitutes a big problem. Since party researchers have made great advances in preference measurement drawing on text analysis, I have discussed several text analysis approaches that could potentially be used for the measurement of interest group influence. I have then conducted a case study in which I compared the applicability of three widely used text analysis approaches for the measurement of policy positions. More specifically, I compared manual hand-coding, *Wordscores*, and *Wordfish*. The policy position estimates obtained by the three techniques correlate highly and therefore largely cross-validate each other.[11]

---

[11] While the three text analysis results highly correlate, there is still a considerable degree of noise given that ideal points are latent variables that are hard to quantify. In order to take

Hence, in theory, all three approaches are applicable to the study of interest group influence. However, one has to keep in mind that each approach has advantages but also disadvantages.

The big advantage of hand-coding is the in-depth knowledge of the content of the submissions and the high validity of the measurement. However, the reliability of the results is relatively low compared to computerized content analysis (Bakker, Edwards, and de Vries 2006; Mikhaylov, Laver, and Benoit 2012). Furthermore, hand-coding is very labor-intensive and time-consuming. Finally, political issues may sometimes be highly technical so that it might be difficult for researchers to understand the content, develop a classification scheme, and allocate the text units to the appropriate categories.

Wordscores has the advantage of being 100 percent replicable and, thus, reliability is not an issue. Furthermore, *Wordscores* allows for the analysis of large amounts of text in short periods of time. However, the usefulness of *Wordscores* for interest group research is limited: Independent policy position estimates are needed as reference values and, unfortunately, no large empirical datasets on the policy positions of interest groups are available yet.

Wordfish is also 100 percent replicable. So, again, reliability is not an issue. Moreover, *Wordfish* also allows for the quick analysis of large amounts of text without requiring reference values. This constitutes an enormous advantage for interest group research owing to the lack of independent policy position estimates. What is, however, often criticized is the lack of validity of computerized content analysis. But, as the case study has shown, the results obtained by *Wordfish* are largely confirmed by hand-coding, which is associated with high validity. So, the validity of the *Wordfish* estimates has also been demonstrated.

To sum up, all three methods offer certain advantages but also suffer from disadvantages. In order to assess interest group influence, hand-coding is only useful if one or just a few issues are studied since it is very time-consuming and cost-intensive. *Wordscores* provides no opportunity to measure interest group influence, at least currently, because reference values are not available. *Wordfish*, by contrast, can be easily applied to the measurement of interest group influence since it enables one to analyze large quantities of text without relying on reference values. Hence, in order to measure interest group influence

into account the measurement error associated with these point estimates, uncertainty estimates can be computed for all three techniques. However, while generalized linear measurement error models include the measurement error associated with independent variables in the estimation (e.g. using the STATA simex command), to my knowledge, there is currently no statistical package that allows for taking into account measurement error associated with the dependent variable. What is more, this book does not use the raw ideal point estimates for the dependent variable, but the dependent variable is computed based on the differences between a set of ideal point estimates (Interest group, Consultation draft, Proposal, Final act). Taking into account the uncertainty around all these estimates simultaneously is at least, to my knowledge, so far not implemented in any statistical package and it would also be extremely demanding in computational terms.

on a large empirical scale, *Wordfish* is clearly the most useful content analysis technique.

In the light of the findings of this case study, I will employ *Wordfish* to measure policy positions of interest groups in this book since it produces valid and reliable policy position estimates and since it allows one to quickly analyze large amounts of texts. *Wordfish* therefore enables me to study interest group influence across a wide variety of policy issues and interest groups. In the next chapter, I illustrate the practical implementation of this measurement approach across a large number of cases in further detail.

4

—————

Mapping European Union Lobbying

In order to explain why some interest groups succeed in influencing European policy-making whereas others fail in their lobbying attempts, chapter 2 has presented an exchange model that identified relative information supply, citizen support, and economic power of lobbying coalitions as the central determinants of interest group influence. As the lack of empirical studies on interest group influence is largely caused by methodological difficulties in measuring influence, chapter 3 has introduced and tested a new measurement approach to interest group influence. Using this approach, a large new dataset on interest group lobbying in the European Union has been constructed which is illustrated in detail in this chapter. I first explain the practical implementation of the new measurement approach to interest group influence across a large number of policy issues and interest groups. I then discuss how I selected the policy issues and interest groups for this study. Afterwards, the operationalization of the explanatory and control variables is laid out and summary statistics of all the variables used in this book are presented. Finally, the statistical model that is estimated to test the theoretical expectations is discussed.

4.1 MEASURING INTEREST GROUP INFLUENCE

Following the preference attainment approach discussed in section 3.1, interest group influence on policy-making in the European Union is measured by comparing the policy preferences of interest groups with the preliminary draft proposal, the official Commission proposal, and the final legislative act in order to draw conclusions about the winners and the losers of the policy-making process. Based on the results of the case study presented in the previous chapter, I decided to use *Wordfish* to measure policy preferences of interest groups. The case study has shown that the policy position estimates obtained by *Wordfish* highly correlate with the position estimates derived from hand-coding and

Wordscores and these three approaches therefore largely cross-validate each other. Due to the demonstrated validity of the *Wordfish* approach and its ability to analyze large quantities of texts without any prior knowledge about the documents, *Wordfish* provides an ideal opportunity for the large-scale measurement of policy positions and ultimately interest group influence.

In order to measure policy positions of interest groups, their submissions in online consultations of the European Commission were analyzed. Being aware that the submissions may reflect "strategic" rather than "true" policy positions (Frieden 2002; Thomson et al. 2006), this should not constitute a problem for the analysis for two reasons: First, since this study focuses on the policy positions that in fact have been transmitted to the European institutions, only transmitted policy positions—even if they over- or understate the "true" ideal policy positions—are taken into account by the legislators and therefore constitute the basis for the influence measurement. Second, it is unlikely that there is a systematic variation of strategically over- or understating preferences across all interest groups in the sample so that the revealed policy position can be taken as a proxy for the true policy position.

The Commission position before the consultation was extracted from the preliminary draft proposal in which the European Commission sets out its preliminary policy position on a given policy issue. The draft proposal can take various forms such as a Green or White Paper, a Communication or a Working Paper. It is a continuous political text which can be easily analyzed with *Wordfish*. The official Commission proposal and the final legislative act, however, have a predefined legal structure including an explanatory memorandum, a preamble, and the actual regulation or directive and they use very specific legal terminology. Due to this particular legal vocabulary, the official legislative proposal and the final act cannot be analyzed directly using *Wordfish*. I therefore draw on summaries of the proposal and the legislative act that are issued by the European Parliament in order to measure their policy positions.[1] These summaries express the same policy position as the actual proposal and legislative act as a hand-coded text analysis of official documents referring to one policy issue demonstrated: On a scale ranging from -100 to $+100$, the EP summary of the legislative proposal received a score of -30.43 whereas the preamble of the proposal scored -28.99. Similarly, the policy position of the final legislative act obtained by coding its EP summary is -31.48 whereas coding the preamble of the final act lead to a policy position estimate of -28.05 (see page 74). Since interest group submissions deal with the same policy issue as the European institution documents on any given policy issue, one can assume that all texts refer to the same policy dimension as required by *Wordfish*. I accordingly assume that policy issues are unidimensional. This

[1] These EP summaries can be downloaded from the European Parliament Legislative Observatory database which is publicly accessible at http://www.europarl.europa.eu/oeil/.

assumption should not constitute a problem for the analysis as the structure of conflict concerning a policy proposal is largely unidimensional. Once a draft proposal is on the table, the general outline of the legislative initiative is defined. Interest groups therefore operate within a clear framework in which they attempt to make the official legislative proposal and the final legislative act even more aggressive or to dilute it. This unidimensional structure of conflict is empirically supported by the findings of Baumgartner et al. (2009, 7) who discovered in an empirical analysis of lobbying in the US that interest groups are opposing each other on the same policy dimension.

Online consultations were introduced in 2000 and have become a regular instrument of consultation for major policy initiatives (European Commission 2002; Quittkat and Finke 2008; Quittkat 2011). Between 2000 and 2008, 554 online consultations were carried out thus providing researchers with a fruitful new data source (Quittkat 2011, 658). Based on a draft proposal which sets out the preliminary Commission position, interest groups have the opportunity to submit comments for an eight-week consultation period before the final policy proposal is decided upon.[2] Being aware that there are other channels for influencing the policy-making process, most interest groups trying to influence the policy outcome should be covered by the analysis since online consultations constitute the easiest form of access. As empirical research accordingly shows, a wide variety of actors indeed participates in online consultations, e.g. business associations, individual companies, and NGOs of international, European, national, and subnational origin (Quittkat and Finke 2008; Quittkat 2011). This is confirmed by an analysis of the submissions received during the consultations for the selected policy issues in this study which is presented later in this chapter. The sample of consultation participants comprises a wide variety of actors which is representative for the overall population of interest groups on the European level as discussed in the following section.

Even though I use online consultations in order to extract interest group preferences from their consultation submissions, I do not assume that consultations are the only channel through which interest groups seek to influence the policy-making process. They might additionally use a variety of inside and outside lobbying tactics such as participation in hearings, informal meetings with decision-makers, or protest activities. However, this does not constitute a problem for the analysis presented in this book as consultations merely serve as a data source for the measurement of interest group preferences. I measure interest group influence by comparing interest group preferences with the policy output without making any assumptions about the lobbying tactics interest groups employ. As influence is, by definition, observed by the convergence of the policy output with an interest group's

[2] Interest group comments are only published once the deadline for submissions has passed so that interest groups are not aware of the comments submitted by other actors when submitting their own response.

policy preference, the measurement approach covers influence that is exercised through a variety of channels. Thus, no matter which other strategies interest groups might use in order to lobby the European institutions, their impact is captured by the influence measurement as lobbying success is, by definition, associated with a convergence of the policy output with an interest group's preference (Dür 2008*c*, 567) (see also figure 1.1).

It is essential for the quality of a quantitative text analysis that the texts draw on a similar pool of words (Proksch and Slapin 2009*a*). It is for instance not possible to simultaneously analyze speeches and laws as the latter use a very specific legal terminology which is not comparable to the words used in speeches. The results of such a *Wordfish* analysis would therefore be seriously flawed. In order to check whether the vocabulary employed by the European institutions is similar to the words used by interest groups, I compared the vocabulary of the interest group and the European institution texts (see table 4.1). On average, 90.77 percent of the stems (words reduced to their roots) that are used in the draft proposal, the legislative proposal, as well as in the final legislative act also appear in the interest group documents. Hence, the vocabulary of the European institution texts is very similar to the vocabulary used in the interest group documents so that the two document types can be compared without concerns. It is therefore not problematic to simultaneously analyze interest group and official documents in the same *Wordfish* analysis.

In order to extract policy preferences from the interest group and official EU documents, the texts had to be preprocessed before running the *Wordfish* analysis. At first, all documents were transformed into *txt* files which is the appropriate format for quantitative text analysis. In a second step, a *PHP* script was applied to the texts in order to automatically remove symbols, to unify British and American spelling, and to transform all words to lowercase.[3] Before the texts could be analyzed using *Wordfish*, several manual modifications were moreover necessary: First, the documents used for the estimation of policy positions need to be encyclopedic statements of the actors' policy positions on a given issue. Accordingly, I manually removed all contact details and self-descriptions of interest groups as they do not express an interest group's policy position on a given policy issue. Second, in semi-standardized consultations interest groups sometimes repeat questions posed by the Commission word-by-word. Without removing these repetitions, these texts would automatically score closer to the Commission position than texts not repeating these questions. I therefore manually eliminated all word-by-word citations of the Commission's consultation paper from the interest group submissions. Third, interest group names were removed from their submissions as recommended by Proksch and Slapin (2009*b*) and all spelling errors were corrected. Fourth, drawing on the computer program *jfreq*,

---

[3] I thank Malte Klüver for assistance in writing the PHP script.

Table 4.1 Vocabulary used by European institutions and interest groups

Policy issue	All stems	Interest group stems	EU institution stems	Common stems
1	1757	1664	682	86.4%
2	1956	1892	519	87.7%
3	2150	2055	774	87.7%
4	2697	2660	423	91.3%
5	1006	975	213	85.5%
6	1351	1312	263	85.2%
7	1495	1361	668	79.9%
8	2268	2183	757	88.8%
9	950	903	271	82.7%
10	2172	2110	641	90.3%
11	3154	3143	400	97.3%
12	2985	2969	514	96.9%
13	3850	3840	611	98.4%
14	4086	4016	1462	95.2%
15	2943	2925	714	97.5%
16	1876	1793	641	87.1%
17	2887	2873	727	98.1%
18	3163	3034	1575	91.8%
19	3383	3348	867	96.0%
20	3290	3183	1229	91.3%
21	3823	3778	984	95.4%
22	2760	2733	654	95.9%
23	3020	2926	1033	90.9%
24	4071	4059	766	98.4%
25	4311	4303	926	99.1%
26	3138	3084	987	99.2%
27	2346	2314	480	93.3%
28	2514	2484	384	92.2%
29	4990	4948	1275	96.7%
30	2516	2240	1298	78.7%
31	3108	2830	1440	80.7%
32	2704	2662	687	93.9%
33	2501	2438	808	92.2%
34	3414	3400	575	97.6%
35	2315	2108	1161	82.2%
36	1849	1811	496	92.3%
37	1123	1028	457	79.2%
38	2512	2417	975	90.3%
39	2279	2136	947	84.9%
40	1926	1805	783	84.6%
41	1982	1922	580	89.7%
42	1255	1128	544	76.7%
43	1988	1917	667	89.4%
44	2262	2183	781	89.9%
45	2557	2539	434	81.8%
46	5366	5327	1333	97.1%
47	1287	1204	507	83.6%
48	2351	2318	525	93.7%
49	2624	2602	465	95.3%
50	2743	2579	1231	86.7%
51	2198	2173	466	94.6%
52	3332	3307	783	96.8%
53	3843	3917	881	97.1%
54	2483	2410	852	91.4%
55	3219	3178	830	95.1%
56	2000	1962	461	91.7%
Mean	2645	2579	757	90.8%

56 issue-specific word frequency matrices were created which are required as input for the *Wordfish* analysis (Lowe 2009*a*). Using *jfreq*, stop words, numbers, and currencies were additionally removed from the documents and the words were stemmed (reduced to their root). At last, all stems that were only mentioned in 15 percent or less of the texts per policy issue were removed from the word frequency matrices as advised by Proksch and Slapin (2009*a*).

Since identification in *Wordfish* is guaranteed by setting the mean of all policy positions to zero and the standard deviation to one, the total variance of policy positions is fixed so that absolute distances cannot be compared across different issues (see the detailed description of the *Wordfish* procedure in section 3.2.3). The absolute distance between interest groups automatically changes with the number of interest group submissions due to the *Wordfish* identification procedure. Hence, interest group influence cannot be measured by looking at the change in absolute distances between interest groups and the European institutions across different policy issues. However, one can simply circumvent this problem by drawing on a dichotomous coding of interest group influence: In line with the preference attainment approach, interest group influence is measured by assessing whether the distance between the policy positions of interest groups and the European institutions decreased over time.

Figure 4.1 illustrates the measurement approach. This book analyzes interest group influence during the policy formulation and the decision-making stage of the European policy-making process. The policy formulation stage begins with the preliminary draft proposal on which basis the European Commission launches a public consultation. This stage ends with the adoption of the official legislative proposal which at the same time marks the beginning of the decision-making stage. During this stage, the Council, the European Parliament, and the European Commission negotiate the design of the final legislative act. The numerical values indicate the policy positions of the draft

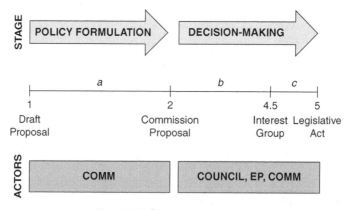

Fig. 4.1 Influence measurement

proposal, the Commission proposal, and the legislative act as well as the policy preferences of the interest group on a given policy dimension. The reference point for the assessment of interest group influence is the preliminary draft proposal as it marks the beginning of the legislative process and therefore sets the agenda for the legislative debate. Interest groups would prefer every policy outcome that is closer to their ideal point than the preliminary draft proposal. The interest group in figure 4.1 is considered to be influential during the policy formulation stage as it was successful in pulling the official Commission proposal closer to its ideal point than the preliminary draft proposal since b is smaller than $a + b$. As the final legislative act is also located closer to the policy preference of the interest group than the preliminary draft proposal since c is smaller than $a + b$, the interest group is also regarded to be influential during the decision-making stage. If one is only interested in the impact of interest group pressure during the decision-making stage, one could potentially choose the Commission proposal as the reference point for the influence analysis. Using this reference point, the interest group would be considered influential during the decision-making stage as c is smaller than b. The results of the empirical analysis are substantially the same no matter whether the draft proposal or the legislative proposal are taken as the reference point. I therefore only present the results based on the draft proposal as the reference point for the influence assessment.

In addition to the validity test of the position measurement conducted in the case study in the previous chapter, I further examined the validity of the *Wordfish* analysis by cross-checking it with information provided by interest groups. One common approach to measure interest group influence is to ask interest groups themselves to report how influential they have been on a specific policy issue (e.g. Dür and De Bièvre 2007a; Mahoney 2007a, 2008; Baumgartner et al. 2009). However, self-reported influence is problematic since it rests on the subjective assessment of interest group leaders and is subject to misleading incentives. I therefore opted not to draw on self-evaluation of interest group influence as a means to cross-validate the results. By contrast, I asked interest groups to name one major opponent and the five most important cooperation partners on the policy issue in question.[4] The information on opponents and cooperation partners was used to check the location of interest groups in the policy space as estimated by *Wordfish*. As the questions referred to the policy formulation stage, the reference point for the location of cooperation partners and opponents is the initial Commission position as reflected in the preliminary draft proposal. If the *Wordfish* estimation is correct, the cooperation partners should be located on the same side of the initial policy position of the European Commission

---

[4] The actual survey questions were: "Was there any interest group or company that had opposing views to you?" and "Could you please provide the names of your five most important cooperation partners on this policy issue?"

Table 4.2 *Wordfish* validity test

Wordfish Estimation	Frequency	Percent
Correct	276	79.54
Incorrect	56	16.14
Ambiguous	15	4.32
Total	347	100.00

whereas the opponents should be located on the opposing side. If the majority of the cooperation partners and opponents is positioned on the correct side of the initial policy position of the European Commission, the *Wordfish* estimation was coded as being correct. If the same number of actors is located on the right and wrong side of the European Commission, the *Wordfish* estimation was coded as being ambiguous. If the majority of actors is located on the wrong side of the European Commission, the *Wordfish* estimation was coded as being incorrect. Out of 347 cases in which opponents and cooperation partners were reported, 79.54 percent were estimated correctly and only 16.14 percent were coded incorrectly (see table 4.2). Hence, the survey data on cooperation partners and opponents strongly support the validity of the *Wordfish* measurement.

In order to check the robustness of the policy position estimation, I conducted further *Wordfish* analyses for word matrices after removing stems that were only mentioned in 10 percent of the texts per issue and for word matrices after removing stems that were only mentioned in 20 percent of the texts per issue. In addition, I performed further analyses after the two most extreme texts at both ends of the policy scale per issue were dropped from the word frequency matrix. The results correlate highly and the policy position estimation is therefore robust to changes in the word frequency matrix.

4.2 SELECTION OF POLICY ISSUES AND INTEREST GROUPS

After having illustrated in detail how interest group influence was operationalized, this section explains how the policy issues and interest groups were selected for this study. The selection of policy issues and interest groups follows a two-stage procedure: I first selected a number of policy proposals and then selected interest groups which participated in Commission consultations preceding the adoption of the selected proposals. The unit of analysis is the lobbying event, defined as the lobbying activity of an interest group concerning a specific policy issue. Hence, an interest group that lobbies on more than one of the selected policy issues appears several times in the dataset. In the following, I first explain how I arrived at the sample of policy issues and I then illustrate the selection of interest groups.

4.2.1 Selection of policy issues

In order to examine possible variation in interest group influence across issues, this book analyzes interest group influence across a wide variety of policy issues. Previous studies on interest group influence on policy-making in the European Union typically focused on one or just a few policy issues (e.g. Cowles 1995; Pollack 1997b; Warleigh 2000; Michalowitz 2007; Woll 2007, 2008). Although case studies provide high internal validity and are well suited for checking rival theories and for generating new hypotheses, the generalizability of the findings is limited. Partly as a result of analyzing one or just a few distinct policy issues, these studies offer a multitude of hypotheses and are characterized by contradictory findings (see also Dür 2008b). Focusing on one or just a few policy issues particularly does not allow for taking into account the effect of issue-related factors such as salience, conflict, or complexity of the policy issue (for an exception, see Mahoney 2007a, 2008; Klüver 2011). To overcome these shortcomings of the literature and to test the hypotheses derived from the theoretical model, this book therefore analyzes interest group influence across a wide variety of policy issues.

In order to select policy issues for a policy-making analysis, one can choose from two different selection procedures. The first procedure is selecting policy issues according to specific criteria (e.g. Thomson et al. 2006; Thomson 2011). This procedure allows one to pick policy issues that meet certain requirements which are of interest for the purpose of the study. The second procedure is randomly selecting a number of policy issues from the entire population of proposals. Even though this strategy leads to a representative subsample of policy proposals, random sampling has several disadvantages: Taking a simple random sample of EU level legislation results in a lot of highly technical policy proposals of minor political importance that caused only little controversy among interest groups. Moreover, simply randomly sampling from the entire population of policy proposals leads to the inclusion of a lot of proposals for legislation which are not legally binding.

In order to avoid the above-mentioned problems, the selection of policy issues is based on four criteria: time period, type of legislation, type of legislative procedure, and whether a consultation was conducted prior to the adoption of the policy proposal. First, in terms of time period, I selected policy proposals that were adopted between 01.01.2000 and 31.12.2008 (Quittkat 2011). I chose this time period since online consultations were introduced in 2000 and since this relatively short period allows interest group representatives to recall their lobbying activities surrounding specific policy issues. This is important in order to be able to question interest groups about their cooperation partners and opponents concerning a policy initiative (see page 99).

Second, in order to control for the impact of policy issues, I only focused on general binding legislation and therefore only directives and regulations were selected for the study. Directives are binding on the member states as to the result to be achieved, but member states can choose the form and method they adopt to realize the objective of the directive. Hence, member states have to transpose the directive into national law. Regulations by contrast are directly applicable which means that they create legislation that takes immediate effect in all the member states. Regulations therefore do not require transposition into national law. Proposals for decisions and recommendations were not included in the analysis as the former are directed at very specific recipients and the latter are not legally binding.

Third, in order to control for the mode of decision-making, I only selected policy proposals which are subject to the Codecision or Consultation procedure. These are the most important legislative procedures in the European Union. The Consultation procedure requires that the European Parliament is consulted before the Council votes on the Commission proposal. The Council is, however, not bound by the Parliament's opinion. By contrast, the Codecision procedure, which was introduced by the Treaty of Maastricht, puts the Council and the European Parliament on an equal footing. If the Council and the Parliament disagree about a Commission proposal, a Conciliation Committee made up of representatives of the two institutions has to arrive at a consensus. The Council cannot adopt legislation without the consent of the European Parliament.

Fourth, I only selected policy proposals for which the European Commission has carried out a consultation. Using consultations as a selection criterion offers two major advantages: First, as the Communication on minimum standards on consultation states, the Commission only consults on "major" policy initiatives (European Commission 2002). The European Commission considers policy issues as "major" if "the proposal will result in substantial economic, environmental and/or social impact on a specific sector," if "the proposal will have a significant impact on major interested parties," and if "the proposal represents a major policy reform in one or several sectors" (European Commission 2002, 15). By drawing solely on policy issues for which the Commission has conducted a consultation, one can therefore focus on policy issues that are politically important and that raised a minimum amount of attention and controversy (for proposal selection according to political importance, see also Thomson et al. 2006). Highly technical issues that are only of minor political importance and that raised little controversy could therefore be avoided. Focusing on policy issues that were preceded by consultations, however, still allows for extensive variance in terms of scope, importance, salience, and conflict of policy issues. For instance, the sample contains highly politically important and far-reaching proposals such as the so-called "health check" proposal that reforms the entire common agricultural policy, but it also contains issues of minor political importance such as the proposal on blind spot mirrors for trucks (see pages 119–122 and section 5.1. for further information about variation across issues). The second major advantage of only choosing policy proposals which have been preceded by stakeholder consultations is the availability of textual data for the influence measurement.

I used the European Union database *PreLex* to produce a list of all Commission proposals for regulations and directives adopted under the Codecision and Consultation procedure between 01.01.2000 and 31.12.2008. Since not every Directorate General (DG) conducted online consultations, I only focused on those having used consultations and whose competence concerns a substantial policy field (n = 19). Due to a lack of competence in a substantial policy field, policy proposals by the Secretariat General were therefore excluded. Between 01.01.2000 and 31.12.2008 these DGs proposed 991 regulations and directives subject to the Consultation and the Codecision procedure. I looked at all these proposals to determine whether an online consultation was conducted during its elaboration by drawing on internet research and the DemoCiv (Democratic Legitimacy via Civil Society Involvement) database kindly provided by Beate Kohler, Christine Quittkat, and Barbara Finke.[5]

In total I identified 162 policy proposals which meet the above-mentioned selection criteria. However, not all of these can be used for the analysis: 41 policy proposals were excluded since the consultations were conducted in a standardized format with given questions and answers and thus textual data are not available. Moreover, 51 policy proposals had to be excluded since the interest group submissions to the preceding consultations were not publicly accessible.[6] I excluded two further policy issues since less than ten submissions were received during the consultations. These two policy issues were excluded for substantial and methodological reasons. Substantially, these issues are not particularly interesting since they raised hardly any response or controversy among interest groups. Methodologically, these issues are problematic since the reliability of *Wordfish* estimates diminishes as the number of texts decreases (Proksch and Slapin 2009*a*). Furthermore, six policy proposals had to be excluded since the Commission did not release any prior position paper and

[5] The DemoCiv database was constructed by the research project on "Democratic Legitimacy via Civil Society Involvement? The Role of the European Commission" conducted by Beate Kohler, Christine Quittkat, and Barbara Finke at the Mannheim Centre for European Social Research.

[6] I submitted an official request to access the unpublished consultation submissions from the European Commission. My request was, however, treated very slowly and the Commission was not very cooperative. Considering time constraints, I therefore concentrate on the published consultations.

five policy issues had to be excluded for other reasons.[7] Thus, 57 policy proposals remain for the analysis.

One of the issues, the policy proposal on "Registration, Evaluation, and Authorization of Chemicals" (REACH) which was adopted by the Commission in October 2003 after extensive stakeholder consultation, raised an extremely high amount of attention. Around 6,000 submissions were received during this single online consultation (Persson 2007). This policy debate constitutes an extraordinary case due to the enormous public attention. As a result, the assumption of unit homogeneity is violated and causal inferences can therefore not be made (King, Keohane, and Verba 1994, 93). In addition, the analysis of this single issue would consume more resources than all other 56 issues together. Due to the violation of the unit homogeneity assumption and given the vast amount of resources needed to analyze this debate, the REACH consultation was excluded from the analysis. Hence, this book analyzes interest group influence on 56 policy proposals. In order to analyze interest group influence during the decision-making stage, the policy proposals had to be officially adopted by the Council and the European Parliament before 31.12.2010 in order to be included in the sample. Out of the 56 selected policy proposals, 42 were adopted within this time frame. Accordingly, the empirical analysis of interest group influence during the policy formulation stage is based on 56 policy issues whereas the analysis of interest group influence during the decision-making stage is based on 42 issues. Section 5.1 provides a detailed overview of the policy issues analyzed in this book.

4.2.2 Selection of interest groups

The second step in the data selection process concerns the selection of interest groups. In the consultations which preceded the adoption of the 56 policy proposals, the European Commission received 4,871 submissions from a wide variety of stakeholders (see table 4.3). I classified all stakeholders that submitted comments to the consultations into nine groups: associations (2,643), companies (775), national public authorities (746), individuals (282), researchers (187), international organizations (55), third states (57), political parties (8), and others (118). In order to keep the workload manageable, I

---

[7] One regulation was excluded since it constitutes a mere recodification of already existing legislation. One directive and one regulation were excluded since they only implement an already signed international convention into European law. Two further issues had to be excluded since the consultation was not based on one single, but on several consultation papers. Interest groups therefore respond to different sub-issues based on the different consultation documents. Thus, it is not possible to determine one single policy dimension using quantitative text analysis.

Table 4.3 Submissions to consultations

Total number of submissions		4,871		100.00%
Associations		2,643		54.26%
Companies		775		15.91%
National authorities		746		15.32%
Individuals		282		5.79%
Researchers		187		3.84%
International organizations		55		1.13%
Third states		57		1.17%
Political parties		8		0.00%
Others		118		2.42%
Sample for analysis	Policy formulation		Decision-making	
Total number	3,202	100.00%	2,131	100.00%
Associations	2,043	63.80%	1,324	62.13%
Companies	653	20.39%	469	22.01%
National authorities	506	15.80%	338	15.86%

only concentrated on associations, companies, and national public authorities.[8] Previous studies have shown that associations and companies are the most active lobbying actors at the European level (e.g. Coen 1997, 1998; Berkhout and Lowery 2008; Wonka et al. 2010) and that they also constitute the biggest groups participating in online consultations (Quittkat and Finke 2008; Quittkat 2011). Comments by national authorities were analyzed in order to control for policy positions of member states.

Since *Wordfish* only works with texts in the same language and with a minimum amount of words, non-English submissions (n = 899) and submissions with less than 100 words (n = 63) were furthermore excluded. Accordingly, 3,202 documents remain for the analysis of which 506 comments are authored by national authorities and 2,696 are submitted by interest groups. Since the European institutions have not adopted legislative acts for all of the 56 selected policy issues during the time frame of the analysis, the sample decreases to 2,131 documents for the decision-making stage out of which 1,793 are authored by interest groups. The distribution of comments across actor types in the policy formulation (n = 3,202) and the decision-making sample (n = 2,131) is fairly similar to the distribution of comments across actor types in the total number of submissions (n = 4,871). Hence, in terms of actor type there is no evidence for selection bias caused by non-English or short submissions. Similarly, as the distribution across actor type is nearly identical in the policy formulation and the decision-making sample, there is also no

[8] National public authorities mainly constitute national ministries that expressed their views on the envisaged policy initiative. These submissions constitute the basis for the measurement of member state positions as discussed in section 4.3.2.

indication for a selection bias induced by legislative proposals that have not been adopted within the time frame of this analysis. Section 5.2 provides a detailed overview of the interest groups studied in this book.

4.3 OPERATIONALIZATION OF INDEPENDENT VARIABLES

In this section, I thoroughly explain the operationalization of the independent variables. In order to measure the explanatory and control variables, several data sources were combined (for an overview of the operationalization, see table 4.12). Data on interest group characteristics were gathered by examining interest group submissions to Commission consultations, by coding the websites of interest groups which participated in the selected consultations, and by conducting a survey of these interest groups. Lobbying coalitions were identified according to the issue-specific alignment of interest groups and the European Commission in the policy space. Data on lobbying coalition characteristics were obtained by aggregating the properties of interest groups that belong to the same coalitions. Issue characteristics were measured drawing on the *EurLex* and *PreLex* databases of the European Commission, on the legislative proposals, and on text analysis of the consultation submissions. In the following, I first illustrate how I measured the explanatory variables information supply, citizen support, and economic power of lobbying coalitions. I then proceed to the measurement of control variables. The section concludes with summary statistics of all the specified variables.

4.3.1 Operationalization of explanatory variables

Information supply, citizen support, and economic power of lobbying coalitions were measured in two steps: Information supply, citizen support, and economic power were first measured on the individual interest group level and then aggregated according to the grouping into lobbying coalitions. I therefore first explain how I operationalized them on the interest group level before illustrating their measurement on the coalition level.

Information supply was measured by the number of words of interest group submissions to the online consultations (see also Klüver 2012). One could argue that the pure number of words only captures the quantity of information, but not its quality. In theory, a very long submission could merely contain information that is useless to the European institutions whereas a short submission might contain information which is very important to the Commission, the Council, and the EP. It is, however, very difficult to empirically assess the quality of information. There is no objective measure that one can rely on in order to measure the quality of information. Hence, any attempt to assess information quality would be based on subjective evaluation and is therefore difficult to justify. Subjective evaluation is likely to vary extensively across different individuals so that reliability of the measurement is therefore hard to achieve. I consequently decided to stick to the number of words as a proxy for the amount of information provided to the European institutions. However, several document preparation measures applied to the texts for the *Wordfish* analysis improve the accuracy of this proxy. These text analytic measures include removing text from the submissions that carries no substantial meaning, more specifically the removal of stopwords such as articles and prepositions as well as all text passages that do not directly convey information to the European institutions such as repetitions of consultation questions or contact details of the interest groups. I then created a word frequency matrix and took the sum of words per text as a measure for the number of words per interest group submission. I checked the validity of this indicator qualitatively in the case study presented in the previous chapter. It indeed turns out that long submissions in general contain much more expertise, technical know-how, and political information about stakeholder preferences than short consultation submissions.

The distribution of absolute information supply across interest groups is illustrated in table 4.4. The vast majority of interest groups supplies up to 1,000 words to the European institutions. This is similar across actor type: About 66 percent of the associations and 64 percent of the companies provided up to 1,000 words in the consultation. The distribution of information supply is highly skewed to the right since the mass of the distribution is concentrated at values of up to 1,000 words and since only very few interest groups supply more than 2,000 words. The distribution of information supply across interest groups is fairly similar in the policy formulation and decision-making sample of interest groups.

Table 4.4 Information supply by interest groups

Information supply	Policy formulation		Decision-making	
	Associations (N = 2,043)	Companies (N = 653)	Associations (N = 1,324)	Companies (N = 469)
up to 1,000 words	66.08%	63.71%	68.58%	61.83%
more than 1,000, up to 2,000 words	21.83%	20.52%	21.15%	19.40%
more than 2,000, up to 3,000 words	7.15%	7.81%	6.80%	8.74%
more than 3,000, up to 4,000 words	2.64%	3.83%	2.27%	4.48%
more than 4,000 words	2.30%	4.13%	1.21%	5.54%
Total	100.00%	100.00%	100.00%	100.00%

Citizen support and economic power were measured by an online survey of the interest groups which participated in the selected consultations. Since online consultations are published on the website of the European Commission and participants are indicated, I developed a list of all associations and companies that submitted contributions. Based on this list, I constructed a dataset in which all interest groups that participated in the 56 consultations are listed once. I term this the "interest group population dataset." The "hierarchical lobbying dataset" by contrast contains interest groups as many times as they participated in the consultations. Hence, an interest group which participated in four different consultations would appear once in the interest group population dataset and four times in the hierarchical lobbying dataset. All together, 1,893 unique interest groups appear in the interest group population dataset while the number of observations in the hierarchical lobbying dataset amounts to 2,696. The interest group population dataset serves as a sampling frame for the survey as it identifies the target population of all interest groups that participated in the consultations prior to the adoption of the selected policy proposals.

In order to carry out the online survey, I checked the submissions and websites of all 1,893 interest groups for email addresses and contact details that were needed to invite these groups to participate in the survey. The survey was conducted in a web format which offers considerable practical advantages, e.g. it is cost and time-efficient, it enables easy data processing as well as administration, and it facilitates follow-ups (Evans and Mathur 2005). In order to implement the web survey, the software *Unipark* was used.[9]

The questionnaire is composed of two parts: The first part comprises questions on permanent interest group characteristics such as membership structure or organizational features. The second part contains eight questions on issue-related variables which were repeated for every consultation in which an interest group participated. I programmed filters for the online questionnaire so that interest groups which only took part in one consultation answered the first part of the questionnaire plus eight questions on the consultation in which they participated. By contrast, an interest group which participated in five consultations answered the first part of the questionnaire plus forty questions on the five consultations in which it took part. I generated a dummy variable that indicates in which of the 56 consultations interest groups participated. The dummy variable is coded "1" if an interest group submitted a response in a consultation and is coded "0" if the interest group did not participate in a consultation. On the basis of this dummy variable, the questionnaire filter was triggered automatically so that interest groups only received issue-specific questions for the consultations in which it participated. Since a variety of questions differed between associations and companies, I programmed two different questionnaires, one for associations

---

[9] The survey software is available at http://www.unipark.info.

and one for companies (see appendices 1 and 2). For the final data analysis, I then combined the two datasets into one single dataset on interest group characteristics.

In order to make it as easy as possible for respondents to fill in the questionnaire, I mostly refrained from using open questions and instead used closed questions with given answer categories so that respondents simply had to tick the appropriate category. Most questions were measured on a five-point ordinal scale which allows for enough variation necessary for the final data analysis and at the same time does not overburden the cognitive abilities of respondents (Cox 1980). In the final analysis, these variables were treated as if they were measured on interval level which is a common procedure in survey research (for an overview, see Borgatta and Bohrnstedt 1980; Kampen and Swyngedouw 2000). Some questions were directly measured on a five-point interval scale for which only value labels for the endpoints of the scales were indicated (see also Porst 2008, 73). In order to avoid non-responses due to refusal to answer sensitive questions (e.g. questions referring to the budget of interest groups), these questions were placed at the end of the questionnaire so that interest groups which reject answering these questions would have at least answered all the previous questions before and would not be lost entirely for the survey.

The survey was conducted in the following way: At first, a pretest of the questionnaire was carried out. Two (former) employees of interest groups as well two interest group researchers were asked to fill in and review the questionnaires.[10] After a thorough review of the questionnaires, an email announcing the launch of the survey and providing background information about the research project was sent to the interest groups. Among other things, interest groups were assured that the responses would be treated confidentially and it was emphasized that their participation was crucial for the success of the research project. One week later, the interest groups received the actual invitation email with a link to the online questionnaire. Where possible, the emails were sent directly to the General Directors of the associations and the Governmental Affairs Directors of companies respectively. In order to tackle the problem of non-response, six reminders were sent to the interest groups in which I kindly asked them again to fill in the questionnaire. The survey was launched in June 2009 and was online until January 2010. The response rate can be calculated in two different ways: First, based on the interest group population dataset which includes every interest group only once, the overall response rate was 38.67 percent, with 43.98 percent of associations and 25.37 percent of the companies participating in the survey. Second, based on the hierarchical lobbying dataset which includes an interest group as many times as it participated in the 56 selected consultations, the overall response rate is 43.40

---

[10] I thank Irina Michalowitz, Tosca Bruno van Vijfeijken, Christine Mahoney, and Beate Kohler for reviewing the questionnaires.

Table 4.5 Survey response rate

	Interest group population dataset	Hierarchical lobbying dataset
Total response rate	38.67%	43.40%
Response rate among associations	43.98%	48.80%
Response rate among companies	25.37%	26.49%
Total population	N = 1,893	N = 2,696

percent with 48.80 percent of associations and 26.49 percent of companies participating in the survey (see table 4.5).[11]

Citizen support was operationalized by the number of represented individuals while *economic power* was measured by the annual turnover and the number of employees of the company and the represented business sector respectively (see table 4.6 for the precise question wording). The number of represented individuals was chosen as an indicator for citizen support as it reflects the number of citizens that an interest group could potentially mobilize for its cause. It therefore provides a heuristic for the European institutions which they use in order to assess the number of potential voters that an interest group represents. The annual turnover and the number of employees were chosen as indicators for economic power as they provide the European institutions with information about the potential impact an interest group can have on overall economic performance. For instance, the European Automobile Manufacturers Association (ACEA) represents the European car industry that employs about 12 million people and that has an annual turnover of over € 500 billion.[12] The European institutions are therefore particularly attentive to the demands raised by ACEA as it represents one of the most important, if not *the* most important industry in Europe and its well-being is crucial for the overall economic performance. I refrained from using market share within a sector as an indicator since it provides information about the ability to alter the market price of a good or service, but it does not convey information about how important an interest group is for the overall state of the economy and the reelection chances of decision-makers.

The indicators for citizen support and economic power were measured on a five-point ordinal scale. In order to provide questions with adequate scales to associations and companies, the category values for companies were lower than those for associations. For instance, the question concerning the number of employees only ranges from "up to 10,000" (category 1) to "more than 500,000" (category 5) in the company questionnaire whereas it ranges from "up to

---

[11] This is a reasonable response rate in interest group research that resembles the survey response rate of other interest group studies (e.g. Hojnacki 1998; Eising 2007a; Dür and Mateo 2009; Klüver 2010).

[12] Source: http://www.acea.be.

Table 4.6 Survey questions for the measurement of citizen support and economic power (association questionnaire)

Variable	Question
Citizen support	How many individuals are members of your organization (and its member organizations)? 0 – 0 1 – up to 10,000 2 – more than 10,000, up to 100,000 3 – more than 100,000, up to 1 million 4 – more than 1 million, up to 5 million 5 – more than 5 million
Economic power	What is the annual revenue of the sector you represent on average? 0 – 0 EUR 1 – up to 10 billion EUR 2 – more than 10 billion, up to 50 billion EUR 3 – more than 50 billion, up to 100 billion EUR 4 – more than 100 billion, up to 500 billion EUR 5 – more than 500 billion EUR How many people does the sector that you represent employ? 0 – 0 1 – up to 50,000 2 – more than 50,000, up to 100,000 3 – more than 100,000, up to 500,000 4 – more than 500,000, up to 1 million 5 – more than 1 million

50,000" (category 1) to "more than 1 million" in the association questionnaire. In order to arrive at one single measure for these variables, I recoded the company categories into the association categories after completion of the survey. Since category 5 was open and it was therefore unclear in which association category these companies should be coded, I conducted internet research to find out the exact value and accordingly coded these companies.

In order to compute one single measure for economic power, I performed a principal component factor analysis using the varimax rotation (see table 4.7) based on the two indicators "annual revenue" and "number of employees." The results of the factor analysis confirm that both indicators measure the same latent underlying factor. According to the Kaiser criterion, which suggests that factors should have an Eigenvalue higher than 1.0, both indicators measure the same latent variable. Correspondingly, the factor loadings of both indicators are very high which also indicates the existence of one underlying factor. I then computed principal component factor scores which directly measure the underlying latent variable and which range from −0.868 to 2.255. I also generated an additive index which simply sums the values of the indicators and divides the sum by the number of indicators. The additive index ranges

Table 4.7 Factor analysis of economic power

Indicator	Factor loading
Annual revenue	0.921
Number of employees	0.921
N	398
Eigenvalue	1.695
Explained variance	84.77%

from 1 to 5 similarly to the indicators. Since the additive index correlates at 0.999 with the principal component factor score, I draw on the index since it allows for easier and more intuitive interpretation as it has the same empirical range as its two indicators.

Table 4.8 presents the distribution of citizen support across associations. By definition, companies do not enjoy any citizen support as they do not have any members and therefore do not represent any individual citizens. The biggest share of associations (about 43 percent) represents up to 10,000 individuals while the rest of the associations are spread relatively evenly across the different categories. The distribution of citizen support across interest groups is nearly identical in the policy formulation and the decision-making sample of interest groups.

Table 4.9 summarizes the economic power of interest groups in the sample. There is a rather big difference in the distribution of economic power across actor types. Whereas economic power of associations is distributed quite evenly across the different categories, most of the companies in the sample only have a very low degree of economic power at their disposal. This is, however, not very surprising as business associations gather a wide variety of companies and their economic power reflects the aggregated economic power of all their member companies. The distribution of economic power is fairly similar across

Table 4.8 Citizen support of interest groups

Citizen support	Policy formulation Associations (N = 432)	Decision-making Associations (N = 267)
up to 10,000	43.06%	41.95%
more than 10,000, up to 100,000	13.43%	12.73%
more than 100,000, up to 1 million	16.67%	16.85%
more than 1 million, up to 5 million	12.04%	13.11%
more than 5 million	14.81%	15.36%
Total	100.00%	100.00%

Table 4.9 Economic power of interest groups

Economic power	Policy formulation		Decision-making	
	Associations (N = 451)	Companies (N = 143)	Associations (N = 293)	Companies (N = 96)
Very low	25.94%	62.24%	26.62%	58.33%
Low	19.51%	20.28%	19.45%	22.92%
Medium	19.07%	16.78%	18.09%	17.71%
High	13.75%	0.70%	14.68%	1.04%
Very high	21.73%	0.00%	21.16%	0.00%
Total	100.00%	100.00%	100.00%	100.00%

interest groups in the policy formulation and the decision-making sample indicating no bias induced by missing policy issues in the latter sample.

As lobbying takes place concerning specific policy issues, information supply, citizen support, and economic power of individual interest groups have to be measured in relation to other interest groups lobbying the EU institutions on the same issues. To illustrate the measurement of relative interest group characteristics using information supply as an example, imagine the following scenario: On a given policy issue, four interest groups A, B, C, and D are lobbying the European institutions. Interest group A provides 5,000 words, interest group B provides 2,000 words, interest group C provides 1,000 words, and interest group D provides 2,000 words. The overall amount of information received by the European institutions amounts to 10,000 words. The relative information information supply z_A by interest group A is then computed by dividing the absolute amount of information x_A provided by interest group A (5,000 words) by the total amount of information supplied by all four interest groups (10,000 words) and multiplying it by 100. For interest group A, the relative information supply accordingly amounts to 50 percent. The values for relative information supply for individual interest groups range from 0 to 100 and the sum of the values for all interest groups lobbying the European institutions on the same policy issue always equals 100. For instance, in this hypothetical example the value for relative information supply is 50 percent for interest group A, 20 percent for interest group B, 10 percent for interest group C, and 20 percent for interest group D which together makes 100. If interest group A would, however, only supply 49 percent of the overall information, one of the other groups would necessarily provide 1 percent more. Consequently, using this measure, a 1 percent increase in the relative information supply by interest group A implies at the same time a one percent decrease in relative information supply by its opposing interest groups B, C and D.

$$z_A = \frac{x_A}{x_A + x_B + x_C + x_D} \cdot 100$$

Table 4.10 summarizes the distribution of the three relative interest group characteristics. Concerning relative information supply, the dataset does not include any missing values. The vast share of interest groups supplies up to 2.5 percent of the overall amount of information provided to the European institutions on a policy issue. Hence, the relative amount of information supplied by interest groups is spread fairly evenly among the different interest groups. There is also no considerable difference in the distribution of relative information supply between associations and companies. Citizen support, which is measured by the number of represented individuals, is by definition only applicable to associations since companies do not have any members. Hence, the (relative) citizen support of companies equals zero for all companies. Relative citizen support of associations is distributed relatively unevenly across associations: About 39 percent of associations in the policy formulation sample and about 49 percent in the decision-making sample represent more than 10 percent of all the citizens represented on a given issue. Concerning relative economic power, the distribution is somewhat different across actor type. Companies have on average less relative economic power than associations. For instance, whereas only about 13 percent of associations in the policy formulation sample have less than 2.5 percent of relative economic power at their disposal, about 30 percent of all companies possess less then 2.5 percent of the overall economic power provided on an issue. By and large, the distribution of relative information supply, citizen support, and economic power is fairly similar in the policy formulation and the decision-making sample of interest groups.

One could potentially argue that information supply, citizen support, and economic power are strongly correlated. The rationale underlying such reasoning is that interest groups that represent a large number of citizens or that have a high degree of economic power should be better able to provide information to the European institutions than interest groups with modest citizen support and economic power. In order to make sure that information supply is not merely a result of the degree of citizen support and economic power, I investigated the correlation between relative information supply, citizen support, and economic power on the individual interest group level (see table 4.11). The correlations between individual information supply and citizen support and individual information supply and economic power on the interest group level are only moderate and it can therefore be concluded that information supply on the individual interest group level is not determined by citizen support and economic power.[13]

---

[13] While information supply, citizen support, and economic power are not correlated on the individual interest group level, they are highly collinear on the lobbying coalition level (see page 129).

Table 4.10 Relative interest group characteristics

Relative interest group characteristic	Policy formulation		Decision-making	
	Associations	Companies	Associations	Companies
Information supply	$N = 2,043$	$N = 653$	$N = 1,324$	$N = 469$
up to 2.5%	79.20%	82.39%	76.51%	77.40%
more than 2.5%, up to 5%	14.05%	12.10%	15.41%	15.14%
more than 5%, up to 7.5%	3.57%	3.83%	4.15%	5.12%
more than 7.5%, up to 10%	1.71%	0.46%	1.89%	0.64%
more than 10%	1.47%	1.23%	2.04%	1.71%
Total	100.00%	100.00%	100.00%	100.00%
Citizen support	$N = 432$	$N = 634$	$N = 267$	$N = 450$
up to 2.5%	8.56%	100.00%	2.25%	100.00%
more than 2.5%, up to 5%	21.30%	0.00%	22.85%	0.00%
more than 5%, up to 7.5%	18.52%	0.00%	16.48%	0.00%
more than 7.5%, up to 10%	12.73%	0.00%	8.99%	0.00%
more than 10%	38.89%	0.00%	49.44%	0.00%
Total	100.00%	100.00%	100.00%	100.00%
Economic power	$N = 451$	$N = 143$	$N = 293$	$N = 96$
up to 2.5%	13.08%	30.07%	8.19%	16.67%
more than 2.5%, up to 5%	25.94%	32.87%	21.84%	32.29%
more than 5%, up to 7.5%	20.18%	10.49%	20.48%	12.50%
more than 7.5%, up to 10%	10.20%	9.09%	11.95%	12.50%
more than 10%	30.60%	17.48%	37.54%	26.04%
Total	100.00%	100.00%	100.00%	100.00%

Table 4.11 Correlation between interest group characteristics

	Information supply	Citizen support	Economic power
Information supply	1.000		
Citizen support	0.251***	1.000	
Economic power	0.307***	0.484***	1.000

***$p \leq 0.01$,**$p \leq 0.05$,*$p \leq 0.10$

4.3.2 Operationalization of lobbying coalition characteristics

I have so far illustrated how information supply, citizen support, and economic power have been measured on the individual interest group level. However, the theoretical model suggests that these variables are decisive on the lobbying coalition level rather than on the level of individual interest groups. In the following, I therefore describe how I aggregated information supply, citizen support, and economic power to measure their supply on the lobbying coalition level.

The first step in operationalizing lobbying coalition characteristics is the identification of lobbying coalitions. Following Baumgartner et al. (2009, 6) I define a lobbying coalition as a "set of actors who share the same policy goal." Since I assumed that all policy issues are characterized by unidimensional policy spaces, I was able to place the European institutions and the interest groups on one straight line representing the policy space of a given policy issue. The location of the different actors on this line depends on their policy position estimates obtained by the quantitative text analysis. I identified the lobbying coalitions according to the alignment of interest groups and the European Commission in the policy space. More specifically, the reference point is the location of the initial draft proposal presented by the European Commission that marks the beginning of the legislative process (COMM1). All interest groups left of the Commission's draft proposal form lobbying coalition *A* and all interest groups right of the initial Commission position constitute lobbying coalition *B* (see figure 4.2). Thus, I do not consider formal, permanent networks of interest groups, but I instead determine lobbying coalitions according to their issue-specific policy preferences. Interest groups that share the same policy objective pull the European institutions towards the same direction and therefore form a lobbying team. The composition of lobbying coalitions can therefore vary extensively across issues as different actors are involved and interest groups that work together on one issue can be opposed on another issue.

The argument supporting this lobbying coalition coding is the following: The starting point of the legislative process is the policy position of the European Commission before the consultation as reflected in the preliminary draft proposal (COMM1). Interest groups are then consulted based on this preliminary position paper before the European Commission adopts its final policy proposal (COMM2). On the basis of this final proposal, the Council, the European Parliament, and the European Commission then negotiate the design of the final legislative act (EP,COU,COMM). The reference point for the identification of lobbying coalitions is the preliminary draft proposal as

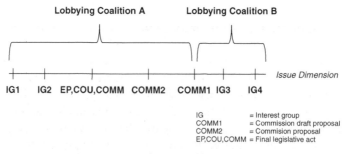

Fig. 4.2 Conceptualization of lobbying coalitions

this sets the framework for the legislative debate. Interest groups would prefer every policy outcome that is closer to their ideal point than the preliminary draft proposal. All interest groups which are located on the same side of the initial Commission position are therefore pushing the European institutions in the same direction and so can be considered as one lobbying team. Since I assumed that all policy issues are characterized by unidimensional policy spaces, there are two lobbying coalitions opposing each other on any given policy issue.[14] This is empirically confirmed by Baumgartner et al. (2009, 7) who found that two lobbying coalitions were opposing each other for most of the 98 policy issues they studied in the United States: One coalition usually supported a policy change whereas the opposing coalition attempted to protect the status quo.

Across the 56 policy issues there are 110 lobbying coalitions. On two policy issues, all interest groups are located on the same side of the preliminary Commission proposal and they therefore all form only one coalition. Since not all policy proposals were transformed into final legislation within the time frame of this analysis, the number of policy issues reduces to 42 while the number of lobbying coalitions decreases to 82 for the analysis of the decision-making stage. In order to measure information supply, citizen support, and economic power on the lobbying coalition level, I first summed the supply of these goods by all members of a coalition to obtain their absolute amount provided by lobbying coalitions. I then measured relative information supply, relative citizen support, and relative economic power of lobbying coalitions in a similar way as the relative characteristics of individual interest groups (see page 113). For instance, the relative information supply z_A by lobbying coalition A equals the absolute information supply x_A by lobbying coalition A divided by the sum of absolute information supply by lobbying coalition A (x_A) and lobbying coalition B (x_B) with both coalitions working on the same policy issue times 100.

$$z_A = \frac{x_A}{x_A + x_B} \cdot 100$$

This measure ranges from 0 to 100. As this is a relative measure, the values for relative information supply by both lobbying coalitions working on the same issue always adds up to 100. For instance, if lobbying coalition A supplies 40 percent of the overall amount of information provided to the European institutions on a policy issue, its opposing lobbying coalition B supplies 60 percent of the information. Similarly, if lobbying coalition A provides 41 percent of the overall amount of information, lobbying coalition B

---

[14] It could, however, be the case that there is only one lobbying coalition if all interest groups and national authorities are located on the same side of the initial policy position of the European Commission.

necessarily provides 59 percent. Thus, an increase in the relative information supply by lobbying coalition *A* by one percentage point implies at the same time a decrease in relative information supply by lobbing coalition *B* by one percentage point. This has to be taken into account when interpreting the regression coefficients in the data analysis.

The distribution of relative information supply, citizen support, and economic power in both the sample of interest groups analyzed in the policy formulation stage and the sample of interest groups analyzed in the decision-making stage is illustrated by the histograms in figure 4.3, figure 4.4, and figure 4.5. The distribution of relative information supply, citizen support, and economic power of lobbying coalitions does not vary systematically between the policy formulation and the decision-making sample of interest groups. In addition, the histograms indicate that the data do not only fall in a narrow range, but that the dataset covers the entire range of possible values for all three independent variables.

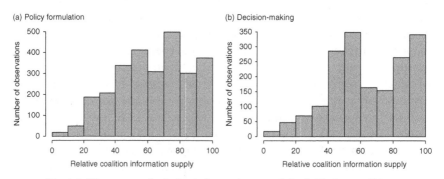

Fig. 4.3 Histogram of relative information supply by lobbying coalitions

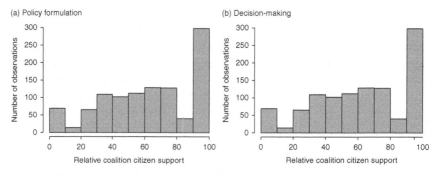

Fig. 4.4 Histogram of relative citizen support of lobbying coalitions

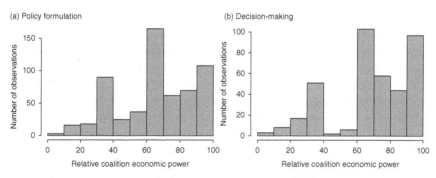

Fig. 4.5 Histogram of relative economic power of lobbying coalitions

4.3.3 Operationalization of control variables

Based on previous findings in interest group and legislative politics research, control variables on the interest group as well as the issue level are included in the analysis. Including these control variables allows for testing the hypotheses formulated in chapter 2 while holding these variables constant that might otherwise affect the dependent variable and therefore bias the results. I first describe the measurement of control variables that have been identified in the interest group literature (Dür and De Bièvre 2007a; Mahoney 2007a; Klüver 2011) before turning to the operationalization of variables discussed in legislative politics studies (e.g. Tsebelis 1994; Thomson et al. 2006; Schneider, Finke, and Bailer 2010; Thomson 2011).

One important control variable on the interest group level is *actor type* which is often associated with interest group influence in the literature (e.g. Bouwen 2002; Dür and De Bièvre 2007a). Actor type was measured by a dummy variable distinguishing between companies, sectional groups, and cause groups. Sectional groups represent a section of society such as farmers or chemical corporations and their membership is usually limited to that section (Stewart 1958, 25). Cause groups by contrast represent some belief or principle and anyone in favor of the principle can become a member of this group (Stewart 1958, 25). Actor type was coded based on organizational statutes and self-descriptions that were gathered on interest group websites and retrieved from consultation submissions.

Based on interest group studies highlighting the importance of issue-related factors for interest group influence (Lowi 1964; Mahoney 2007a, 2008; Baumgartner et al. 2009; Klüver 2011), several issue-level variables are included in the analysis. The *salience* of policy issues was measured by the number of submissions received during the online consultation preceding the adoption of a policy proposal. By salience of policy issues, I mean the broader public salience of issues, that is, the attention that policy issues raise in general. The underlying assumption for using this indicator is that policy issues which are highly salient among stakeholders should evoke a high number of consultation submissions. One drawback of using consultation submissions as an indicator for issue salience is that I can only rely on the number of published submissions in online consultations. However, it is plausible to assume that the number of overall submissions highly correlates with the number of published submissions per consultation. As the impact of each additional actor involved in the legislative debate is expected to decrease as the number of actors increases, I use the logarithm of the number of consultation submissions as a measure for salience (Long and Freese 2001, 42). Taking the logarithm in addition decreases the impact of outliers on the regression coefficients.

The *complexity* of policy issues was measured relying on the number of recitals of policy proposals (see also Kaeding 2006). Recitals are paragraphs in the preamble of a policy proposal which state the purpose of the proposal and summarize its main provisions (Kaeding 2006, 236). The rationale for using this indicator is the assumption that the number of recitals increases with the complexity of a policy proposal. Similar to salience, I also expect that the size of the effect of complexity decreases as complexity increases and I therefore use the logged number of recitals as a measure for complexity. In addition, the log transformation pulls outliers closer to the rest of the data and therefore decreases their impact on the regression coefficients.

The *degree of conflict* over an issue was measured by dividing the number of interest groups forming the smaller lobbying coalition by the number of interest groups constituting the bigger coalition on an issue. This measure ranges from 0 to 1 with 0 indicating no conflict at all and 1 indicating maximum conflict. The rationale for using this indicator is the following: The degree of conflict is understood as the dispersion of actors' policy preferences over an issue. Policy issues that are characterized by a strong degree of conflict create a difficult environment for interest groups as countervailing forces attempt to push the policy output in opposing directions. Interest groups should therefore find it very difficult to successfully lobby policy-making since they are fighting against a strong opposition. By contrast, if the majority of interest groups shares the same policy goal, it should be relatively easy for an interest group to be successful in its lobbying attempts since all actors are pushing the legislator in the same direction. Thus, if the majority of interest groups on a given policy issue belong to the same lobbying coalition, they fight for the same policy issue and only face a small opposition. The conflict measure is accordingly close to 0. By contrast, if a relatively equal number of interest groups have opposing views on a policy issue, it is highly polarized as similarly strong coalitions pull decision-makers in opposing directions. The conflict measure is accordingly close to 1.

The importance of member state preferences, the legislative procedure, the voting rule, and the status quo for the policy outcome have been discussed extensively in the legislative politics literature and these variables are therefore also included as control variables (e.g. Tsebelis 1994; Thomson et al. 2006; Schneider, Finke, and Bailer 2010; Thomson 2011). In order to test whether member states determined the outcome of the legislative debate independent of the influence exerted by interest groups, I included an additional variable controlling for *member state support* in the final regression model. In order to measure member state support, I measured the preferences expressed by national governments in the Commission consultations. The European Commission has not only received comments by interest groups in its legislative consultations, but also national governments have communicated their views on the proposed policy initiative. In addition to the 2,696 consultation submissions by interest groups, I therefore also extracted policy preferences from 506 comments that were submitted by individual member state governments. When measuring member state support it is important to take into account that not all member state governments are equally powerful in the EU as for instance Germany has a much bigger say on European affairs than Malta. I therefore measure member state support by the number of member states supporting the policy objective of each lobbying coalition weighted by their voting power in the Council.

Whether the policy proposal constitutes new legislation or whether there was already a European level *status quo* (SQ) was assessed by drawing on the EU database *EurLex* which indicates for every policy proposal whether it is a modification to prior EU legislation. Ideally, it would also be worthwhile to control for the location of the status quo. However, measuring the location of the status quo is not feasible due to two difficulties. First, if there is no prior European legislation, the status quo corresponds to national legislation adopted in the 27 member states of the European Union. There is therefore not a single status quo, but 27 different domestic ones. As a result, it is very difficult to precisely identify the location of the status quo as it is unclear how the different national status quos should be weighted in order to arrive at one single European-wide estimate. Second, even if there is prior European legislation, it is difficult to locate the position of the status quo using the text analysis approach employed in this book. It is very often the case that prior legislation that is linked to a proposal does not deal with the same specific policy issue, but that it is merely a very general legislative framework regulating an entire policy area. For instance, the regulation on roaming which regulates the pricing for mobile phone calls abroad amends the directive that set up the regulatory framework for telecommunications which regulates the entire telecommunications market. The two policy proposals therefore differ extensively in terms of scope and they do not refer to the same single issue dimension as required by *Wordfish*.

The *legislative procedure* was coded according to information gathered from the *PreLex* database that denotes the legislative procedure for every

Table 4.12 Operationalization of independent variables

Variable	Indicator
General concepts	
Information supply	– No. of words per submission
Citizen support	– No. of represented individuals
Economic power	– Annual turnover
	– No. of employees
Lobbying coalitions	
Relative information supply	– Share of aggregated information supply per issue
Relative citizen support	– Share of aggregated citizen support per issue
Relative economic power	– Share of aggregated economic power per issue
Interest groups	
Actor type	– Coding according to configuration of actor
Relative information supply	– Share of aggregated information supply per issue
Relative citizen support	– Share of aggregated citizen support per issue
Relative economic power	– Share of aggregated economic power per issue
Policy issues	
Salience	– No. of consultation submissions
Complexity	– No. of recitals per proposal
Degree of conflict	– Ratio of no. of interest groups per coalition on an issue
Existence of EU status quo	– Existence of prior binding legislation as reported in *EurLex*
Legislative procedure	– Legislative procedure as reported in *PreLex*
Voting rule	– Legal basis specifying the voting rule as indicated in *EurLex*
Member state support	– No. of states supporting a coalition weighted by Council votes

single policy proposal that the European Commission introduces to the legislative process. The *voting rule* was coded according to the legal basis of policy proposals which indicates what voting rule applies to a specific policy proposal. The legal basis of a policy proposal was determined from information provided by the *EurLex* database. Table 4.12 presents an overview of the operationalization of the independent variables used in this book. Summary statistics of the dependent, the explanatory, and the control variables can be found in table 4.13.

4.4 SPECIFICATION OF THE STATISTICAL MODEL

In order to test the hypotheses laid out in chapter 2, the special structure of the dataset has to be taken into account. The data are hierarchical in nature since interest groups are nested into policy issues (see figure 4.6). This is reflected in the two-stage selection procedure that underlies the dataset: As explained earlier in this chapter, I first selected 56 policy proposals. I then selected 2,696

Table 4.13 Summary statistics of variables

Variable	N	Mean	Standard deviation	Minimum	Maximum
Dependent variable					
Influence (Policy formulation)	2696		Influential: 53.08%, Not influential: 46.92%		
Influence (Decision-making)	1793		Influential: 49.53%, Not influential: 50.47%		
Lobbying coalition characteristics					
Relative information supply by lobbying coalitions	110	50.909	28.677	3.989	100
Relative citizen support of lobbying coalitions	106	50.943	37.126	0	100
Relative economic power of lobbying coalitions	110	50.909	34.083	0	100
Interest group characteristics					
Actor type	2696	Companies: 24.22%, Sectional groups: 55.68%, Cause groups: 20.10%			
Relative information supply by interest groups	2696	1.738	2.432	0.047	45.237
Relative citizen support of interest groups	1066	5.066	11.078	0	100
Relative economic power of interest groups	594	9.428	12.456	1.058	100
Issue characteristics					
Salience	56	4.274	0.650	2.639	5.727
Complexity	56	3.190	0.685	1.792	5.004
Conflict	56	0.418	0.299	0.000	0.971
Existence of status quo	56	Yes: 67.86%, No: 32.14%			
Legislative procedure	56	Codecision: 87.50%, Consultation: 12.50%			
Voting rule	56	Qualified Majority (QM): 92.86%, Unanimity: 7.14%			
Member state support	56	16.226	16.062	0	82.759

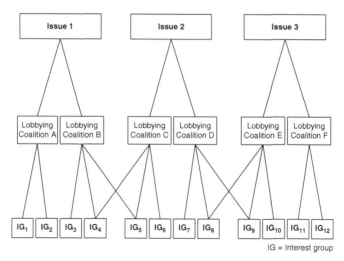

Fig. 4.6 Data structure

interest groups which submitted comments to consultations that the European Commission conducted before it officially adopted the legislative proposals. Interest groups which participated in the same consultations are subject to the same contextual characteristics and therefore not completely independent as assumed by ordinary regression analysis.

Due to the hierarchical nature of the dataset, the variables vary on different levels. Some variables vary on the individual interest group level, some vary with lobbying coalitions, and some vary only with the policy issues. Interest groups which lobby the European institutions concerning the same policy proposal are therefore subject to the same contextual characteristics. While interest group properties vary across all individual interest groups in the sample, issue-specific variables such as the degree of conflict or complexity are held constant for all interest groups participating in the same legislative debate. However, recent literature suggests that lobbying success varies not only with individual characteristics, but also with the issue context (Mahoney 2007a, 2008; Klüver 2011). As a result, issue-specific variables are held constant for all interest groups involved in the same policy debate, but these contextual characteristics vary across policy issues and therefore lead to on average lower or higher success probabilities for all interest groups lobbying the same proposal. For instance, if a policy issue is highly complex and if all interest groups involved in this debate largely agree, the probability to successfully lobby the European institutions is relatively high for all interest groups as the European institutions require a lot of information and because there is no counterlobbying taking place.

In order to take into account the hierarchical nature of the data, I analyzed the data using multilevel modeling. Multilevel models are very popular in educational statistics and sociology and have recently spread into political science. There are various substantive and methodological reasons for the use of multilevel models (Steenbergen and Jones 2002; Gelman and Hill 2007): First, multilevel analysis allows combining predictors located on different levels of analysis to account for variation in the dependent variable. Complex theoretical models suggesting simultaneous effects of explanatory variables located on different levels of analysis can therefore be tested empirically. Accordingly, using multilevel modeling I can test the hypothesized effects of information supply, citizen support, and economic power of interest groups while controlling for characteristics of policy issues. Second, using multilevel analysis one can examine causal heterogeneity, that is, testing whether a causal effect is the same across different subpopulations or whether an effect is moderated by contextual characteristics. For instance, I can examine whether the effect of information supply varies with the complexity of the policy issue as hypothesized in chapter 2.

Apart from substantive motivations, there are also important methodological advantages of multilevel modeling (Steenbergen and Jones 2002; Gelman and Hill 2007): Traditional alternatives to multilevel modeling are complete pooling in which the data are analyzed as if there was no hierarchical clustering and no pooling in which different subpopulations are analyzed separately. These approaches have serious problems (Gelman and Hill 2007, 253–254): No pooling overstates the differences between subpopulations whereas complete pooling ignores differences between subpopulations. Multilevel models by contrast compromise between pooled and unpooled estimates by taking the hierarchical structure into account and thus producing estimates that are weighted by the sample size of the clusters and the variation within and between clusters. I am accordingly able to test the theoretical model across different policy issues by taking into account variation within and across policy issues and by weighting the estimates according to the number of interest groups which lobbied on each policy issue. Another important advantage of multilevel models concerns the estimation of standard errors (Steenbergen and Jones 2002, 219–220): Ignoring the hierarchical nature and thereby the clustering of the data may result in deflated standard errors and inflated Type I error rates. Hence, ignoring the multilevel structure of the data leads to a misspecification of the model so that predictors seem to have a significant effect even though they do not.

I therefore draw on multilevel modeling to analyze the data by distinguishing between the interest group (first) level and the issue (second) level. As the dependent variable interest group influence is of binary nature,

I estimate multilevel logistic regression models.[15] For all analyses, I present a variance decomposition and a random intercept model. The variance decomposition model does not include any predictors and is solely presented in order to be able to assess the fit of the random intercept model. In order to illustrate the nature of the models, I shortly present the model equations and discuss their elements. The logistic variance decomposition model can be noted as follows:[16]

$$logit\{Pr(y_{ij} = 1)\} = \beta + \zeta_j$$

$$\zeta_j \sim N(0, \psi)$$

The variance decomposition model, which is also often termed the "empty model," is the standard model which does not include any covariates. The probability of an interest group i to influence policy-making on issue j $Pr(y_{ij} = 1)$ is modeled as depending on an overall mean β and a second level residual ζ_j for issue j. The random intercept ζ_j is assumed to be normally distributed with mean 0 and variance ψ.

The random intercept model by contrast includes explanatory variables and also allows the intercept to vary across the different second level units so that the average value of the dependent variable can vary across the different clusters. The probability of an interest group to influence policy-making $Pr(y_{ij} = 1)$ depends on an overall mean β_0, on covariates x_{1ij} through x_{kij}, and on the error term ζ_j located on the issue level (second level). The random intercept ζ_j is again assumed to be normally distributed with mean 0 and variance ψ. The logistic random intercept model can be noted as follows:

$$logit\{Pr(y_{ij} = 1)\} = \beta_0 + \beta_1 x_{1ij} + \ldots + \beta_k x_{kij} + \zeta_j$$

$$\zeta_j | \mathbf{x}_{ij} \sim N(0, \psi)$$

Potentially one could also conceptualize the data structure as cross-classified since several interest groups do not only participate in one single consultation, but lobby on several policy issues in the dataset (see table 4.14). The unit of analysis is the lobbying event defined as the lobbying activity of an interest group concerning a specific policy issue. Hence, if an interest group lobbies on more than one of the 56 policy issues in the dataset, the same interest group appears several times in the dataset. One could therefore conceptualize lobbying events as clustered into interest groups on the one hand and as clustered into policy issues on the other hand. However, since 78.55 percent of the interest groups only participated in one single consultation, a

---

[15] As discussed on pages 98–99, interest group influence is measured by assessing whether the distance between the policy positions of interest groups and the European institutions decreased over time.

[16] The notation employed in this study was adapted from Rabe-Hesketh and Skrondal (2008).

Table 4.14 Participation of interest groups in consultations

Number of participations	Number of interest groups	Percent of interest groups
1	1,487	78.55
2	237	12.52
3	82	4.33
4	34	1.80
5	27	1.43
6	11	0.58
7	3	0.16
8	4	0.21
9	2	0.11
10	1	0.05
11	2	0.11
13	2	0.11
23	1	0.05
Total	1,893	100.00

cross-classified model would be based on estimating random effects for only one single case for the vast majority of interest groups.

In addition to the cross-classification, one could think of estimating a three-level model with interest groups being the first level, lobbying coalitions the second level, and issues the third level. However, due to survey non-response, the number of interest groups per lobbying coalition is also relatively small. For some of the models discussed in this chapter, the majority of the lobbying coalitions are only represented by one single interest group so that estimating random effects would only be based on one single case. Due to the relatively small number of cases, it was therefore not possible to estimate cross-classified or three-level models for all the models presented in this chapter. Where it was, however, possible to estimate these models, the results do not substantially differ from the results obtained by two-level models. I therefore refrain from presenting cross-classified and three-level models and concentrate on two-level models

I decided to cluster the data according to policy issues to have a sufficiently large number of cases in each cluster to estimate the multilevel model and to still be able to capture the hierarchical nature of the dataset. Clustering the data according to policy issues is also theoretically important as lobbying coalitions are not independent of each other. As discussed earlier, it is decisive how much information, citizen support, and economic power lobbying coalitions provide in relation to their opposing coalition working on the same issue. Hence, lobbying coalitions are always issue-specific and cannot be treated as randomly distributed across the entire sample of policy issues analyzed in this book.

In order to evaluate the overall model fit, models are compared to the variance decomposition model using the Akaike information criterion (AIC), the Bayesian information criterion (BIC), and the likelihood ratio test. Models with smaller AIC and BIC should be preferred over models with larger AIC and BIC. Whereas the log likelihood can simply be improved by adding a new predictor to the model, the AIC and BIC penalize for adding new predictors to the model with the BIC being more conservative than the AIC (Gelman and Hill 2007, 524–525).

Due to survey non-response, the dataset unfortunately includes a lot of missing values on the explanatory variables. As explained earlier in this chapter, I conducted an online survey of interest groups which participated in consultations on the 56 selected policy issues in order to measure interest group characteristics. The response rate of the survey was 38.67 percent (see table 4.5). In addition to unit non-response, there are, however, also a lot of missing values due to item non-response. The missing value structure for the variables of interest is illustrated in table 4.15.

In order to deal with missing values, one can draw on different strategies of which listwise deletion and multiple imputation have proven most promising (Allison 2000, 2002). Multiple imputation is, however, only appropriate if the number of missing values is not too high. Even though there is no rule of thumb about the minimum number of observed values, Royston (2004, 240) suggests that multiple imputation should be avoided for variables that have 50 percent or more missing values. Since both citizen support, and economic power have about 50 percent of missing values after removal of all unit non-responses, I therefore refrained from using multiple imputation and instead analyze the dataset using listwise deletion. Listwise deletion excludes all observations which have missing values on at least one of the variables in the model. The major problem of listwise deletion is an extensive reduction of the sample size. The standard errors are therefore larger in the reduced dataset due to the smaller number of cases. Analyzing the effect of information supply, citizen support, and economic power simultaneously using listwise deletion would accordingly reduce the sample size extensively: For the policy formulation stage, the sample would shrink from 2,696 interest groups and 56 policy issues to 291 interest groups and 48 issues. For the decision-making stage, the sample would be reduced from 1,793 interest groups and 42 issues to 177 interest groups and 35 issues.

Table 4.15 Missing values

Variables	Missing values	
	Original sample (n = 2,696)	Without unit non-response (n = 1,170)
Citizen support	59.76%	48.29%
Economic power	77.97%	49.23%

What is more, relative information supply, citizen support, and economic power on the lobbying coalition level are highly collinear. Relative information supply and citizen support correlate at 0.65, relative information supply and relative economic power correlate at 0.68, and relative citizen support and relative economic power of lobbying coalitions correlate at 0.75. Collinearity leads to unstable regression coefficients and larger standard errors (Fox 1991, 10–11). If two variables are strongly collinear, the data contain little information about the impact of the first variable when the second is held constant since there is little variation in the first variable when the second is fixed (Fox 2005, 354). The estimation problems caused by collinearity are furthermore aggravated by the small number of cases that are available if all three predictors are included simultaneously in the model. It is therefore not possible to estimate the effect of all three lobbying coalition characteristics simultaneously. Due to the collinearity of the predictors and in order to keep as many observations as possible for the empirical analysis, I therefore test the effects of relative information supply, relative citizen support, and relative economic power of lobbying coalitions one after the other.

A plausible source for the high degree of collinearity between the lobbying coalition characteristics is the size of lobbying coalitions. One could argue that the size of a lobbying coalition crucially affects the relative information supply, the relative citizen support, and the relative economic power of lobbying coalitions so that larger coalitions on average provide more information, citizen support, and economic power to decision-makers than smaller lobbying coalitions. However, from a theoretical point of view, information supply, citizen support, and economic power are distinct and independent concepts. Information supply describes the technical and political information that interest groups provide to the European institutions. Citizen support refers to the degree to which interest groups can directly mobilize citizens and voters. Economic power is the ability of interest groups to control business investments and job creation. In addition, lobbying coalitions composed of a large number of interest groups are not necessarily able to supply more information, citizen support, and economic power to the European institutions than small coalitions. It could for instance be the case that a lobbying coalition is larger in size than its opposing coalition, but that all its members are relatively weak in terms of information supply, citizen support, and economic power which are needed by the European institutions whereas its opposing coalition is only made up of very few, but very powerful groups. In order to test whether information supply, citizen support, and economic power of lobbying coalitions can be solely explained by coalition size, I have estimated three regression models predicting relative information supply, relative citizen support and relative economic power by the relative size of lobbying coalitions. If information supply, citizen support, and economic power are solely a function of the size of a lobbying coalition, the R^2 should be approximately 1.00. The average R^2, however, only amounts to 0.66. This indicates that coalition size is positively related to relative information supply, citizen support, and economic power of lobbying coalitions and that all three characteristics are therefore collinear, but that approximately 34 percent of the variance remains unexplained by the pure size of coalitions. The three goods are therefore distinct and have an independent effect on interest group influence.

Evaluating and comparing the size of the effects across different logistic regression models cannot be carried out by simply assessing the coefficients due to arbitrary variance normalization required in binary outcome models (Mroz and Zayats 2008; Mood 2010). However, the effects of explanatory variables can be compared across different models drawing on predicted probabilities and first differences as these quantities are not affected by the variance normalization. Accordingly, Mroz and Zayats (2008, 413) argue:

> While direct comparisons and interpretations of arbitrarily scaled coefficients from different estimation approaches for binary outcomes can be quite problematic, nearly all interesting magnitudes related to probabilities and impacts of covariates on predicted probabilities can be compared across models and estimation approaches.

I therefore present the results of the analyses in three different ways. I first display the results of the multilevel logistic regression in regression tables using odds ratios. In order to compare the effects across different models and to illustrate the effects in a more intuitive manner, I then use statistical simulation to compute predicted probabilities and first differences (King, Tomz, and Wittenberg 2000). These quantities are estimated in three steps: First, after performing the regression analysis, the coefficients and the variance covariance matrix are obtained. Second, the independent variables are set to specific values, e.g. to the mean and the median. Third, a large number of values is drawn from a multivariate normal distribution which has a vector containing the regression coefficients as its mean and the variance covariance matrix as its variance. I then summarize these simulated draws in order to obtain predicted probabilities and first differences together with their appropriate degrees of uncertainty.[17] As overlapping confidence intervals cannot be used to evaluate statistical significance (e.g. Schenker and Gentleman 2001; Austin 2002; Payton, Greenstone, and Schenker 2003), first differences are inspected to assess whether the differences in the predicted probabilities are statistically significant.

---

[17] I estimate these quantities using the *R* software package *Zelig* developed by Imai, King, and Lau (2006).

5

Policy Debates, Interest Groups,
and the Structure of Conflict

The last chapter has illustrated in detail how the dataset was constructed on which basis the theoretical claims developed in chapter 2 are tested. This chapter now turns the focus to the universe of policy issues and interest groups that are studied in this book. As there are hardly any large-scale empirical studies of interest group lobbying in the European Union, we know little about the nature of policy debates and the characteristics of interest groups. What are the issues that are talked about in Brussels? Who mobilizes in these policy debates? Which interest groups form coalitions and what is the underlying structure of conflict? In order to shed light on interest group influence in the European Union, it is crucial to answer these questions to enhance our understanding about the major players and the context of the lobbing process.

This chapter therefore studies the nature of policy debates in the European Union. The chapter proceeds as follows: The first section sheds light on the characteristics of the policy issues that are dealt with in Brussels. The second section then focuses on the population of interest groups that mobilized on these issues. Finally, section three examines the structure of conflict and the composition of lobbying coalitions in EU policy debates.

5.1 THE UNIVERSE OF ISSUES

Over the past decades, a large number of policy competences have been transferred to the European level. In some policy areas such as agricultural policy, the European Union enjoys exclusive competences and virtually all important policy decisions are therefore taken in Brussels. However, at the same time the European Union has hardly any say in other policy domains such as taxation. In terms of policy issues, the European Union is therefore not a political system like any other. What are the issues that are typically subject to legislative debate in Brussels? What policy areas are most important and how many interest groups mobilize in these debates? What are the levels of conflict? Are policy debates largely consensual or are interest groups largely divided? This section presents information about the policy issues analyzed in this book to shed light on the nature of policy debates in the European Union (see Table 5.1 (a) and (b) for a list of all 56 issues).

Table 5.1 (a) Summary of policy issues

Issue	Issue description	Primarily responsible DG	Submissions
1	Advanced therapies	Enterprise & Industry	44
2	Euro 5 emisssion standards	Enterprise & Industry	51
3	Residues in foodstuffs of animal origin	Enterprise & Industry	41
4	Units of measurement	Enterprise & Industry	143
5	Protection of pedestrians	Enterprise & Industry	17
6	Hydrogen powered motor vehicles	Enterprise & Industry	19
7	Circulation of defense products	Enterprise & Industry	24
8	Cosmetic products	Enterprise & Industry	45
9	Better regulation of pharmaceuticals	Enterprise & Industry	22
10	Advanced safety features & tires	Enterprise & Industry	81
11	Information to patients	Enterprise & Industry	185
12	Pharmacovigilance	Enterprise & Industry	81
13	Counterfeit medicines	Enterprise & Industry	127
14	Payment services	Internal Market & Services	94
15	Shareholder rights	Internal Market & Services	129
16	Defense & security procurement	Internal Market & Services	37
17	Simplifying the business environment	Internal Market & Services	129
18	UCITS	Internal Market & Services	61
19	Copyright	Internal Market & Services	118
20	Food safety	Health & Consumers	86
21	Consumer protection	Health & Consumers	163
22	Nutrition & health claims made on food	Health & Consumers	85
23	Timeshare	Health & Consumers	96
24	Food information to consumers	Health & Consumers	178
25	Consumer rights	Health & Consumers	307
26	Emissions trading scheme	Environment	92
27	Environmental liability	Environment	73
28	Batteries	Environment	132
29	Waste	Environment	205
30	Use of pesticides	Environment	78
31	Mercury	Environment	55
32	Reducing CO_2 emissions from cars	Environment	75
33	Restriction of hazardous substances	Environment	59
34	Waste: electrical and electronic equipment	Environment	130
35	Rights & obligations of intern. rail passengers	Energy & Transport	39
36	Road infrastructure safety management	Energy & Transport	49
37	Blind spot mirrors for trucks	Energy & Transport	38
38	Access to road transport markets	Energy & Transport	69
39	Computerized reservation schemes	Energy & Transport	44
40	Road safety	Energy & Transport	51

(*continued*)

Table 5.1 (a) Continued

41	Energy labeling	Energy & Transport	74
42	Labeling of tires	Energy & Transport	14
43	Rights of passengers in intern. bus transport	Energy & Transport	57
44	Reuse of public sector information	Information Society & Media	76
45	Roaming	Information Society & Media	49
46	Electronic communication networks & services	Information Society & Media	194
47	European network & information security agency	Information Society & Media	31
48	Competition rules to maritime transport	Competition	52
49	Fundamental rights agency	Justice, Freedom, & Security	112
50	Rome I	Justice, Freedom, & Security	83
51	Divorce matters	Justice, Freedom, & Security	68
52	Economic migration	Justice, Freedom, & Security	144
53	Common European asylum system	Justice, Freedom, & Security	100
54	Excise duty on tobacco products	Taxation	89
55	Health check	Agriculture & Rural Development	75
56	School fruit scheme	Agriculture & Rural Development	101

Table 5.1 (b) Summary of policy issues

Issue	Proposal type	Legislative procedure	Draft date	Proposal date	Date of legislative act
1	Regulation	Codecision	04.05.2005	16.11.2005	13.12.2007
2	Regulation	Codecision	15.07.2005	21.12.2005	20.06.2007
3	Regulation	Codecision	18.12.2003	17.04.2007	06.05.2009
4	Directive	Codecision	22.12.2006	10.09.2007	11.03.2009
5	Regulation	Codecision	06.2005	03.10.2007	14.01.2009
6	Regulation	Codecision	13.07.2006	10.10.2007	14.01.2009
7	Directive	Codecision	21.03.2006	05.12.2007	06.05.2009
8	Regulation	Codecision	12.01.2007	05.02.2008	30.11.2009
9	Directive	Codecision	10.07.2007	04.03.2008	18.06.2009
10	Regulation	Codecision	23.08.2007	23.05.2008	13.07.2009
11	Both	Codecision	05.02.2008	10.12.2008	–
12	Both	Codecision	05.12.2007	10.12.2008	–
13	Directive	Codecision	11.03.2008	10.12.2008	–
14	Directive	Codecision	02.12.2003	01.12.2005	13.11.2007
15	Directive	Codecision	13.05.2005	05.01.2006	11.07.2007
16	Directive	Codecision	23.09.2004	05.12.2007	13.07.2009
17	Directive	Codecision	10.07.2007	17.04.2008	–
18	Directive	Codecision	22.03.2007	16.07.2008	13.07.2009
19	Directive	Codecision	19.07.2004	16.07.2008	–
20	Regulation	Codecision	12.01.2000	08.11.2000	28.01.2002
21	Directive	Codecision	02.10.2001	18.06.2003	11.05.2005
22	Regulation	Codecision	28.05.2001	16.07.2003	20.12.2006

(*continued*)

Table 5.1 (b) Continued

Issue	Proposal type	Legislative procedure	Draft date	Proposal date	Date of legislative act
23	Directive	Codecision	01.06.2006	07.06.2007	14.01.2009
24	Regulation	Codecision	13.03.2006	30.01.2008	–
25	Directive	Codecision	08.02.2007	08.10.2008	–
26	Directive	Codecision	08.03.2000	23.10.2001	13.12.2003
27	Directive	Codecision	25.07.2001	23.01.2002	21.04.2004
28	Directive	Codecision	25.02.2003	21.11.2003	06.09.2006
29	Directive	Codecision	27.05.2003	21.12.2005	19.11.2008
30	Directive	Codecision	01.07.2002	12.07.2006	21.10.2009
31	Both	Codecision	15.03.2004	21.02.2006	25.09.2007
32	Regulation	Codecision	07.02.2007	19.12.2007	23.04.2009
33	Directive	Codecision	13.12.2007	03.12.2008	–
34	Directive	Codecision	11.04.2008	03.12.0008	–
35	Regulation	Codecision	04.10.2002	03.03.2004	23.10.2007
36	Directive	Codecision	12.04.2006	05.10.2006	19.11.2008
37	Directive	Codecision	12.04.2006	05.10.2006	11.07.2007
38	Regulation	Codecision	09.06.2006	01.06.2007	21.10.2009
39	Regulation	Codecision	23.02.2007	15.11.2007	14.01.2009
40	Directive	Codecision	06.11.2006	19.03.2008	–
41	Directive	Codecision	20.12.2007	13.11.2008	19.05.2010
42	Directive	Codecision	28.04.2008	13.11.2008	25.11.2009
43	Regulation	Codecision	14.07.2005	04.12.2008	–
44	Directive	Codecision	23.10.2001	05.06.2002	17.11.2003
45	Regulation	Codecision	03.04.2006	12.07.2006	27.06.2007
46	Both	Codecision	29.06.2006	13.11.2007	25.11.2009
47	Regulation	Codecision	01.06.2007	20.12.2007	24.09.2008
48	Regulation	Consultation	13.10.2004	14.12.2005	25.09.2006
49	Regulation	Consultation	25.10.2004	30.06.2005	15.02.2007
50	Regulation	Codecision	14.01.2003	15.12.2005	17.06.2008
51	Regulation	Consultation	14.03.2005	17.07.2006	–
52	Directive	Consultation	11.01.2005	23.10.2007	–
53	Both	Codecision	06.06.2007	03.12.2008	–
54	Directive	Consultation	30.03.2007	16.07.2008	16.02.2010
55	Regulation	Consultation	20.11.2007	20.05.2008	19.01.2009
56	Regulation	Consultation	18.12.2007	08.07.2008	18.12.2008

Table 5.2 presents information about the Directorates General responsible for the policy proposals analyzed in this book. The European Commission is divided into several departments known as Directorates General (DGs). The DGs are responsible for different policy portfolios very much like ministries at the national level. Relying on the primarily responsible DG is therefore a good proxy for the policy area in which a proposal falls. Thirteen (23.21 percent) proposals were developed by DG Enterprise and Industry. DG Environment and DG Energy and Transport were each responsible for nine (16.07 percent) policy initiatives while DG Health and Consumers and

Table 5.2 Distribution of policy issues across Directorates General

Primarily responsible Directorat General	Frequency	Percent
Enterprise & Industry	13	23.21
Environment	9	16.07
Energy & Transport	9	16.07
Internal Market & Services	6	10.71
Health & Consumer Protection	6	10.71
Justice, Freedom, & Security	5	8.93
Information Society & Media	4	7.14
Agriculture & Rural Development	2	3.57
Competition	1	1.79
Taxation	1	1.79
Total	56	100.00

DG Internal Market and Services each directed six (10.71 percent) policy proposals. DG Justice, Freedom, and Security coordinated the elaboration of five (8.93 percent) initiatives and DG Information Society and Media drafted four (7.14 percent) policy proposals. Finally, DG Agriculture and Rural Development was responsible for two (3.57 percent) policy initiatives while DG Competition and DG Taxation each coordinated one (1.79 percent) policy proposal.

Even though the sample of policy debates studied in this book is not a random sample and therefore not representative for the entire population of issues dealt with in Brussels, the sample captures a wide variety of policy areas typically regulated by the European Union. The largest number of policy issues in the sample (about 35 percent) deal with economic issues which is not surprising given the large number of competences that the European Union controls in this domain. In addition, about 27 percent of the policy debates studied in this book deal with regulatory issues concerning environmental protection, health, and consumer protection. Since agricultural policy constitutes one of the most important policy areas in the EU, it might seem surprising that only two proposals fall in the agricultural domain. However, one of these initiatives is the so-called "Health Check" proposal which reformed the entire Common agricultural policy and is therefore probably the most important agricultural proposal in the past decade.

How salient are policy issues in the European Union? How many interest groups mobilize to lobby the European institutions in these policy debates? Figure 5.1 indicates the number of submissions that the European Commission received during the consultations preceding the adoption of the 56 selected proposals. On average, the European Commission received 87 submissions per consultation. Typical policy debates that raised an average amount of attention among interest groups are the policy debate revolving around the introduction

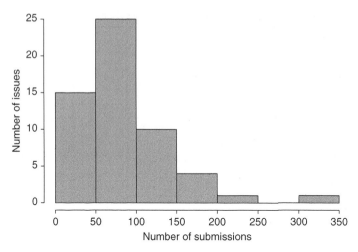

Fig. 5.1 Mobilization of interest groups

of the emissions trading scheme (92 submissions), the stakeholder debate concerning food safety (86 submissions), or the legislative debate on tobacco taxation (89 submissions). The most salient policy debate in the sample of policy issues studied in this book is the stakeholder debate on the policy proposal on consumer rights which affects the entire single market (307 consultation submissions). By contrast, a policy initiative that triggered very little response from interest groups is the policy proposal concerning the protection of pedestrians (17 submissions). Hence, the number of submissions varies considerably and it can therefore be inferred that policy debates in the European Union vary extensively in terms of salience. Some issues mobilize a large number of interest groups while other debates receive hardly any attention.

How complex are policy proposals that are discussed in Brussels? Given that it is often argued that lobbying is about information transmission as decision-makers require policy expertise, it is important to examine how complex policy issues are. Figure 5.2 illustrates the complexity of the policy proposals analyzed in this book. As discussed on page 120, the complexity of policy issues was measured by the number of recitals of legislative proposals. Typical proposals with an average degree of complexity are the legislative proposal on roaming (31 recitals), the policy proposal regulating nutrition and health claims made on food (28 recitals), or the Commission proposal on the reduction of CO_2 emissions from cars (28 recitals). A policy issue that is particularly complex is the previously mentioned "Health Check" proposal which reformed the common agricultural policy of the EU (91 recitals). By contrast, a policy proposal with a very low level of complexity is the proposal

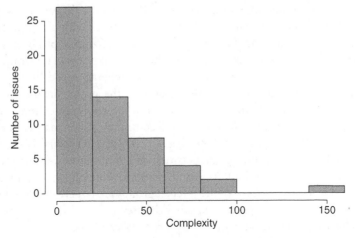

Fig. 5.2 Complexity of policy issues

on units of measurement which harmonizes the use of measurement units for expressing quantities in the European Union (7 recitals). The complexity of policy issues in the European Union therefore varies considerably. Some issues are highly complex while other policy issues are very simple in nature.

What is the nature of conflict in policy debates in the European Union? Are policy debates consensual or are legislative debates characterized by a large degree of conflict between the different interest groups? Figure 5.3 illustrates the degree of conflict underlying the 56 policy debates studied in this book. The measure of conflict ranges from 0 to 1 whereby 0 indicates no conflict

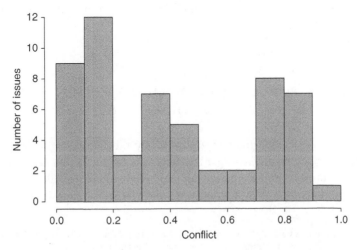

Fig. 5.3 The degree of conflict

at all and 1 indicates maximum conflict. The average degree of conflict is 0.42 with a standard deviation of 0.30. Policy debates with a typical level of conflict are the debate about residues in foodstuffs of animal origin (0.44), the debate on regulating copyright (0.48), or the legislative debate reforming units of measurement (0.38). A policy debate that is characterized by high levels of conflict between different interest groups is the policy debate about the review of the regulatory framework for electronic communication networks and services which regulates the entire telecommunications market in Europe (0.87). By contrast, a policy debate that was largely consensual is the debate about establishing the European network and information security agency (0.07). Policy debates in the European Union are therefore also characterized by varying levels of conflict. While interest groups are largely divided on some policy issues, consensus prevails in other debates.

Finally, what is the legal nature of the proposals and under which legislative procedure are they adopted? Out of the 56 legislative proposals studied in this book, 28 (50.00 percent) are directives, 23 (41.07 percent) are regulations, and 5 (8.93 percent) of the drafts resulted in the adoption of policy proposals for both, a regulation and a directive.[1] As mentioned previously, directives are binding on the member states as to the result to be achieved, but member states can choose the form and method they adopt to realize the objective of the directive. Hence, member states have to transpose the directive into national law. Regulations by contrast are directly applicable which means that they create legislation that takes immediate effect in all the member states. The sample of policy issues is fairly balanced between directives and regulations. In terms of legislative procedure, 49 (87.50 percent) of the policy proposals are subject to the Codecision and 7 (12.50 percent) are subject to the Consultation procedure. The majority of legislative proposals studied in this book therefore require the approval of both the Council and the European Parliament in order to enter into force.

5.2 THE POPULATION OF MOBILIZED INTEREST GROUPS

Who mobilizes? Which interest groups lobby the European institutions? Is there a bias with regard to organized interests in the European Union? Do business interests dominate policy debates in Brussels or are different types of organized interests equally represented? How large are these interest groups

---

[1] In cases where a consultation resulted in the adoption of more than one policy proposal, I collapsed the Parliament's summaries of these proposals and the resulting legislative acts into one single document in order to measure their policy position.

and how much do they spend on lobbying? This section answers these questions and sheds light on the population of interest groups that mobilized on the 56 policy issues that are studied in this book.

First, which interest groups mobilize in Brussels? Table 5.3 presents information on the composition of the population of mobilized interest groups. Business associations, which comprise all membership organizations related to business affairs such as sectoral industry associations, employers' associations, and chambers of commerce, constitute by far the largest share of actors participating in Commission consultations. Business associations account for 42 percent of all interest groups that mobilized in the 56 policy debates. The second largest group of advocates in the EU lobby process are companies which make up approximately 24 percent of all interest groups in the selected policy debates. Cause groups, which are defined as interest groups that represent some belief or principle and whose membership is not restricted (Stewart 1958, 25), represent the third largest group of actors. Cause groups include for instance environmental and consumer NGOs such as Greenpeace and the European Consumers' Organization (BEUC). Professional associations, which are organizations that represent the interests of certain professions such as the Committee of Professional Agricultural Organisations (COPA), constitute about 9 percent of the population of mobilized interest groups. Trade unions participated only to a marginal extent in the selected policy debates. Finally, public authority associations such as for instance the Council of European Municipalities and Regions constitute about 2 percent of all interest groups that mobilized on the 56 policy issues.

The population of interest groups which lobbied the European institutions in the selected policy debates is strongly biased in favor of European business. Interest group representation in the European Union is not balanced between different societal interests, but economic interests strongly dominate the lobbying game in Brussels. On the one hand, we observe an enormous

Table 5.3 Population of mobilized interest groups by actor type

Actor type	Frequency	Percent
Business associations	1,140	42.28
Companies	653	24.22
Cause groups	541	20.07
Professional associations	241	8.94
Public authority associations	46	1.71
Trade unions	28	1.04
Other	47	1.74
Total	2,696	100.00

imbalance between capital and labor. While industries and employers account for about 66 percent of all the lobbyists in the European Union, trade unions only constitute 2 percent of all interest organizations which mobilized in the selected policy debates. On the other hand, lobbying in the European Union is characterized by an imbalance between economic and diffuse interests. While cause groups fighting for a diffuse cause or belief such as environmental protection or human rights only make up about 20 percent of all mobilized advocates, sectional groups and companies representing concentrated, economic interests constitute about 76 percent of the mobilized interest group population. The dominance of economic interest groups in the 56 policy debates studied in this book largely corresponds to their overall weight in the entire population of interest groups at the EU level (see for instance Wonka et al. 2010).[2] Hence, policy debates in the European Union are clearly dominated by economic interests and interest group representation in Brussels is therefore heavily biased.

Second, the European Union is a multilevel political system in which different levels of government are intertwined. Accordingly, interest groups organize at different geographical levels, more precisely at the subnational, the national, and the European level. Do nationally organized interest groups dominate politics in the European Union or have interest groups evolved into truly European organizations? Figure 5.4 illustrates the territorial origin of interest groups that mobilized on the 56 policy issues studied in this book. The largest share of associations originate from the national level directly followed by European-wide associations. Most of the companies that mobilized in the selected policy debates are international companies which have subsidiaries in at least one European and one non-European or in two non-European countries.[3] The smallest group of consultation participants are associations or companies which are organized at the subnational level or which are based in a third state. The distribution of territorial origin in the population of interest groups that mobilized in the 56 policy debates studied in this book also corresponds nicely to the distribution of territorial origin in the entire population of interest groups at the European level (see Wonka et al. 2010).

---

[2] Wonka et al. (2010) identify the population of interest groups that lobby the European institutions based on three different sources: the Commission's voluntary "Consultation, the European Commission and Civil Society" (CONECCS) database in which interest groups could register that have participated in Commission committees or hearings, the accreditation registry of the European Parliament which contains all interest groups and representatives that obtained a special entry pass, and the Landmarks European Public Affairs Directory which is a commercial directory listing interest groups that operate on the European level.

[3] Companies are classified as international companies if they have have subsidiaries in at least one European and one non-European or in two non-European countries. If companies are only based in one foreign country, they are classified as third country companies. European firms are companies that are based in at least two different EU member states without having a subsidiary in a third state.

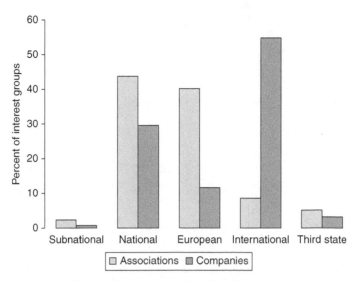

Fig. 5.4 Territorial origin of interest groups

In terms of interest group type and territorial origin, there is therefore no indication of a selection bias.

In terms of territorial origin, it can be concluded that lobbying in the European Union is neither dominated by national interests nor is it exclusively a European game. National interest groups and interest groups which organize at the European level are more or less equally represented in Brussels. Forty-four percent of all mobilized associations are national-level interest groups and 40 percent are organized at the European level. While interest groups have considerably Europeanized over the years by founding and joining European-wide organizations, interest representation is not exclusively European. Given the considerable heterogeneity and diversity in the 27 member states of the European Union, European federations can only provide interest representation on the lowest common denominator. In order to express their specific national views, national associations therefore simultaneously spill over to the European level and also lobby the European institutions directly (Klüver 2010). In addition, we observe considerable large firm lobbying in the European Union. Out of the 2,696 interest groups that mobilized on the policy issues studied in this book, 653 are companies. The vast majority of these companies are large European or international firms which directly seek to influence the European Commission, the Council, and the European Parliament.

How large are the interest groups that lobby the European institutions? How many lobbyists do they employ? Table 5.4 indicates the staff size of the interest groups that mobilized on the policy issues that are analyzed in

Table 5.4 Staff numbers of interest groups

Lobbying staff	Companies	Business groups	Professional groups	Trade unions	Cause groups	Public authority groups	Other	Total
1–5	53.49%	58.49%	61.54%	29.41%	62.89%	38.10%	88.46%	59.18%
6–10	15.50%	19.14%	16.35%	29.41%	17.94%	28.57%	3.85%	18.07%
11–25	15.50%	13.55%	7.69%	5.88%	13.36%	19.05%	7.69%	12.99%
26–50	9.30%	6.24%	11.54%	35.29%	3.05%	0.00%	0.00%	6.54%
more than 50	6.20%	2.58%	2.88%	0.00%	2.67%	14.29%	0.00%	3.22%
Total	100.00%	100.00%	100.00%	100.00%	100.00%	100.00%	100.00%	100.00%
N	129	465	104	17	262	21	26	1,024

Note: Cramer's V = 0.130

this book. The staff level was measured drawing on a survey question with answer categories provided on a five-point ordinal scale.[4] The vast majority of interest groups only employ one to five people that are in charge of lobbying decision-makers. Out of all interest groups, about 59 percent only employ up to five lobbyists. The small number of lobbying staff is not unique to a particular type of interest group, but nearly all interest groups exhibit similar staff numbers. About 63 percent of all cause groups and 62 percent of all professional associations solely rely on up to five people to lobby the European institutions. Similarly, approximately 58 percent of all business associations and 53 percent of all companies run their lobbying activities with only up to five employees. The distribution of staff numbers across different interest group types is similarly comparable with regard to a larger number of staff. For instance, about 3 percent of all cause groups, business associations, and professional associations employ more than 50 lobbyists. Trade unions and public authority associations employ on average a slightly larger number of staff while other groups rely on fewer people. However, overall the distribution of lobbying staff is fairly similar across different types of interest groups. Accordingly, the correlation coefficient only indicates a moderate association between staff number and interest group type. Hence, cause groups and trade unions are not disadvantaged in comparison to business groups or companies. By contrast, interest groups in the European Union are similarly equipped with lobbying staff.

Finally, how much do interest groups in the European Union spend on lobbying decision-makers? Table 5.5 provides information about the amount of money that interest groups which participated in the 56 selected policy debates spend on lobbying per year. Lobbying expenses were measured by a survey question with answer categories provided on a five-point ordinal scale.[5] The largest share of interest groups spends up to 50,000 euros on lobbying decision-makers. The second largest group of advocates pays between 100,000 and 500,000 euros per year for lobbying activities. About 20 percent of all interest groups that mobilized on the 56 selected policy issues invest more than 500,000 euros per year on lobbying and 10 percent spend even more than one million euros per year on lobbying activities. Lobbying expenses follow a fairly similar distribution across interest group type. About 43 percent of all companies, 40 percent of all professional associations and 37 percent of all cause groups spend up to 50,000 euros per year on lobbying the European

---

[4] The precise wording of the question is as follows: "How many of these employees are dealing with monitoring and commenting on public policy at least half their working time? Monitoring and commenting on public policy refers to all activities that aim at influencing legislation at the EU level such as participation in hearings and consultations, informal contacts with representatives of the EU institutions, demonstrations or media campaigns." See also appendices 1 and 2.

[5] The wording of the question is as follows: "How much do you spend on monitoring and commenting on public policy per year?" See also appendices 1 and 2.

institutions. Similarly, between 28 and 29 percent of all companies, business associations, and cause groups spend between 100,000 and 500,000 euros per year for lobbying activities. Finally, 6 percent of all companies, 11 percent of all business associations, and 14 percent of all cause groups spend more than one million euros a year for lobbying decision-makers. Thus, lobbying expenses do not vary systematically with interest group type. Accordingly, the correlation coefficient only indicates a moderate association. Hence, there are no interest group types that are generally disadvantaged with regard to lobbying staff or lobbying expenses. Business interests do not systematically have more money or more staff than other organized interests in the European Union.

5.3 THE STRUCTURE OF CONFLICT

Lobbying is a collective enterprise. Interest groups do not lobby alone, but they collectively mobilize on policy issues. There is probably not a single policy debate on which only one interest group attempts to lobby decision-makers. By contrast, a multitude of interest groups simultaneously lobbies the European institutions. In order to understand why some interest groups succeed and others fail in their lobbying activities, it has therefore been argued in this book that it is crucial to take into account how interest groups position themselves on an issue. Interest groups that pursue the same policy objective pull the European institutions in the same direction and therefore form a lobbying team. What is decisive for the lobbying success of interest groups is therefore not their own individual supply of information, citizen support, and economic power, but it is crucial how much of these goods is provided by their entire lobbying coalition. This section therefore investigates the structure of conflict in the European Union by examining the composition and the characteristics of lobbying coalitions.

First of all, how big are lobbying coalitions? How many interest groups typically come together in a coalition? The size of the different lobbying coalitions on the 56 policy issues studied in this book is illustrated in figure 5.5. On average, lobbying coalitions have about 29 members with a standard deviation of approximately 23. The size of the lobbying coalitions is to some extent correlated with the overall number of interest groups which mobilized in a policy debate. The larger the number of interest groups that participate in a debate, the larger the potential number of interest groups in a lobbying coalition. However, the Pearson correlation coefficient only amounts to 0.66 which indicates that the size of lobbying coalitions is far from being perfectly proportional to the overall number of mobilized interest groups. The size of lobbying coalitions is not only related to the pool of interest groups which

Table 5.5 Lobbying expenses of interest groups per year

Lobbying expenses	Companies	Business	Professional	Trade unions	Cause groups	Public authority	Other	Total
up to 50,000 EUR	43.44%	31.85%	40.24%	50.00%	37.02%	47.06%	47.83%	36.52%
more than 50,000, up to 100,000 EUR	11.48%	18.54%	17.07%	0.00%	13.19%	17.65%	17.39%	15.78%
more than 100,000, up to 500,000 EUR	28.69%	28.72%	21.95%	50.00%	27.66%	29.41%	30.43%	28.00%
more than 500,000, up to 1 million EUR	10.66%	9.92%	18.29%	0.00%	7.66%	0.00%	0.00%	9.68%
more than 1 million EUR	5.74%	10.97%	2.44%	0.00%	14.47%	5.88%	4.35%	10.02%
Total	100.00%	100.00%	100.00%	100.00%	100.00%	100.00%	100.00%	100.00%
N	122	383	82	6	235	17	23	868

Note: Cramer's V = 0.106

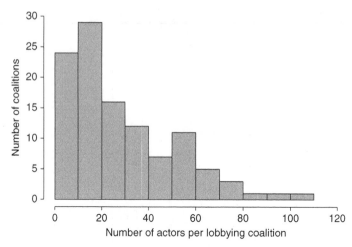

Fig. 5.5 Histogram of lobbying coalition size

participated in a legislative debate, but also to the distribution of interest groups across different coalitions and the underlying structure of conflict of a policy debate.

Second, how are interest groups distributed across lobbying coalitions? Are policy debates dominated by one large coalition or are two equally strong coalitions typically opposing each other? Table 5.6 reports information about the size of the larger coalition active in a policy debate. As it was assumed that policy debates are unidimensional, there are always two lobbying coalitions opposing each other in a debate. Hence, if one lobbying coalition assembles 60 percent of all interest groups active in a debate, the opposing coalition necessarily brings together 40 percent of the interest groups. The minimum relative size of the larger coalition is therefore just above 50 percent while a size of 50 percent signals perfectly equal lobbying coalitions. It is therefore sufficient to only focus on the larger coalitions to illustrate the size and the composition of lobbying coalitions as they are perfectly related to the smaller opposing coalitions.

Table 5.6 Size of larger coalition

Interest groups per issue	Frequency	Percent
up to 60%	16	28.57
60% to 70%	9	16.07
70% to 80%	9	16.07
80% to 90%	13	23.21
90% to 100%	9	16.07
Total	56	100.00

About 30 percent of all policy debates in the sample are characterized by more or less equally strong coalitions in which the larger coalition assembles up to 60 percent of all interest groups that mobilized in a policy debate. However, at the same time about 40 percent of all legislative debates studied in this book are dominated by a lobbying coalition that comprises between 80 and 100 percent of all interest groups that mobilized on these issues. Similarly, about 32 percent of the issues are characterized by a structure of conflict in which the larger coalition brings together between 60 and 80 percent of all interest groups that lobby the European institutions. Hence, policy debates in the European Union are usually not characterized by equally strong lobbying coalitions. We can only observe a tie between two opposing coalitions in about 30 percent of the debates studied in this book. By contrast, most legislative debates are dominated by one large lobbying coalition that assembles the vast majority of interest groups that mobilized on an issue.

What is the nature of lobbying coalitions? How are they composed? Do lobbying coalitions bring together a unique set of actors? Is a lobbying coalition of business groups for instance opposing a lobbying coalition of NGOs? Or are lobbying coalitions instead heterogeneous teams of different types of interest groups? Figure 5.6 illustrates the average composition of lobbying coalitions analyzed in this book. The typical lobbying coalition in the European Union is not restricted to one type of actor. By contrast, lobbying coalitions are heterogeneous entities that bring together a diverse set of actors. On average, lobbying coalitions in the European Union include 23 percent companies, 41 percent business associations, 9 percent professional associations, 1 percent trade unions, 21 percent cause groups, and 4 percent other groups. The

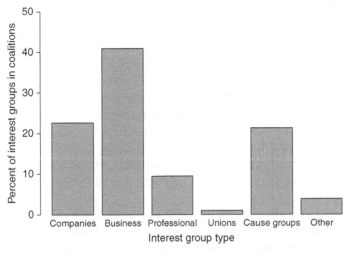

Fig. 5.6 Average composition of lobbying coalitions

majority of interest groups represent economic interests which is a result of the better representation of economic interest groups in the European Union more generally. At the same time, lobbying coalitions, however, also bring together a wide variety of other actors and therefore form heterogeneous entities.

Solely looking at the average composition might, however, still hide issue-specific differences in the composition of lobbying coalitions. It might be the case that distinct camps of interest groups are opposing each other in the different policy debates and that differences in the composition are simply overlooked by merely looking at the aggregate level. Table 5.7 therefore provides information about the issue-specific composition of opposing lobbying coalitions. Rather than solely focusing on the aggregate composition of all coalitions in the sample, the table indicates how the different interest group types are distributed across the two coalitions directly opposing each other on the same issue. On average, the larger coalition on a given policy issue comprises 75 percent of all companies, 73 percent of all business associations, 67 percent of all professional associations, 73 percent of all trade unions, 65 percent of all cause groups, and 83 percent of all other actors active in a policy debate. Hence, lobbying coalitions include a very diverse set of actors. In addition, none of the 56 policy debates analyzed in this book are characterized by a clear-cut opposition of business interests and cause groups. The empirical analysis reveals that there is not a single legislative debate on which companies and business associations formed a united front against cause groups. Lobbying coalitions are by contrast heterogeneous entities that bring together a variety of different actors.

Policy debates in the European Union are not characterized by a clear opposition of business versus public interests. It is often argued that lobbying is a two-sided game in which economic interests fight against citizen interests. However, the empirical analysis in this book shows that there is no clear divide between business interests and cause groups. One cannot find any policy debate in which all economic interest groups collectively fight against a united alliance of cause groups. By contrast, lobbying coalitions bring together a variety of different economic and citizen interest groups. Interest groups which are generally considered to have opposing interests often lobby together for a common policy objective. The heterogeneous nature of lobbying coalitions in the European Union largely corresponds to the findings of Baumgartner et al. (2009) who analyzed interest group lobbying in the United States across 98 policy issues. In line with the analysis presented in this section, they find that lobbying coalitions are by no means homogeneous entities, but that they have a very diverse set of members.

The heterogeneous composition of lobbying coalitions is a result of the nature of policy debates in the European Union. Policy proposals affect diverse constituencies, creating heterogeneous lobbying teams. Interest groups that might be aligned on one issue, might oppose each other on another issue.

Table 5.7 Composition of lobbying coalitions in percent of interest group type per issue

Issue	Larger coalition						Smaller coalition					
	Company	Businesss	Professional	Trade	Cause	Other	Company	Businesss	Professional	Trade	Cause	Other
1	100.00	42.86	66.67	—	0.00	100.00	0.00	57.14	33.33	—	100.00	0.00
2	66.67	93.33	0.00	—	9.09	—	33.33	6.67	100.00	—	90.91	—
3	0.00	93.33	100.00	—	100.00	—	100.00	6.67	0.00	—	0.00	—
4	100.00	79.10	100.00	—	57.14	—	0.00	20.90	0.00	—	42.86	—
5	100.00	100.00	—	—	100.00	—	0.00	0.00	—	—	0.00	—
6	100.00	66.67	—	—	0.00	—	0.00	33.33	—	—	100.00	—
7	100.00	100.00	—	—	100.00	—	0.00	0.00	—	—	0.00	—
8	83.33	94.12	100.00	—	0.00	—	16.67	5.88	0.00	—	100.00	—
9	50.00	88.89	100.00	—	100.00	100.00	50.00	11.11	0.00	—	0.00	0.00
10	43.75	64.29	0.00	—	44.44	100.00	56.25	35.71	100.00	—	55.56	0.00
11	55.56	68.75	100.00	—	88.37	100.00	44.44	31.25	0.00	—	11.63	0.00
12	93.33	76.92	0.00	—	0.00	0.00	6.67	23.08	100.00	—	100.00	100.00
13	51.67	53.33	75.00	—	37.50	80.00	48.33	46.67	25.00	—	62.50	20.00
14	22.22	48.28	100.00	100.00	100.00	—	77.78	51.72	0.00	0.00	0.00	—
15	43.24	61.54	55.56	—	60.00	—	56.76	38.46	44.44	—	40.00	—
16	100.00	100.00	—	—	100.00	100.00	0.00	0.00	—	—	0.00	0.00
17	27.27	56.52	61.90	—	50.00	—	72.73	43.48	38.10	—	50.00	—
18	100.00	100.00	—	—	100.00	—	0.00	0.00	—	—	0.00	0.00
19	60.00	69.70	83.33	100.00	42.86	33.33	40.00	30.30	16.67	0.00	57.14	66.67
20	85.71	70.83	66.67	33.33	85.71	100.00	14.29	29.17	33.33	66.67	14.29	0.00
21	37.50	49.12	71.43	100.00	61.11	50.00	62.50	50.88	28.57	0.00	38.89	50.00
22	100.00	77.78	77.78	—	94.44	—	0.00	22.22	22.22	—	5.56	—
23	100.00	71.43	80.00	—	85.71	100.00	0.00	28.57	20.00	—	14.29	0.00
24	92.86	75.51	70.00	0.00	75.00	100.00	7.14	24.49	30.00	100.00	25.00	0.00
25	26.67	53.42	91.67	—	69.23	0.00	73.33	46.58	8.33	—	30.77	100.00
26	90.00	96.55	100.00	—	83.33	100.00	10.00	3.45	0.00	—	16.67	0.00
27	83.33	93.55	100.00	—	100.00	100.00	16.67	6.45	0.00	—	0.00	0.00
28	100.00	94.44	100.00	—	80.00	100.0	0.00	5.56	0.00	—	20.00	0.00

(continued)

Table 5.7 Continued

Issue	Larger coalition						Smaller coalition					
	Company	Business	Professional	Trade	Cause	Other	Company	Business	Professional	Trade	Cause	Other
29	53.85	80.60	28.57	—	23.08	53.85	46.15	19.40	71.43	—	76.92	46.15
30	83.33	100.00	100.00	—	0.00	100.00	16.67	0.00	0.00	—	100.00	0.00
31	44.44	85.71	100.00	—	0.00	—	55.56	14.29	0.00	—	100.00	—
32	100.00	50.00	—	100.00	44.44	—	0.00	50.00	—	0.00	55.56	—
33	50.00	64.86	100.00	—	100.00	—	50.00	35.14	0.00	—	0.00	—
34	77.42	69.39	100.00	—	66.67	61.54	22.58	30.61	0.00	—	33.33	38.46
35	50.00	80.00	50.00	—	36.36	—	50.00	20.00	50.00	—	63.64	—
36	66.67	20.00	0.00	—	44.44	100.00	33.33	80.00	100.00	—	55.56	0.00
37	50.00	83.33	—	—	100.00	—	50.00	16.67	—	—	0.00	—
38	66.67	60.00	—	100.00	50.00	100.00	33.33	40.00	—	0.00	50.00	0.00
39	94.74	90.00	0.00	—	50.00	—	5.26	10.00	100.00	—	50.00	—
40	100.00	100.00	100.00	—	100.00	—	0.00	0.00	0.00	—	0.00	—
41	100.00	91.30	0.00	—	50.00	—	0.00	8.70	100.00	—	50.00	—
42	100.00	0.00	—	—	100.00	—	0.00	100.00	—	—	0.00	—
43	100.00	100.00	33.33	—	100.00	100.00	0.00	0.00	66.67	—	0.00	0.00
44	90.00	100.00	100.00	—	100.00	85.71	10.00	0.00	0.00	—	0.00	14.29
45	94.74	80.00	0.00	—	0.00	—	5.26	20.00	100.00	—	100.00	—
46	55.88	63.41	33.33	0.00	7.14	100.00	44.12	36.59	66.67	100.00	92.86	0.00
47	100.00	83.33	—	—	100.00	—	0.00	16.67	—	—	0.00	—
48	94.12	93.33	—	—	0.00	—	5.88	6.67	—	—	100.00	—
49	—	100.00	100.00	100.00	82.86	100.00	—	0.00	0.00	0.00	17.14	0.00
50	100.00	70.59	25.00	—	100.00	—	0.00	29.41	75.00	—	0.00	—
51	—	—	100.00	—	100.00	—	—	—	0.00	—	0.00	—
52	—	20.00	50.00	100.00	96.55	100.00	—	80.00	50.00	0.00	3.45	—
53	—	100.00	100.00	—	100.00	66.67	—	0.00	0.00	—	0.00	33.33
54	18.75	25.00	100.00	—	91.30	100.00	81.25	75.00	0.00	—	8.70	0.00
55	—	15.38	50.00	—	100.00	75.00	—	84.62	50.00	—	0.00	0.00
56	100.00	50.00	66.67	—	95.83	—	0.00	50.00	33.33	—	4.17	25.00
Mean	74.58	73.03	67.49	73.33	65.40	82.97	25.42	26.97	32.51	26.67	34.60	17.03

Similarly, organized interests of the same type might be divided on some issues even though they work together on most of the other issues. For instance, the automobile industry was divided on the Commission proposal reducing CO_2 emissions from cars discussed in chapter 3. The European Commission intended to reduce CO_2 emissions from passenger cars to 120 grams per kilometre by 2012. Manufacturers such as Volkswagen and General Motors as well as their industry associations opposed the Commission initiative and attempted to water down the proposal. By contrast, manufacturers of electric or hybrid vehicles and producers of alternative fuels teamed up with environmental groups and supported the Commission initiative. The somewhat surprising lobbying coalition between parts of the automotive industry and environmental groups can be explained by the differential impact of the Commission initiative on different industry sectors. While more traditional manufacturers that produce petrol-based cars are negatively affected by the CO_2 emission targets, the alternative automobile industry sector in fact benefits from the Commission initiative as it strengthens its competitiveness vis-à-vis the traditional automobile manufacturers by increasing the demand for electric and hybrid cars.

A very different example is the policy debate revolving around the Commission initiative to enhance pedestrian protection. In June 2005, The European Commission published a preliminary draft proposal in which it proposed several measures to increase the protection of pedestrians. Amongst others, the Commission suggested that brake assist systems should be mandatory for all new vehicles from 1 July 2008 in order to increase the safety of pedestrians in European traffic. In contrast to the CO_2 emissions debate, this issue united the entire automobile industry. All car manufactures collectively opposed the Commission proposal and advocated for longer lead times for making brake assistant systems mandatory. Car manufacturers argued that vehicles have a production cycle that goes way beyond 2008. As a result, cars coming on the market in 2008 would have already been designed and their production would have already been implemented so that adjusting these models at such short notice would cause costly adaptation processes that would harm the competitiveness of the European automobile industry. Car producers therefore fought together in one single lobbying coalition trying to water down the Commission proposal in their favor.

These examples make clear that there are no universal lobbying fronts. The structure of conflict varies across policy debates. Policy proposals are complex and have a differential impact on constituencies. Even though interest groups are similar in nature, it does not necessarily mean that they also work together. For instance, it is very often the case that economic interest groups are divided on an issue. A policy proposal might have negative implications for the productivity of one economic sector while another sector might benefit from the same initiative. Interest groups that fight together on one issue, might therefore oppose each other in the next policy debate. Lobbying teams are therefore not universal. The composition of lobbying coalitions varies from one issue to the next. In order to understand lobbying success, it is therefore crucial not to assume an a priori structure of conflict, but to empirically examine the composition of lobbying coalitions for every single policy debate.

5.4 CONCLUSION

This chapter has provided an overview of the nature of policy issues, the population of mobilized interest groups, and the underlying structure of conflict in policy debates in the European Union. The chapter has first of all demonstrated that policy issues in the EU are diverse. Policy debates revolve mostly around economic issues, but also regulatory issues related to environmental protection, health, or consumer protection are very common. Similarly, distributive issues, most importantly related to agriculture, play an important role in EU politics. Policy issues furthermore vary in salience, complexity, and the degree of conflict. There are policy debates which receive a large amount of attention from interest groups, but there are also other issues which trigger hardly any response. Similarly, some policy proposals are highly complex in nature whereas other proposals deal with relatively simple matters. In addition, some policy debates are largely consensual whereas other policy issues divide the interest group community. Hence, policy debates in the European Union vary considerably in a number of important characteristics and it is therefore crucial to take into account the specific issue-context in which interest groups lobby the European institutions.

The analysis presented in this chapter has furthermore shed light on the population of mobilized interest groups. The vast majority of interest groups that lobby the European institutions are economic interests. Lobbying in the European Union is therefore not a balanced activity in which different types of organized interests seek to feed their ideas into the policy-making process. By contrast, interest group lobbying is strongly biased in favor of economic interests. In the words of Schattschneider (1960, 35), interest group representation in the European Union "is skewed, loaded and unbalanced in favor of a fraction of a minority" and "the flaw in the pluralist heaven is that the heavenly chorus sings with a strong upper-class accent." With regard to the territorial origin of interest groups, this chapter has demonstrated that lobbying in the European Union is dominated neither by national level nor by European level organizations. Lobbying in the European is instead a truly multilevel endeavor in which both national and European interest groups are equally active. Finally, with regard to staff numbers and lobbying expenses the analysis presented in this chapter has indicated that there are no systematic differences across interest group type.

This chapter has furthermore investigated the structure of conflict and the nature of lobbying coalitions in the European Union. Policy debates in the European Union are dominated by one large coalition. Most policy issues analyzed in this book are characterized by a structure of conflict in which one coalition dominates the debate. This chapter has moreover demonstrated that lobbying coalitions are not homogeneous. We hardly find any policy debates in which lobbying coalitions emerge that only bring together interest groups of the same kind. By contrast, lobbying coalitions are characterized by a very diverse and heterogeneous membership cutting across various actor types. Hence, policy debates in the European Union are not characterized by an overarching cleavage between for instance business and citizen interests. On the contrary, the structure of conflict is highly issue-specific and varies from one issue to the next.

6

The Policy Formulation Stage: Interest Groups and the European Commission

Why are some interest groups able to influence policy-making in the European Union while others are not? This is the crucial question this book aims to answer. In order to understand why some interest groups succeed in lobbying decision-makers while others fail, chapter 2 presented a theoretical model of interest group influence in the European Union. It was argued that lobbying has to be conceptualized as a complex collective enterprise in which information supply, citizen support, and economic power of entire lobbying coalitions account for variation in lobbying success. In order to test these theoretical expectations, chapter 3 introduced a new measurement approach to interest group influence which allows one to overcome the methodological difficulties that have long prevented scholars from addressing the question of influence. Using this measurement approach and combining it with a survey of interest groups and data gathered from EU databases, a new dataset on interest group lobbying in the European Union was constructed which was illustrated in chapter 4. Chapter 5 then provided a thorough overview of the nature of the issues, the population of mobilized interest groups, and the structure of conflict in the 56 selected policy debates. This chapter now tests the hypotheses derived from the theoretical model on the basis of the data collected about the 56 policy debates for the policy formulation stage in which the European Commission drafts the legislative proposal.

The chapter proceeds as follows: It first provides a short summary of the policy formulation stage in the European Union. Afterwards, the hypotheses derived from the theoretical model are tested for the policy formulation stage using multilevel logistic regression. The hypotheses are tested one after the other as the dataset suffers from high collinearity of the predictors and from a lot of missing values so that the sample would otherwise shrink from 2,696 interest groups and 56 policy issues to 291 interest groups lobbying the European Commission concerning 48 issues (see section 4.4). I therefore first test the effect of relative information supply by lobbying coalitions on interest group influence. I then examine whether the strength of this effect varies with the complexity of policy issues. Second, I test whether relative citizen support of lobbying coalitions has a positive effect on the ability of interest groups to shape policy outcomes. Finally, I examine the effect of relative economic power of lobbying coalitions on interest group influence on policy formulation in the European Union. Effect sizes are compared using predicted probabilities and first differences (Mroz and Zayats 2008, see also page 130).

6.1 POLICY FORMULATION BY THE EUROPEAN COMMISSION

The policy formulation stage constitutes the start of any legislative debate in the European Union. During the policy formulation stage the European Commission develops its legislative proposal that is passed on to the Council and the European Parliament for legislative discussion. The European Commission has the monopoly of initiative in the first pillar which is arguably the most important one. Every legislative debate in this pillar is therefore based on a legislative initiative of the European Commission. The legislative process only starts once a proposal is tabled by the Commission. The European Commission is thus solely responsible for the elaboration of a policy proposal that forms the basis for the discussion between the Council and the European Parliament.

The elaboration of a policy proposal is a complex and lengthy process in which several actors within and outside the Commission are involved. The responsibility of drafting a legislative proposal lies with the Directorate General (DG) that is primarily concerned with the policy area in which the proposal falls. The lead DG consults with other DGs that are affected by the policy proposal to reach consensus within the European Commission (Nugent 2001, 242–243; Hartlapp, Metz, and Rauh 2010*a*). In order to obtain policy-relevant information and to safeguard support for its proposals among stakeholders, the European Commission also consults external actors such as interest groups, experts, national officials and also the general public (Nugent 2001, 246–249; Gornitzka and Sverdrup 2008; Hartlapp, Metz, and Rauh 2010*b*). In an effort to enhance the transparency and accountability of European policy-making, consultations of the general public were recently institutionalized (Kohler-Koch and Finke 2007; Quittkat and Finke 2008): The European Commission conducts public consultations on all "major" policy initiatives (European Commission 2002). Policy issues are considered as "major" if "the proposal will result in substantial economic, environmental and/or social impact on a specific sector," if "the proposal will have a significant impact on major interested parties," and if "the proposal represents a major policy reform in one or several sectors" (European Commission 2002, 15). Once the draft proposal is ready for legislative discussion, the responsible DG takes it to the College of Commissioners which has to agree on the proposal if necessary by simple majority vote before it is forwarded to the Council and the European Parliament.

The monopoly of legislative initiative provides the European Commission with an important agenda-setting function: It determines the terms and conditions of any legislative debate as it is up to the Commission to design the content of a legislative proposal on which basis the other institutions bargain about the final legislative act. It is accordingly more difficult for the Council and the European Parliament to modify than to accept the policy proposal (Thomson and Hosli 2006, 14–15). Practitioners as well as interest group scholars have therefore argued that the policy formulation stage constitutes the most promising stage to influence the outcome of a legislative debate (Hull 1993; Bouwen 2009). A former Secretary General of the European Commission commented that "for interest groups in particular, the proposal stage often offers the most fertile opportunities for exerting influence" (Thomson and Hosli 2006, 15). Bouwen (2009, 25) reasons in a similar vein: "It is common knowledge among lobbyists that as long as no formal written documents are produced during the policy development stage, changes to the policy proposals can be made much more swiftly and easily." Similarly, Austen-Smith (1993, 813) asserts that lobbying is most successful in early stages of the policy cycle. Hence, the policy formulation stage is of crucial importance to interest groups in order to influence the final policy outcome.

6.2 THE EFFECT OF INFORMATION SUPPLY

Table 6.1 shows the results of the multilevel logistic regression testing the effect of coalition information supply on interest group influence on policy formulation in the European Union. The model in column one is the empty model which is displayed in order to evaluate the explanatory power of the other models. Column two contains the results of the basic model including relative information supply as a predictor for interest group influence. The model in column three in addition contains several control variables on the interest group and issue level. Finally, column four includes the results of the full multilevel model that additionally comprises an interaction effect between relative information supply by lobbying coalitions and the complexity of policy issues. As none of the variables in the model suffers from missing values, the analysis could be performed for the complete sample consisting of 2,696 interest groups and 56 policy issues.

Table 6.1 Multilevel analysis examining the effect of information supply on interest group influence during the policy formulation stage

Variables	Empty	Basic	With controls	Full
Fixed effects				
LOBBYING COALITION CHARACTERISTICS				
Rel. information supply		1.022***	1.027***	0.993
		(0.003)	(0.003)	(0.014)
Rel. information supply * complexity				1.011**
				(0.005)
CONTROLS: INTEREST GROUP LEVEL				
Type: Sectional group			1.062	1.071
			(0.125)	(0.126)
Type: Cause group			0.924	0.913
			(0.139)	(0.138)
Rel. information supply			0.985	0.984
			(0.023)	(0.023)
CONTROLS: ISSUE LEVEL				
Salience			1.321	1.345
			(0.476)	(0.480)
Complexity			1.452	0.723
			(0.446)	(0.307)
Conflict			0.409	0.403
			(0.298)	(0.291)
Existence of EU SQ			0.839	0.859
			(0.378)	(0.384)
Legislative procedure: Codecision			2.788	2.702
			(2.479)	(2.380)
Voting rule: QM			2.718	2.897
			(3.149)	(3.330)
Member state support			0.979***	0.976***
			(0.005)	(0.005)
Random effects				
Issue level variance	2.377	2.128	1.930	1.892
Model fit				
N / Issues	2696 / 56	2696 / 56	2696 / 56	2696 / 56
Log likelihood	−1592	−1556	−1539	−1536
AIC	3187	3117	3104	3101
BIC	3199	3135	3181	3183
LR Test, Prob > Chi2		0.000	0.000	0.021

***$p \leq 0.01$,**$p \leq 0.05$,*$p \leq 0.10$, coefficients represent odds ratios, standard errors in parentheses, sectional and cause groups are compared to companies, Codecision is compared to Consultation, qualified majority voting is compared to unanimity, the reference model for the likelihood ratio test is the model left of the model in question.

In both versions of the multilevel model with and without control variables, relative information supply by lobbying coalitions has a statistically significant positive effect on interest group influence. A 1 percent increase in relative information supply by a lobbying coalition *A*, which at the same time implies a 1 percent decrease in relative information supply by its opposing lobbying coalition *B*, increases the chance of interest groups which belong to lobbying coalition *A* to influence policy formulation by 2.2 percent (2.7 percent when control variables are included).[1] Hence, the multilevel analysis indicates that the probability to influence policy formulation increases with the information that lobbying coalitions provide to the European Commission.

The multilevel analysis furthermore demonstrates that individual group characteristics cannot account for variation in interest group influence on European policy formulation. Neither actor type nor information supply by individual interest groups has a systematic effect on lobbying success. In addition, none of the issue-level control variables except for member state support has a statistically significant effect. Member state support is surprisingly negatively associated with lobbying success whereas none of the other issue characteristics has a systematic effect on interest group influence. Thus, what seems to matter most is the issue-specific grouping of interest groups into lobbying coalitions rather than the attributes of the issue itself. All model fit measures accordingly indicate that the inclusion of relative information supply by lobbying coalitions significantly increases the explanatory power of the model whereas adding the control variables does not increase the model fit according to the BIC.

In order to present the effect of relative information supply in a more intuitive fashion, I simulated predicted probabilities and first differences (King, Tomz, and Wittenberg 2000). Figure 6.1 displays the predicted probabilities of interest group influence as relative information supply by lobbying coalitions changes from its minimum (0) to maximum value (100) while holding all other variables constant. The solid line presents the point estimate for the predicted probability and the broken lines indicate the 95 percent confidence interval. The probability to influence the policy proposal of the European Commission steadily increases with a rise in relative information supply by lobbying coalitions. Hence, a higher value of relative information supply is associated with a higher probability to influence policy formulation across the entire range of possible values.

---

[1] As explained in section 4.3.2, the values of the coalition characteristics of two lobbying coalitions working on the same issue always add up to 100 since these are relative measures and there are only two coalitions on each issue. If lobbying coalition *A* provides 40 percent of the information, lobbying coalition *B* provides 60 percent. Similarly, if lobbying coalition *A* provides 41 percent, lobbying coalition *B* necessarily supplies 59 percent of the information provided to the European Commission. A 1 percent increase in relative information supply by one lobbying coalition therefore always implies a 1 percent decrease in relative information supply by its opposing lobbying coalition.

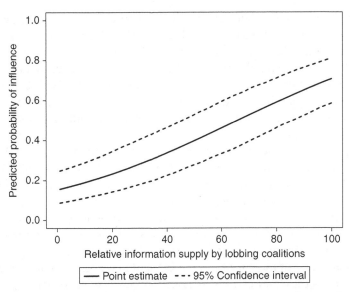

Fig. 6.1 Effect of relative information supply on interest group influence during the policy formulation stage

In order to further illustrate the size of the effects, I simulated first differences to demonstrate how the probability to influence policy formulation changes when relative information supply by lobbying coalitions is altered (see table 6.2). The first column contains the change in relative information supply and the second column indicates the associated predicted change in the probability to influence policy formulation together with a 95 percent confidence interval. If relative information supply by lobbying coalitions increases from 0 to 25 percent, the probability to influence policy formulation rises by approximately 10.3 percentage points. Similarly, if a lobbying coalition *A* provides 25 percent of all the information provided on an issue, whereas lobbying coalition *C* provides 50 percent on another issue, the probability to

Table 6.2 First differences: Effect of relative information supply on interest group influence during the policy formulation stage

Change: Information supply	Change: Influence probability	95% Confidence interval	
0–25%	0.103	0.073	0.137
25–50%	0.141	0.106	0.175
50–75%	0.160	0.125	0.196
75–100%	0.148	0.112	0.184
0–100%	0.555	0.451	0.643

influence the content of the Commission proposal is 14.1 percentage points higher for members of coalition C than for interest groups which belong to coalition A. The effect is strongest when relative information supply augments from 50 to 75 percent: The associated change in the probability to influence policy formulation amounts to 16.0 percentage points. Overall, if relative information supply increased from its minimum (0) to its maximum value (100), the probability to influence policy formulation would increase by about 55.5 percentage points.

A typical example for the positive effect of information supply is the policy debate about the mercury strategy of the European Commission.[2] Mercury is highly toxic to humans, animals, and ecosystems. In March 2004, the European Commission therefore released a policy document which laid out a new mercury strategy that envisaged a number of actions to protect citizens' health and the environment. Amongst others, the European Commission has suggested restrictions on the sale of measuring devices containing mercury, a ban on exports of mercury from the EU, and new rules on safe storage. The publication of the Commission's envisaged strategy has led to major opposition from the electric, the chemical, and the steel industry. Industry groups argued that additional measures reducing the use of mercury would impose costs on European industries that seriously harm their competitiveness. It has furthermore been stated that several EU initiatives such as as the Greenhouse Gas Emissions Trading Scheme (ETS) have already sufficiently reduced the use of mercury so that additional measures are not necessary.

The opposing lobbying coalition on this issue was composed of environmental NGOs, health groups, as well as groups representing the water industry which supported the Commission initiative. These groups have submitted very detailed position papers in which they thoroughly discuss the impact of mercury on human health and the environment. They present the results of scientific studies examining the effect of mercury exposure on the human body, on animals, and on entire ecosystems. While the industry lobby largely based their demands on general claims regarding the competitiveness of European industry, the environmental, health, and water groups provided the European Commission with important technical policy expertise. Accordingly, the industry lobby supplied only 38 percent of the information while the lobbying coalition in favor of the Commission strategy supplied 62 percent of all information transmitted to the European Commission in this policy debate. The European Commission adopted a legislative framework in 2006 which followed the reasoning of the environmental, the health, and the water lobby while the demands of the industry have not been taken up. This indicates that

---

[2] The following discussion is based on responses submitted to the Commission consultation on the development of an EU mercury strategy and the associated consultation document, legislative proposals (COM (2006) 69, COM (2006) 636), and final legislative acts (Directive 2007/51/EC, Regulation (EC) No. 1102/2008).

the policy expertise provided by environmental, health, and water groups has led the Commission to follow their line of argumentation.

The empirical analysis has thus far shown that high levels of information supply by lobbying coalitions increases the likelihood that interest groups are able to influence policy formulation. However, hypothesis 4 suggested that this effect varies with issue complexity. It was argued that this effect should increase with the complexity of policy issues as the European institutions need much more information for issues that are highly complex than for issues of low complexity. In order to test this hypothesis, I included a cross-level interaction effect between relative information supply and complexity of policy issues in the model.[3] The results are indicated in column four of table 6.1. The multilevel analysis indicates that the effect of relative information supply indeed varies with the complexity of policy issues as there is a statistically significant interaction at play. When complexity is 0, the effect of a 1 percent increase of relative information supply by lobbying coalition *A*, which at the same time implies a decrease in relative information supply by lobbying coalition *B*, on interest group influence is 0.993. Similarly, the effect of complexity on interest group influence is 0.723 when relative information supply by lobbying coalitions is 0. All model fit measures except the BIC, which is the most conservative measure, accordingly indicate that including the interaction term has considerably enhanced the explanatory power of the model.

In order to illustrate how the effect of relative information supply by lobbying coalitions varies across issues, I computed a marginal effects plot (see figure 6.2) as recommended by Brambour, Clark, and Golder (2006). The solid line indicates how the effect of relative information supply by lobbying coalitions varies with the degree of complexity. The broken lines represent the 95 percent confidence interval allowing one to determine the significance of the interaction term. It is statistically significant when the lower and upper bounds of the confidence intervals are both below or above the zero line. Since the upper and the lower bound of the confidence interval are both above zero for the entire range of complexity, there is a statistically significant interaction effect between information supply and issue complexity across all policy issues: The size of the positive effect of relative information supply by lobbying coalitions steadily increases with the complexity of policy issues.[4]

In conclusion, the multilevel analysis has provided empirical support for hypothesis 1 and hypothesis 4. Relative information supply by lobbying coalitions has indeed a statistically significant positive effect on interest group

---

[3] Ideally, this interaction should be tested drawing on a random slope model. However, the number of cases is not sufficient to estimate a random slope model and the analysis is therefore limited to a random intercept model which only allows for variation of the intercept across policy issues.

[4] The marginal effect steadily increases, but it does so at decreasing increments. This indicates that the European institutions need more information as the complexity increases, but that there is at the same time a saturation effect at play as the additional information needs get smaller.

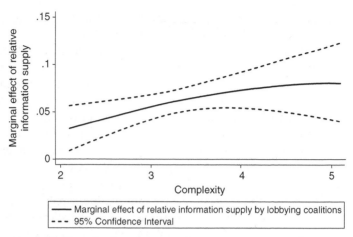

Fig. 6.2 Marginal effect of information supply on interest group influence during the policy formulation stage

influence. Thus, interest groups that belong to a lobbying coalition that on the aggregate supplies a high amount of information to the European Commission have a much better chance to influence policy formulation than interest groups belonging to a lobbying coalition which only provides little information to the Commission. In addition, this effect is particularly strong for highly complex issues as the European Commission requires a lot of information for the drafting of a policy proposal. By contrast, if a policy issue is of very low complexity, the European Commission hardly needs any external expertise and information supply can therefore barely increase the probability to influence policy formulation.

6.3 THE EFFECT OF CITIZEN SUPPORT

After having tested the effect of information supply on interest group influence on EU policy formulation, I now turn to the hypothesized effect of citizen support. Table 6.3 presents the results of the multilevel analysis examining the effect of relative citizen support of lobbying coalitions on interest group influence during the policy formulation stage. The first column contains the results of the empty model, the basic model in the second column includes relative citizen support as a predictor, and the third model additionally comprises various control variables on the interest group and issue level. Due to survey non-response, the sample is reduced to 1,066 interest groups and 54 policy issues.

Table 6.3 Multilevel analysis examining the effect of citizen support on interest group influence during the policy formulation stage

Variables	Empty	Basic	Full
Fixed effects			
LOBBYING COALITION CHARACTERISTICS			
Rel. citizen support		1.044***	1.047***
		(0.004)	(0.005)
CONTROLS: INTEREST GROUP LEVEL			
Type: Sectional group			1.215
			(0.295)
Type: Cause group			1.021
			(0.302)
Rel. citizen support			0.971***
			(0.010)
CONTROLS: ISSUE LEVEL			
Salience			1.104
			(0.511)
Complexity			1.508
			(0.580)
Conflict			0.530
			(0.491)
Existence of EU SQ			0.971
			(0.549)
Legislative procedure: Codecision			5.995
			(7.722)
Voting rule: QM			4.037
			(6.483)
Member state support			0.990
			(0.009)
Random effects			
Issue level variance	2.635	3.465	2.503
Model fit			
N / Issues	1066 / 54	1066 / 54	1066 / 54
Log likelihood	−627	−551	−539
AIC	1258	1109	1104
BIC	1268	1124	1168
LR Test, Prob > Chi2		0.000	0.005

***$p \leq 0.01$, **$p \leq 0.05$, *$p \leq 0.10$, coefficients represent odds ratios, standard errors in parentheses, sectional and cause groups are compared to companies, Codecision is compared to Consultation, qualified majority voting is compared to unanimity, the reference model for the likelihood ratio test is the model left of the model in question

Across both model specifications, relative citizen support of lobbying coalitions has a statistically significant positive effect on interest group influence on policy formulation as suggested by hypothesis 2. A 1 percent increase in relative citizen support of a lobbying coalition *A*, which again implies a 1 percent decrease in relative citizen support of its opposing lobbying coalition *B*, increases the chance of interest groups which are members of lobbying coalition *A* to influence the policy proposal by 4.4 percent (4.7 percent when control variables are included). Hence, interest groups which belong to lobbying coalitions that enjoy a large degree of citizen support find it easier to influence the drafting of policy proposals than interest groups which belong to lobbying coalitions that largely lack citizen support. All the other control variables on the interest group and issue level by contrast do not have a statistically significant effect on interest group influence with the exception of citizen support provided by individual interest groups. Citizen support of individual interest groups in fact has a statistically significant negative effect on interest group influence. Thus, citizen support only increases the chance to influence policy formulation if provided on the aggregate coalition level. All model fit measures indicate that the inclusion of relative citizen support of lobbying coalitions has significantly improved the fit of the model whereas the BIC denotes that incorporating the control variables has not enhanced the explanatory power of the model.

In order to illustrate the effect of citizen support, I have again simulated predicted probabilities and first differences (King, Tomz, and Wittenberg 2000). Figure 6.3 presents the predicted probabilities of interest group influence as relative citizen support of lobbying coalitions changes from its minimum (0) to maximum value (100) while holding all other variables constant. The probability to influence policy formulation again rises steadily as relative citizen support of lobbying coalitions increases. Accordingly, a

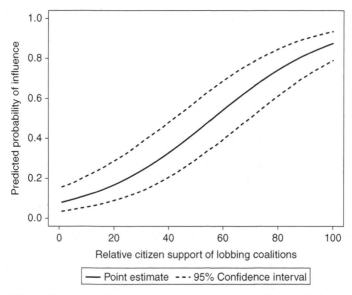

Fig. 6.3 Effect of relative citizen support on interest group influence during the policy formulation stage

Table 6.4 First differences: Effect of relative citizen support on interest group influence during the policy formulation stage

Change: Citizen support	Change: Influence probability	95% Confidence interval	
0–25%	0.124	0.072	0.184
25–50%	0.230	0.170	0.281
50–75%	0.266	0.213	0.316
75–100%	0.177	0.118	0.243
0–100%	0.797	0.716	0.864

higher value of relative citizen support of lobbying coalitions leads to a higher probability to influence policy formulation across the entire range of possible values. While both information supply and citizen support have a positive effect on interest group influence on policy formulation, a comparison of figures 6.1 and 6.3 indicates that the effect of citizen support is much stronger than the effect of information supply.

To demonstrate the size of the effect more profoundly, I also simulated first differences to demonstrate how the probability to influence formulation changes when relative citizen support of lobbying coalitions is altered. Table 6.4 contains the differences in relative citizen support in the first column and the associated change in the probability to influence policy formulation in column two together with a 95 percent confidence interval. If relative citizen support of a lobbying coalition increases from 25 to 50 percent, the probability to influence the content of the Commission proposal rises by approximately 23.0 percentage points. Similarly, if relative citizen support augments from 75 to 100 percent, the probability to influence policy formulation rises on average by 17.7 percentage points. The effect of citizen support is strongest for the difference between 50 and 75 percent as this difference leads to an increase in the probability to influence policy formulation by approximately 26.6 percentage points. Finally, if citizen support increased from its minimum (0) to its maximum (100) value, the probability to influence policy formulation would increase by 79.7 percentage points. The effect of citizen support is therefore much stronger than the effect of information supply which only leads to an increase of 55.5 percentage points when information supply rises on the same scale.

The policy debate revolving around the Commission strategy on pesticides nicely illustrates the effect of citizen support on interest group influence.[5] In July 2002, the European Commission published a communication

[5] The following discussion is based on responses submitted to the Commission consultation on the thematic strategy on the sustainable use of pesticides and the associated consultation document (COM (2002) 349), legislative proposal (COM (2006) 373), and final legislative act (Directive 2009/128/EC).

in which it set out a policy initiative that aimed at reducing the impact of pesticides on human health and the environment. Amongst others, the Commission suggested improving controls on the use and distribution of pesticides, encouraging the use of pesticide free crop farming, and establishing transparent monitoring systems. The publication of the Commission communication led to the mobilization of numerous interest groups that lobbied the European institutions on this issue. Two lobbying coalitions emerged that had opposing views on how the Commission should proceed with its pesticides strategy: first, a lobbying coalition bringing together industry representatives and second, a lobbying coalition consisting of consumer and environmental groups.

The industry coalition consisted of various interest groups representing the chemical and the crop industry as well as the agricultural sector. The industry lobby opposed the policy measures suggested by the European Commission and tried to water down the proposal. By contrast, environmental and consumer groups fought on the other side of the policy debate. They supported the envisaged pesticide strategy of the Commission and even asked for stricter regulations on the use of pesticides. An important point of the debate between industry representatives and NGOs was the ban of aerial spraying of pesticides. Industry groups strongly opposed the ban of aerial spraying and tried to prevent the Commission from including this measure in its legislative framework. For instance, the British, the French, and the European Crop Protection Association stated in their consultation submissions that they are opposed to a general ban of aerial spraying. They argued that aerial spraying was the only instrument through which crops could be protected and that it was a safe procedure as only certified and well-trained pilots could carry out aerial spraying. By contrast, the Pesticides Action Network, the European Environmental Bureau, and the European Consumers' Organization strongly supported a ban of aerial spraying as the practice would have an impact far beyond the intended crop area and would therefore pose unnecessary risks to the environment and human health.

The European Commission largely moved forward with its strategy despite the opposition of the industry lobby. For instance, the ban of aerial spraying remained an important element in the legislative proposal irrespective of the concerns raised by industry groups. The environmental and consumer NGOs successfully lobbied the European Commission while the industry lobby largely failed in its lobbying activities. The success of the environmental and consumer NGOs can be explained by the relative amount of citizen support they provided to the Commission. While the citizen support of the lobbying coalition opposing the pesticides strategy was only 26 percent, the environmental and consumer groups together represented about 74 percent of all citizens represented in this policy debate. At the same time, the information supply and economic power of the NGO coalition was relatively low. This policy debate therefore provides a good example of the effect of citizen support on interest group influence on policy formulation in the European Union.

In conclusion, the empirical analysis has also provided empirical support for hypothesis 2: Relative citizen support of lobbying coalitions has a statistically significant positive effect on interest group influence during the policy formulation stage. Hence, interest groups which enjoy the backing of a lobbying coalition that is supported by a large number of citizens find it much easier to succeed in their lobbying attempts than interest groups whose coalitions suffer from a lack of citizen support. Thus, the European Commission is more likely to be responsive to interest group demands if they are brought forward by a coalition that represents a large number of citizens. The size of the effect is in addition considerably stronger than the effect of relative information supply. Thus even though information supply and citizen support are both important exchange goods, citizen support seems to be more valuable to the European Commission than information supply.

6.4 THE EFFECT OF ECONOMIC POWER

In this section, I test whether relative economic power of lobbying has a positive effect on the ability of interest groups to influence policy-making as suggested by hypothesis 3. Table 6.5 presents the results of the multilevel logistic regression. As in the case of information supply and citizen support, I estimated an empty model, a basic model including only relative economic power of coalitions as predictor for interest group influence, and a model controlling in addition for several interest group and issue characteristics. Due to survey non-response, the sample reduces from 2,696 interest groups and 56 policy issues to 594 interest groups lobbying the European Commission concerning 56 policy issues.

The relative economic power of lobbying coalitions also has a statistically significant positive effect on interest group influence. A 1 percent increase in relative economic power of a lobbying coalition A, which implies a 1 percent decrease in relative economic power of its opposing lobbying coalition B, raises the chance of interest groups which belong to lobbying coalition A to influence policy formulation by 4.4 percent (4.7 percent when control variables are included). Hence, interest groups benefit considerably from belonging to a lobbying coalition that represents powerful economic actors who control business investments and job creation. The European Commission has an

Table 6.5 Multilevel analysis examining the effect of economic power on interest group influence during the policy formulation stage

Variables	Empty	Basic	Full
Fixed effects			
LOBBYING COALITION CHARACTERISTICS			
Rel. economic power		1.044***	1.047***
		(0.006)	(0.007)
CONTROLS: INTEREST GROUP LEVEL			
Type: Sectional group			1.045
			(0.278)
Rel. economic power			0.989
			(0.012)
CONTROLS: ISSUE LEVEL			
Salience			1.531
			(0.653)
Complexity			1.553
			(0.529)
Conflict			0.531
			(0.446)
Existence of EU SQ			1.139
			(0.586)
Legislative procedure: Codecision			1.173
			(1.191)
Voting rule: QM			11.993
			(19.421)
Member state support			0.989
			(0.012)
Random effects			
Issue level variance	1.771	2.150	1.711
Model fit			
N / Issues	594 / 56	594 / 56	594 / 56
Log likelihood	−377	−345	−339
AIC	759	696	701
BIC	768	709	754
LR Test, Prob > Chi2		0.000	0.187

***$p \leq 0.01$,**$p \leq 0.05$,*$p \leq 0.10$, coefficients represent odds ratios, standard errors in parentheses, sectional and cause groups are compared to companies, Codecision is compared to Consultation, qualified majority voting is compared to unanimity, the reference model for the likelihood ratio test is the model left of the model in question

open ear for the demands of big business as their support increases the chance that the proposal will be approved by the Council and the European Parliament. By contrast, neither the interest group nor the issue characteristics have a systematic effect on interest group influence. Accordingly, all model fit measures indicate that the inclusion of relative economic power of lobbying coalitions has significantly improved the model fit whereas adding the control variables has not enhanced the explanatory power of the model.

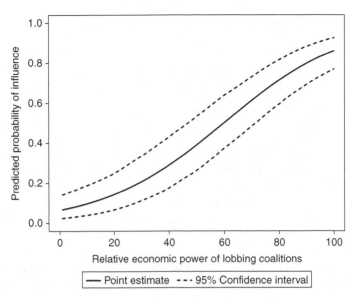

Fig. 6.4 Effect of relative economic power on interest group influence during the policy formulation stage

Figure 6.4 graphs the predicted probabilities of interest group influence for the range of possible values of relative economic power of lobbying coalitions. As relative economic power of a lobbying coalition rises, the probability of its member groups to influence the policy proposal of the European Commission steadily increases. Thus, a higher value of relative economic power of lobbying coalitions is associated with a higher probability of their member groups to exert influence. The empirical analysis therefore also provides empirical support for hypothesis 3: Relative economic power of lobbying coalitions is positively related to interest group influence.

In order to shed further light on the size of the effect of relative economic power of coalitions, I also simulated first differences for this effect. Table 6.6

Table 6.6 First differences: Effect of relative economic power on interest group influence during the policy formulation stage

Change: Economic power	Change: Influence probability	95% Confidence interval	
0–25%	0.109	0.066	0.160
25–50%	0.220	0.162	0.276
50–75%	0.274	0.195	0.348
75–100%	0.193	0.134	0.255
0–100%	0.796	0.670	0.876

contains the difference in relative economic power in the first column and the associated change in the probability to influence policy formulation in column two together with the 95 percent confidence interval. If relative economic power of a lobbying coalition augments from 25 to 50 percent, the probability that member groups succeed in their lobbying activities increases by 22.0 percentage points. Furthermore, if relative economic power of a lobbying coalition increases from 50 to 75 percent, the probability that interest groups which belong to this coalition indeed are able to shape the design of the Commission proposal rises by approximately 27.4 percentage points. The size of the effect slightly decreases if relative economic power further augments: When relative economic power increases from 75 to 100 percent, the probability to influence policy formulation increases only by 19.3 percentage points. Overall, the probability to shape the content of the policy proposal increases by 79.6 percentage points if economic power rises from its minimum (0) to its maximum (100) value. While the effects of citizen support and economic power are nearly identical in size, the effect of information supply is much smaller indicating that electoral resources are much more important to the Commission than policy expertise.

The policy debate on the so-called "Health Check" is a typical example of the influence of economically powerful interest groups.[6] In November 2007, the European Commission released a communication in which it laid out its plans to reform the Common Agricultural Policy (CAP). Building on previous reforms of the CAP that were launched in 2003, the European Commission suggested several policy measures designed to make the agricultural policy regime more efficient while at the same time confronting new challenges such as climate change, increasing biofuel production, water management, and the protection of biodiversity. The European Commission suggested a number of measures to simplify the direct aid system to farmers and to adapt the Common Agricultural Policy to the extended scope of the EU-27. For instance, the Commission proposed to further decouple agricultural production from direct payments, to establish upper limits for subsidies, and to improve cross-compliance standards which farmers have to comply with in order to receive financial support from Brussels.

The proposed policy initiative lead to a vibrant debate among stakeholders. The envisaged Health Check was strongly opposed by a lobbying coalition consisting of farmers and agricultural industries. However, the European Commission has also received support. A lobbying coalition that united environmental NGOs welcomed the Commission initiative and even

---

[6] The following discussion is based on responses submitted to the Commission consultation on the "Health Check" reform of the Common Agricultural Policy (CAP) and the associated consultation document (COM (2007) 722), legislative proposal (COM (2008) 306), and final legislative acts (Regulation (EC) No 73/2009, Regulation (EC) No 72/2009, Regulation (EC) No 74/2009).

demanded a more wide-ranging reform. An important point of debate between the two lobbying coalitions was the reform of the cross-compliance framework. The Committee of Professional Agricultural Organisations (COPA), which is the representative of European farmers, argued that farmers have already made great efforts to meet cross-compliance requirements, but that these are far too bureaucratic and would endanger production standards. As a result, COPA demanded the simplification of the cross-compliance framework and it rejected any further measures. By contrast, Birdlife International and the World Wide Fund For Nature (WWF) argued that cross-compliance is an important policy tool which helps to achieve sustainable agriculture. They therefore supported the Commission proposal and even demanded further cross-compliance measures. Agricultural and environmental groups furthermore disagreed about upper limits for agricultural subsidies. The European Commission suggested gradually reducing the support level as overall payments to individual farmers increase. COPA strongly objected to such upper limits for agricultural subsidies and argued that these would effectively constitute penalties for large farms. Upper limits would penalize farmers who have made efforts to modernize and they would discourage further progress. By contrast, environmental groups such as WWF, the Coalition Clean Baltic, and Birdlife International supported the Commission initiative to introduce maximum support levels for large farms.

The European Commission largely followed the reasoning of the agricultural lobby on most issues discussed in the communication. For instance, cross-compliance measures have been simplified to make it easier for farmers to comply with them while not suffering productivity losses. Similarly, the European Commission abandoned general upper limits for agricultural subsidies in line with the demands raised by the agricultural lobby. The lobbying success of agricultural interest groups can be explained by their considerable economic power. Even though the environmental NGOs have been supported by some food industry groups, the economic power of their coalition is only moderate as they can hardly control investments or employment. By contrast, farmers are very well organized and the agricultural lobby therefore has a considerable impact on business investments and jobs in the agricultural sector. For instance, COPA represents over 13 million farmers and their families whilst its partner organization, the General Committee for Agricultural Cooperation in the European Union (COGECA) represents the interests of 38,000 agricultural cooperatives. Together, their members are responsible for over 40 million jobs in Europe. It is therefore hardly surprising that the European Commission was responsive to the concerns raised by the agricultural lobby.

To conclude, the analysis has demonstrated that relative economic power of lobbying coalitions also has a positive effect on interest group influence. Thus, the European Commission is not only in need of external information and citizen support, but it also requires economic power from interest groups. Interest groups which represent powerful economic actors are important allies in promoting a new legislative initiative towards the Council and the European Parliament. The European Commission is therefore particularly responsive to demands raised by lobbying coalitions that represent these powerful economic actors. The size of the effect is by and large comparable to the effect of relative citizen support. Hence, the European Commission is similarly attentive to lobbying coalitions with a high degree of economic power and lobbying coalitions which are supported by a large number of citizens.

6.5 LOBBYING COALITIONS: INFLUENCE OR FREE-RIDING?

I have demonstrated so far that information supply, citizen support, and economic power of lobbying coalitions have an important effect on the ability of interest groups to influence policy formulation in the European Union. Based on the observable implications illustrated in figure 1.1, it can therefore be concluded that interest groups indeed influenced European policy formulation since a systematic effect of lobbying coalition characteristics as theoretically expected could be detected. However, it is not clear why the lobbying coalition characteristics matter. There are two primary explanations for the effect of lobbying coalition characteristics: First, it is possible that only few powerful interest groups influence policy-making. Hence, other members of a lobbying coalition could benefit from the influence that a few strong interest groups exert which share the same policy goal. Accordingly, weak interest groups could simply "free-ride" on the influence of others and are therefore merely lucky to get what they want. Second, it is also possible that the sum of the characteristics of all interest groups which form a lobbying coalition makes the difference. Accordingly, the convergence of policy preferences with the policy outcome would be caused by the sum of the characteristics of each individual member of the coalition. Hence, the question is whether the sum of the characteristics of all coalition members is causing the convergence or whether just a few powerful groups influence the policy-making process while the majority of groups just free-rides on their efforts. In order to empirically disentangle the two explanations, I draw on the observable implications illustrated in figure 6.5 (see also Klüver 2013).

The effect of lobbying coalition characteristics can be caused by the sum of characteristics of all coalition members or by the characteristics of a few powerful groups. In both scenarios, the characteristics of lobbying coalitions

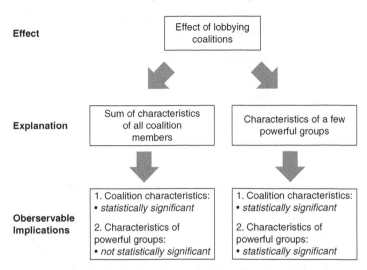

Fig. 6.5 Conceptualization of lobbying coalition effects

exhibit a systematic, that is, statistically significant effect on interest group influence. This systematic effect, however, does not allow us to judge whether only a few powerful groups within the coalition influenced policy-making or whether all interest groups simultaneously exerted influence. In order to empirically distinguish between the two explanations, I took a sample of the dataset which only contains the strongest interest groups in terms of relative information supply, relative citizen support, or relative economic power. More specifically, I only selected interest groups which belonged to the strongest 15 percent on a given policy issue. Thus, I did not select the strongest 15 percent of the overall sample, but the strongest 15 percent on each policy issue since the strength relative to other interest groups on an issue is decisive. To classify as the strongest 15 percent, interest groups have to belong to the strongest 15 percent in terms of relative information supply, relative citizen support, or relative economic power on a given policy issue.

If indeed only a few powerful interest groups influence policy formulation while their coalition partners simply free-ride, their individual characteristics must have a systematic, that is, statistically significant effect on interest group influence when these powerful groups are analyzed separately.[7] By contrast, if one finds that the individual characteristics of powerful interest groups do not have a statistically significant effect on policy-making, one can conclude that the effect of lobbying coalition characteristics cannot be explained by a few

---

[7] If one by contrast analyzed all interest groups simultaneously, the positive effects for the powerful interest groups would be canceled out by the effects for the weak groups so that the overall effect would not be statistically significant.

Table 6.7 Lobbying success of the 15% strongest groups in the policy formulation stage

Successful interest groups	Not successful interest groups
58.24% (Strongest groups)	41.76% (Strongest groups)
50.65% (Other groups)	49.35% (Other groups)

Pearson's r: 0.071, $p \leq 0.01$, N = 2,696

powerful interest groups so that weak interest groups cannot simply free-ride on the efforts of a few strong groups.

Table 6.7 presents descriptive information about the strongest 15 percent pooled across all policy issues. If the positive effect of lobbying coalition characteristics is indeed only due to characteristics of individual interest groups, there should be a systematic pattern that shows that strong interest groups are particularly able to influence policy formulation. However, out of the 862 strongest interest groups during the policy formulation stage, only 58.24 percent were successfully lobbying the European Commission. In addition, the share of successful interest groups does not vary considerably according to individual strength of the interest groups since also 50.65 percent of the groups that did not belong to the strongest 15 percent were successful. Accordingly, the Pearson correlation coefficient only indicates a very small association between belonging to the 15 percent strongest groups and being influential.

In order to further test whether the specific individual characteristics of strong interest groups can account for interest group influence on EU policy formulation, I estimated multilevel regression models only based on the sample of strong interest groups. Due to the significantly smaller number of cases, I only estimated bivariate regression models. Table 6.8 presents the results for the policy formulation stage. As illustrated in figure 6.5, one can empirically distinguish whether the positive effect of lobbying coalitions is due to the attributes of a few strong groups or whether it is due to the sum of the characteristics of all coalition members: If a few strong interest groups are responsible for the positive effect of lobbying coalition characteristics, there must be a systematic effect of their individual characteristics on interest group influence when these actors are analyzed separately. By contrast, if the sum of the characteristics of all coalition members accounts for the positive effect of lobbying coalition characteristics, there is no systematic pattern that links the properties of a few strong groups with interest group influence.

The multilevel analyses provide no evidence in favor of the argument that only a few strong groups exert influence whereas others are free-riding.

Table 6.8 Multilevel logistic regression testing the free-riding hypothesis for the policy formulation stage

Variables	Information	Citizen support	Economic power
Relative information supply	0.981		
	(0.037)		
Relative citizen support		0.982*	
		(0.010)	
Relative economic power			0.993
			(0.009)
Random effects			
Issue level variance	3.174	3.238	0.093
Model fit			
N / Issues	456 / 56	428 / 54	139 / 56
Log likelihood	−268	−229	−96
AIC	542	463	197
BIC	554	475	206
LR Test, Prob > Chi2	0.610	0.067	0.427
Pearson's r	−0.003	−0.175	−0.071

***$p \leq 0.01$, **$p \leq 0.05$, *$p \leq 0.10$, coefficients represent odds ratios, standard errors in parentheses

None of the individual group characteristics has a statistically significant positive effect on interest group influence on policy formulation. One could of course argue that statistically significant effects are quite unlikely given the small number of cases. However, not even the direction of the effects of information supply, citizen support, or economic power provides support for the free-riding explanation. In addition, the last row of table 6.8 indicates the correlation between interest group properties and interest group influence for the sample of strong interest groups. The correlations do not reveal any positive association between the individual interest group characteristics and interest group influence which also does not provide any support for the free-riding explanation. These results are robust across different thresholds for strength: I repeated the analysis for the 20 percent, 10 percent, 5 percent, and 1 percent strongest groups and could also not detect any systematic pattern that links individual interest group properties and interest group influence. Hence, the positive effect of lobbying coalition characteristics cannot be explained by the properties of a small number of strong groups. I could not find any evidence that provides support to the hypothesis that only the most powerful interest groups in fact exert influence on policy formulation while weaker groups free-ride on their impact. The positive effect of lobbying coalition characteristics during the policy formulation stage can therefore not solely be attributed to a few powerful groups.

Table 6.9 Comparison of effect sizes in the policy formulation stage

Change in supply of exchange good: 0–100%	Change: Influence probability	95% Confidence interval	
Information supply	0.555	0.451	0.643
Citizen support	0.797	0.716	0.864
Economic power	0.796	0.670	0.876

6.6 CONCLUSION

This chapter has demonstrated that lobbying at the policy formulation stage can be conceptualized as an exchange relationship between interdependent actors: The European Commission needs information, citizen support, and economic power from interest groups which in turn demand influence on policy formulation. The empirical analysis furthermore confirmed that lobbying is a collective enterprise in which the aggregated information supply, citizen support, and economic power of entire lobbying coalitions are decisive for preference attainment during the policy formulation stage. It is therefore crucial to take into account how interest groups position themselves in policy debates and how they come together in lobbying coalitions. The empirical analysis provided in this chapter furthermore demonstrated that the information needs of the European Commission vary across proposals and that the positive effect of information supply therefore increases with the complexity of a policy issue.

Finally, table 6.9 compares the effects of information supply, citizen support, and economic power of lobbying coalitions drawing on first differences (Mroz and Zayats 2008, see also page 130). The table indicates how the probability to influence policy formulation changes when information supply, citizen support, and economic power change from their minimum (0) to their maximum (100) value. While the effects of citizen support and economic power are nearly identical, the effect of information supply is much smaller. Hence, the European Commission relies on information provided by interest groups, but they are most importantly a source of legitimacy and electoral resources for the Commission. At the same time, citizen support and economic power are equally important for lobbying success which indicates that policy formulation is not dominated by European business, but that both business as well as citizen interests have similar chances to influence policy formulation in the European Union.

7

The Decision-Making Stage: Bringing the Council and the European Parliament in

While previous studies have largely provided a static view focusing either on an aggregate analysis of the entire policy-making process or on just one stage of the policy cycle, this book compares interest group influence at different stages of the policy-making process. In the preceding chapter, the hypotheses derived from the theoretical model have been tested for the policy formulation stage in which the European Commission drafts the legislative proposal. This chapter now shifts the focus from the policy formulation to the decision-making stage of the European policy-making process. During the decision-making stage, the Council, the European Parliament, and to some extent the European Commission bargain on the basis of the Commission proposal about the design of the final legislative act. This chapter asks whether we find the same patterns during the decision-making stage that we found in the previous stage of the policy cycle. Are information supply, citizen support, and economic power of lobbying coalitions equally important drivers of lobbying success or are other factors at play when the Council and the European Parliament are involved?

In order to investigate the determinants of interest group influence during the decision-making stage, the chapter proceeds as follows: After a brief summary of the formal legislative process in the European Union, the hypotheses derived from the theoretical model are tested for the decision-making stage. Similar to the empirical analysis conducted for the previous stage, I test the hypotheses step by step given the high collinearity of the predictors and a considerable reduction of the sample size due to survey non-response if all effects were tested simultaneously (see section 4.4). Drawing on multilevel logistic regression, I first analyze the effect of information supply, I then investigate the effect of citizen support, and I finally assess the effect of economic power on interest group influence on decision-making in the European Union. In order to study lobbying success during the decision-making stage, the policy proposal needed to be adopted before 31 December 2010 to be included in the sample. Out of the initial sample of 56 policy proposals, 42 were adopted by the Council and the European Parliament during this time frame. The empirical analysis is therefore based on 1,793 interest groups lobbying the European institutions concerning 42 policy issues. Effect sizes are compared using predicted probabilities and first differences (Mroz and Zayats 2008, see also page 130).

7.1 DECISION-MAKING BETWEEN THE COUNCIL, THE EP, AND THE EUROPEAN COMMISSION

The decision-making stage begins with the formal adoption of the legislative proposal by the European Commission. The Council, the European Parliament, and the European Commission bargain about the final legislative act on the basis of the Commission proposal. There are mainly three different legislative procedures (for a detailed description, see Hix 2005, 99–102): Consultation, Cooperation, and Codecision.[1] Consultation is the traditional legislative procedure whose importance has diminished over the years with the introduction of the Cooperation and most importantly the Codecision procedure. The Cooperation procedure was established by the Single European Act, but was over time also replaced by the Codecision procedure which was introduced with the Treaty of Maastricht and now applies to the vast majority of legislative acts. As the policy proposals studied in this book are only subject to Consultation or Codecision and since Cooperation only applies to a very small number of proposals, the following discussion concentrates on the Consultation and the Codecision procedure (see figure 7.1 and figure 7.2 for a graphical illustration of these decision-making procedures).

Under both legislative procedures, the European Parliament comments during the *first reading* stage on the Commission proposal and suggests possible amendments to the text. The European Commission then drafts a revised proposal based on the EP opinion in which it states which amendments it accepts and which it rejects. Afterwards, the Council examines the revised proposal. Under the Consultation procedure, the Council can autonomously decide whether to accept or to reject the amendments suggested by the European Parliament and the legislative process ends at the first reading stage.

---

[1] The Treaty of Lisbon, which entered into force in December 2009, only distinguishes two different procedures: the "ordinary legislative procedure" which was formerly the Codecision procedure and "special legislative procedures" which replace amongst others the former Consultation and Cooperation procedure. As all proposals analyzed in this book have been adopted by the European Commission between 2000 and 2008 and therefore under the old legislative regime, the Consultation and Codecision procedure are illustrated in this section.

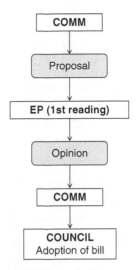

Fig. 7.1 The Consultation procedure

If the European Parliament does not propose any amendments to a proposal that is subject to Codecision or if all its amendments are accepted by the Council, the proposal similarly enters into force after approval by the Council. If the Council, however, disagrees with amendments made by the EP to a Codecision proposal, the Council adopts a Common Position and the legislative process reaches the *second reading* stage. The European Parliament has three opportunities at the second reading: First, it can accept the Common Position and the legislative act can be adopted by the Council. Second, it can reject the Common Position which leads to the failure of the legislative act under Codecision. Finally, the European Parliament can also suggest amendments to the Common position.

If the European Parliament suggested amendments, the European Commission enters the legislative arena again. It can decide whether to accept or reject the amendments proposed by the European Parliament before resubmitting the text to the Council. If the European Commission incorporates the EP amendments, the Council can adopt the legislative act with qualified majority. If the European Commission does not include the EP amendments, the Council needs to decide with unanimity in order to adopt the legislative act. If the Council fails to reach the necessary quorum or if it rejects the amendments, the Conciliation Committee consisting of an equal number of representatives of both the Council and the EP is convened. If the Conciliation Committee does not reach an agreement, the proposal fails. If it comes to an agreement, the committee adopts a Joint Text which launches the *third reading* stage. The Council has to adopt the Joint Text by

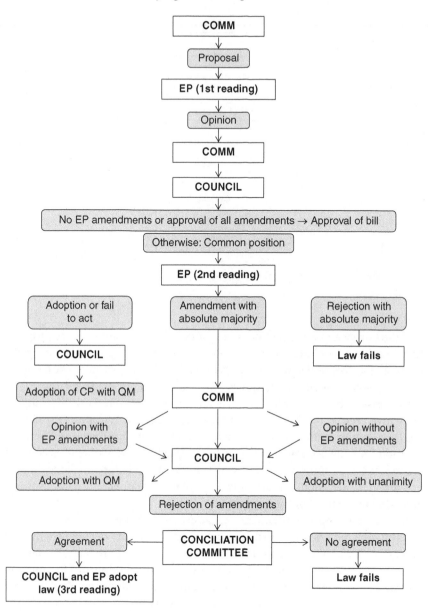

Fig. 7.2 The Codecision procedure

qualified majority and the EP by absolute majority in order to approve the final legislative act.

The decision-making stage thus involves three institutional bodies: the Council, the European Parliament, and the European Commission. Under the Consultation procedure, the Council can autonomously decide about whether a legislative proposal enters into force or not after consulting the European Parliament. Under the Codecision procedure, the European Parliament has a veto right so that proposals cannot enter into force without its assent. Even though the European Commission is not involved in the final adoption of a legislative act, it retains important powers throughout the decision-making stage (Nugent 2001, 254–257; Hooghe and Nugent 2006, 152): Under Consultation, the Council can only introduce amendments to a proposal which are opposed by the European Commission if it decides unanimously. Even more important, the Commission can change and even withdraw a proposal at any stage of the legislative process. Under Codecision, the right to withdraw a proposal only applies until the Conciliation Committee is convened.

Interest groups enjoy multiple access points during the decision-making stage. They can establish informal and formal contacts with the Council, the European Parliament, and the European Commission to shape the final legislative act. In order to affect the final policy outcome through the Council channel, interest groups can for instance lobby national ministries, the Permanent Representations of the member states in Brussels, or the preparatory bodies that consist of national officials which prepare the discussions at the ministerial level in the Council (Schneider and Baltz 2005; Hayes-Renshaw 2009; Saurugger 2009). To shape the design of the legislative act through the European Parliament, interest groups can for instance lobby the rapporteur who is in charge of drafting the EP report on the proposal, they can try to make their voice heard in the committees or they can get in touch with Intergroups that consist of MEPs from different political groups that share an interest in a particular political theme (Bouwen 2003, 2004b; Lehmann 2009; Marshall 2010; Kluger Rasmussen 2011). Finally, interest groups can also attempt to affect the policy outcome through the European Commission as it is involved in making amendments to proposals and as it retains the right to withdraw proposals as long as the Conciliation Committee is not convened.

7.2 THE EFFECT OF INFORMATION SUPPLY

Table 7.1 presents the results of the multilevel logistic regression analysis examining the effect of coalition information supply on interest group

Lobbying in the European Union

Table 7.1 Multilevel analysis examining the effect of information supply on interest group influence during the decision-making stage

Variables	Empty	Basic	With controls	Full
Fixed effects				
Lobbying coalition characteristics				
Rel. information supply		1.018***	1.009**	0.762***
		(0.004)	(0.004)	(0.022)
Rel. information supply * complexity				1.100***
				(0.011)
Controls: Interest group level				
Type: Sectional group			0.993	1.078
			(0.152)	(0.173)
Type: Cause group			1.159	1.098
			(0.225)	(0.225)
Rel. information supply			1.038	1.032
			(0.027)	(0.028)
Controls: Issue level				
Salience			2.319*	2.349
			(1.018)	(1.419)
Complexity			1.138	0.003***
			(0.413)	(0.002)
Conflict			0.430	1.609
			(0.385)	(2.022)
Existence of EU SQ			0.685	0.671
			(0.361)	(0.494)
Legislative procedure: Codecision			2.877	1.337
			(2.852)	(1.913)
Voting rule: QM			1.248	4.452
			(1.839)	(9.343)
Member state support			1.049***	1.032***
			(0.008)	(0.008)
Random effects				
Issue level variance	3.086	2.950	2.140	4.414
Model fit				
N / Issues	1793 / 42	1793 / 42	1793 / 42	1793 / 42
Log likelihood	−984	−970	−940	−840
AIC	1971	1947	1907	1708
BIC	1982	1963	1978	1785
LR Test, Prob > Chi2		0.000	0.000	0.000

***$p \leq 0.01$, **$p \leq 0.05$, *$p \leq 0.10$, coefficients represent odds ratios, standard errors in parentheses, sectional and cause groups are compared to companies, Codecision is compared to Consultation, qualified majority voting is compared to unanimity, the reference model for the likelihood ratio test is the model left of the model in question

influence during the decision-making stage. The table contains the empty model in the first column, the basic model including relative information supply by lobbying coalitions in the second column, and a third model that additionally contains several control variables on the interest group and issue level. The full model furthermore contains a cross-level interaction effect between complexity and relative information supply by lobbying coalitions in order to test whether the strength of the effect of information supply also varies with issue complexity during the decision-making stage.

Information supply by lobbying coalitions has a statistically significant positive effect on interest group influence during the decision-making stage no matter whether additional control variables are added to the model or not. A 1 percent increase in relative information supply by a lobbying coalition A, which at the same time implies a 1 percent decrease in relative information supply by its opposing lobbying coalition B, increases the chance of interest groups which belong to lobbying coalition A to influence decision-making by 1.8 percent (0.9 percent when control variables are included). Hence, information supply does not only increase the likelihood that interest groups succeed in lobbying the European Commission during the policy formulation stage, but it also increases the chance that interest groups can shape the design of the final legislative act negotiated during the decision-making stage. The empirical analysis furthermore indicates that salience and member state support have a statistically significant effect on interest group influence. Hence, the more interest groups try to shape the final policy outcome and the more member states support the policy objective of an interest group, the higher the probability that this interest group succeeds in its lobbying attempts. All model fit measures similarly indicate that including relative information supply by lobbying coalitions significantly increases the explanatory power of the model. Adding the control variables only increases the model fit according to the AIC and the likelihood ratio test.

In order to further illustrate the effect of relative information supply on interest group influence during the decision-making stage, I simulated predicted probabilities illustrated in figure 7.3. The solid line indicates the point estimates of the predicted probabilities whereas the broken lines represent a 95 percent confidence interval. Relative information supply also has a steady positive effect on lobbying success during the decision-making stage. The increase in the probability to influence the outcome of the decision-making stage is, however, considerably smaller than during the policy formulation stage. This suggests that even though information supply also matters during the decision-making stage, it is more important for lobbying success during the policy formulation stage.

In order to further investigate the size of the effect, I also simulated first differences to illustrate how the probability to influence the final policy outcome changes as relative information supply by lobbying coalitions increases (see table 7.2). If relative information supply by a lobbying coalition rises from 25 to 50 percent, the predicted probability to succeed in shaping the design of the final legislative act increases by approximately 5.0 percentage points. Similarly, if relative information supply augments from 50 to 75 percent, the probability to influence decision-making on average

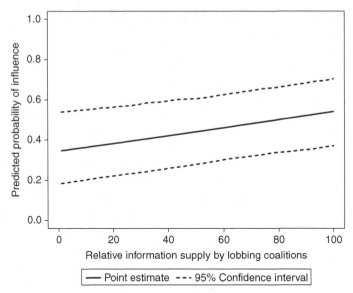

Fig. 7.3 Effect of relative information supply on interest group influence during the decision-making stage

Table 7.2 First differences: Effect of relative information supply on interest group influence during the decision-making stage

Change: Information supply	Change: Influence probability	95% Confidence interval	
0–25%	0.046	0.005	0.088
25–50%	0.050	0.005	0.092
50–75%	0.051	0.004	0.094
75–100%	0.051	0.001	0.099
0–100%	0.195	0.027	0.359

increases by 5.1 percentage points. The changes in the predicted probabilities are statistically significant as none of the confidence intervals includes zero. Overall, the probability to influence the final policy outcomes increases by 19.5 percentage points if information supply rises from its minimum (0) to its maximum (100) value. The effect of information supply is therefore considerably smaller during the decision-making stage than during the policy formulation stage where a similar increase in information supply leads to an increase in the influence probability by 55.5 percentage points.

The policy debate concerning the Commission strategy to reduce CO_2 emissions from cars nicely illustrates the importance of information supply for lobbying success (see also chapter 3).[2] In February 2007, the European Commission adopted a communication in which it proposed a legislative framework aimed at the reduction of CO_2 emissions from cars. The Commission suggested a variety of measures such as an emission limit of 120 grams of CO_2 per kilometer, the inclusion of vans in this legislative framework, and improved car labeling to indicate emission levels. On the basis of this communication, the European Commission launched a public consultation which has mobilized various organized interests. After consulting the public, the European Commission adopted its legislative proposal in December 2007 and the Council and the European Parliament approved the final legislative act in April 2009. The mobilized interest groups were divided into two lobbying coalitions: First, a coalition consisting of environmental NGOs and manufacturers of electric and hybrid cars as well as alternative fuel producers and second, a coalition bringing together the traditional automobile manufacturers in Europe and beyond.

The two coalitions had opposing views on most of the issues discussed in the Commission communication. For instance, while the environmental and alternative industry groups fully supported the proposed reduction target of 120 grams per kilometer until 2012, the traditional industry strongly rejected it. Environmental groups such as Greenpeace, WWF, and the Finnish Association of Nature Conservation welcomed the Commission initiative to implement an obligatory emission reduction target and even claimed that the 120g/km target was not ambitious enough. By contrast, the automobile industry lobby advocated for more flexibilities in reducing CO_2 emissions. Manufacturers argued that car development and production cycles take a number of years and that the models for 2012 have already been designed and implemented. Adjusting the car models to comply with the proposed reduction target would be extremely costly and would therefore harm the competitiveness of the European automobile industry. Industry representatives such as the European Automobile Manufacturers' Association or Volkswagen therefore demanded longer lead times to meet the emission reduction target. In addition, the automobile industry rejected a general reduction target that applies to every single vehicle. Instead, car producers suggested averaging the reduction target across the entire fleet so that they can compensate cars with higher emissions by cars with lower emissions. Finally, environmental groups supported the suggestion of the European Commission to include vans in the legislative framework while traditional car manufacturers opposed this idea given that vans are entirely different vehicles.

---

[2] The following discussion is based on responses submitted to the Commission consultation on the review of the Community strategy to reduce CO_2 emissions from passenger cars and light-commercial vehicles and the associated consultation document (COM (2007) 19), legislative proposal (COM (2007) 856), and final legislative act (Regulation (EC) No 443/2009).

The European institutions largely responded to the demands raised by the traditional automobile industry. The reduction target was kept at 120g/km and no additional long-term limits have been envisaged. In addition, flexibility measures suggested by car manufacturers were included in the legislative framework. The reduction target does not have to be met by each individual car, but only the average of the entire fleet has to comply with the 120g/km emissions limit. Finally, the legislative framework only applies to passenger cars while vans were excluded from the framework. The legislative debate revolving around the policy initiative to reduce CO_2 emissions is a typical example for the importance of information supply for lobbying success. While the lobbying coalition composed of environmental and alternative industry groups only provided about 29 percent of all the information transmitted in the consultation, the traditional automobile industry supplied 71 percent of the information provided by lobbyists in this policy debate. Environmental NGOs and manufacturers of electric and hybrid cars submitted policy papers with an average length of 724 words while the automobile industry lobby submitted comments with an average length of 1,302 words. The automobile industry moreover provided very profound technical expertise about the production processes and the impact on market shares and productivity levels while the opposing coalition largely focused on conveying their political message rather than providing expert knowledge. It is therefore hardly surprising that the European institutions were more responsive to industry demands than to concerns raised by the environmental lobby.

In conclusion, the provision of information does not only play an important role during the policy formulation stage when the European Commission drafts the policy proposal, but it also matters during the decision-making stage. The higher the amount of information that a lobbying coalition provides to the European institutions, the higher the probability that interest groups belonging to this lobbying coalition are able to have an impact on the final legislative act. However, the size of the effect of information supply is considerably smaller during the decision-making stage than during the policy formulation stage. This suggests that information supply is much more important at the beginning of the legislative process when the main features of the legislative initiative are laid down in the proposal. Once the proposal is drafted, the general outline of the legislative framework is already sketched and bargaining between the European institutions is limited to modifications of the existing draft. Information supply therefore has the strongest effect on lobbying success during the policy formulation stage.

In order to test whether the size of the effect of information supply also varies with the complexity of policy issues during the decision-making stage, a cross-level interaction term between relative information supply by lobbying coalitions and issue complexity was included in the fourth model of table 7.1. The multilevel analysis indicates that the effect of information supply indeed changes with the complexity of policy issues as there is a statistically significant interaction effect at play. All model fit measures accordingly confirm that the introduction of the cross-level interaction has significantly improved the explanatory power of the model.

As interaction terms are difficult to interpret simply based on the regression coefficients, I computed a marginal effect plot to demonstrate how the effect of relative information supply by lobbying coalitions changes as issue complexity increases (see figure 7.4). The solid line indicates the point estimate of the marginal effect of relative information and the broken lines mark the 95 percent confidence interval. The marginal effect of information supply steadily increases with the complexity of policy issues. While information supply has a negative effect if complexity is below approximately 3.0, the effect is positive and steadily increases once complexity exceeds that threshold as the lower and upper bound of the confidence interval are both above zero. Hence, the analysis of the decision-making stage also provides empirical support for hypothesis 4: The size of the effect of relative information supply on interest group influence during the decision-making stage increases with the degree of complexity. The higher the complexity of a policy issue, the stronger the effect of relative information supply by lobbying coalitions.

The empirical findings confirm that information supply also plays an important role for lobbying success during the decision-making stage. Interest groups that belong to lobbying coalitions which supply a large amount of information to the European institutions find it easier to shape the policy outcome than interest groups whose lobbying coalitions provide only little information to legislators. As suggested by hypothesis 4, the effect varies

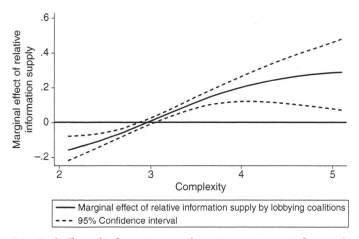

Fig. 7.4 Marginal effect of information supply on interest group influence during the decision-making stage

with the complexity of policy issues as the information needs differ: The size of the effect of relative information supply by lobbying coalitions increases with the complexity of policy issues as the European institutions require more external information when a highly complex issue is discussed than for issues of low complexity. However, the overall size of the effect of information supply is considerably smaller in the decision-making than in the policy formulation stage. The general outline of a legislative act is already designed at the beginning of the legislative process when the policy proposal is drafted so that the need for external information is considerably smaller during the decision-making than during the policy formulation stage.

7.3 THE EFFECT OF CITIZEN SUPPORT

In this section, the effect of citizen support of lobbying coalitions on the ability of interest groups to exert influence during the decision-making stage is empirically examined. Table 7.3 presents the results of the multilevel analysis, more specifically the empty model, the basic model including only citizen support, and the full model containing in addition several control variables on the interest group and issue level. Due to survey non-response, the sample reduces to 717 interest groups lobbying on 40 issues.

Across both model specifications, relative citizen support of lobbying coalitions has a statistically significant positive effect on interest group influence during the decision-making stage. A 1 percent increase in relative citizen support of a lobbying coalition *A*, which again implies a 1 percent decrease in relative citizen support of its opposing lobbying coalition *B*, increases the chance of interest groups which are members of lobbying coalition *A* to influence the design of the final legislative act by 2.2 percent (1.6 percent when control variables are included). Hence, interest groups which belong to a lobbying coalition that represents a large number of citizens find it much easier to exert influence on the decision-making process than interest groups which lack citizen support. Accordingly, all model fit measures indicate that including relative citizen support of lobbying coalitions has significantly enhanced the explanatory power of the model. Thus, hypothesis 2 was confirmed by the analysis of interest group influence during the policy formulation stage and also during the decision-making stage. Hence, not only the European Commission, but also the European Parliament and the Council are responsive to demands raised by a large number of citizens and voters. The multilevel analysis furthermore shows that member state support has a positive effect on lobbying success: The more member states support the policy objective advocated by an interest group, the higher the

Table 7.3 Multilevel analysis examining the effect of citizen support on interest group influence during the decision-making stage

Variables	Empty	Basic	Full
Fixed effects			
LOBBYING COALITION CHARACTERISTICS			
Rel. citizen support		1.022***	1.016***
		(0.005)	(0.005)
CONTROLS: INTEREST GROUP LEVEL			
Type: Sectional group			1.098
			(0.345)
Type: Cause group			1.505
			(0.528)
Rel. citizen support			0.988
			(0.011)
CONTROLS: ISSUE LEVEL			
Salience			1.983
			(1.077)
Complexity			1.339
			(0.569)
Conflict			0.337
			(0.365)
Existence of EU SQ			0.616
			(0.386)
Legislative procedure: Codecision			1.270
			(1.685)
Voting rule: QM			2.870
			(5.135)
Member state support			1.051***
			(0.013)
Random effects			
Issue level variance	3.647	3.906	2.516
Model fit			
N / Issues	717 / 40	717 / 40	717 / 40
Log likelihood	−389	−377	−364
AIC	781	759	753
BIC	790	773	813
LR Test, Prob > Chi2		0.000	0.004

***$p \leq 0.01$, **$p \leq 0.05$, *$p \leq 0.10$, coefficients represent odds ratios, standard errors in parentheses, sectional and cause groups are compared to companies, Codecision is compared to Consultation, qualified majority voting is compared to unanimity, the reference model for the likelihood ratio test is the model left of the model in question

likelihood that this interest group succeeds in shaping the content of the final legislative act.

In order to further illustrate the effect of citizen support on interest group influence during the decision-making stage, I simulated predicted probabilities displayed in figure 7.5. The solid line indicates the point estimate and the

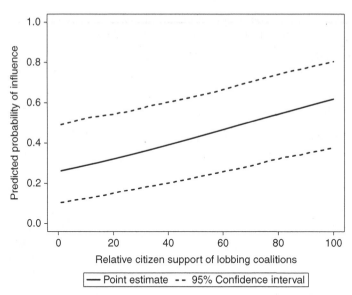

Fig. 7.5 Effect of relative citizen support on interest group influence during the decision-making stage

Table 7.4 First differences: Effect of relative citizen support on interest group influence during the decision-making stage

Change: Citizen support	Change: Influence probability	95% Confidence interval	
0–25%	0.078	0.038	0.119
25–50%	0.090	0.036	0.141
50–75%	0.095	0.037	0.151
75–100%	0.094	0.038	0.149
0–100%	0.355	0.158	0.538

broken lines represent the 95 percent confidence interval. Relative citizen support of lobbying coalitions has a steady positive effect. Hence, a higher value of relative citizen support is associated with a higher probability to influence the outcome of the legislative process.

The size of the effect of citizen support during the decision-making stage is further demonstrated by simulated first differences. Table 7.4 presents the difference in relative citizen support in the first column and the associated change in the predicted probability to influence decision-making in the second column along with values for the 95 percent confidence interval for the predicted changes. As relative citizen support of a lobbying coalition increases from 25 to 50 percent, the probability that interest groups which belong to this lobbying coalition manage to have an impact on the final policy outcome rises by approximately 9.0 percentage points. Likewise, if relative citizen support augments from 50 to 75 percent, the likelihood that interest groups which are members of this coalition affect the design of the legislative act increases on average by 9.5 percentage points. Overall, the probability to exert influence on the final policy outcome increases by 35.5 percentage points if citizen support by lobbying coalitions rises from its minimum (0) to its maximum (100) value. The effect of citizen support is therefore smaller at the decision-making stage than at the policy formulation stage. At the same time, citizen support is more important for lobbying success than information supply at the decision-making stage.

A good example for the effect of citizen support on lobbying success during the decision-making stage in the EU is the policy debate regarding tobacco taxation.[3] In March 2007, the European Commission published a working paper in which it suggested several policy measures designed to simplify and modernize tobacco taxation with a particular view on the health implications of tobacco consumption. Amongst others, the European Commission discussed an increase in tobacco taxation rates and an inclusion of other tobacco products into the legislative framework. After a lively stakeholder debate, the European Commission adopted its legislative proposal in July 2008 and the Council finally approved the directive in February 2010. The policy debate concerning tobacco taxation mobilized a large number of interest groups which can be divided into two lobbying coalitions that were opposing each other. On the one hand, health groups lobbied European decision-makers and on the other hand, the tobacco industry sought to influence the policy process on this issue.

A variety of health organizations formed a united lobbying coalition that supported the legislative initiative on tobacco taxation. Health groups like the European Heart Network, the Standing Committee of European doctors, Finland's Action on Smoking and Health and Cancer Research UK welcomed the policy measures proposed by the Commission. The health lobby highlighted the crucial importance of tobacco taxation for society given the large number of deaths and serious illnesses that can be traced back to tobacco consumption and the huge costs this imposes on European health systems. Health NGOs therefore asked for an increase in tobacco taxation in order to reduce the affordability and availability of cigarettes. For instance, the British Medical Association cited a World Bank Study that showed that a 10 percent increase in price leads to a 4 percent reduction in demand and that particularly young people would reduce their tobacco consumption as a result of price increases. Higher taxation levels would therefore be an ideal instrument to

---

[3] The following discussion is based on responses submitted to the Commission consultation on the structure and rates of excise duty applied on cigarettes and other manufactured tobacco and the associated consultation document, legislative proposal (COM (2008) 459), and final legislative act (Directive 2010/12/EU).

reduce tobacco consumption. In addition, health NGOs furthermore argued that all tobacco products should be taxed equally as there is no justification for differential treatment given that tobacco has a general negative impact on human health irrespective of its form.

By contrast, the tobacco industry including actors such as Philip Morris, the European Smoking Tobacco Association, and British American tobacco largely opposed the Commission initiative on tobacco taxation. With regard to an increase in tobacco tax rates, the German association of tobacco industries argued that tobacco taxes would first and foremost be an instrument to fill the holes in state budgets rather than a measure to enhance human health. It was furthermore stated that an increase in tobacco taxation would solely lead to higher levels of cigarette smuggling and an increase in counterfeit tobacco products with harmful implications for the human body. Similarly, cigar manufacturers strongly opposed aligning the cigarette and the cigar taxation rates. The European Cigar Manufacturers Association for instance argued that applying the same tax rate to cigars would have a disastrous effect on the cigar industry as cigar manufacturing is a very labor-, time- and resource-intensive small-scale activity. In addition, in contrast to cigarettes which have a widespread negative effect on the population and in particular young people, cigar smokers would only constitute 1 percent of the entire European population and they would usually be mature male adults.

Despite the opposition from the tobacco industry, the European institutions largely moved forward with their envisaged tobacco taxation initiative. While the official legislative proposal and the final directive are in line with most of the demands raised by the health coalition, the concerns raised by the tobacco industry were hardly taken up. For instance, the directive increases cigarette taxation in order to reduce cigarette consumption by 10 percent in a five-year period. In addition, the legislative framework also raised taxation rates on other tobacco products in order to avoid substituting cigarettes with other equally harmful tobacco products. The policy debate on tobacco taxation is a prime example for a legislative debate in which citizen interests have won over economic interests. While the tobacco industry coalition is clearly the more important economic actor, the coalition of health NGOs and medical professionals is much stronger when it comes to citizen support. The health coalition represents 75 percent of all the citizens that interest groups reported to represent in this policy debate. It can therefore be concluded that the high level of citizen support seems to have caused the lobbying success of the health coalition.

In conclusion, relative citizen support of lobbying coalitions also has a positive effect on interest group influence during the decision-making stage. The probability that an interest group is able to influence the final legislative act therefore increases with the number of citizens that are represented by its lobbying coalition. However, the size of the effect during the decision-making stage is considerably smaller than during the policy formulation stage. Thus, the European Commission seems to be more receptive to citizen demands at early stages of the policy-making process than the Council and the European Parliament during the decision-making stage. However, citizen support is more important than information supply for lobbying success during the decision-making stage as the effect of citizen support is considerably larger than the effect of information supply.

7.4 THE EFFECT OF ECONOMIC POWER

In this section, I turn to the empirical analysis of the effect of economic power on interest group influence during the decision-making stage. Hypothesis 3 suggested that the relative economic power of their lobbying coalitions has a positive effect on the ability of interest groups to shape the outcome of a legislative debate. Table 7.5 presents the results of the multilevel analysis examining this effect. Column one contains the results of the empty model, the basic model including relative economic power of lobbying coalitions is presented in column two, and column three contains the results of the full model which additionally includes several control variables on the interest group and issue level. As the dataset suffers from a considerable number of missing values due to survey non-response, the sample shrinks to 389 interest groups that lobby the European institutions concerning 42 policy issues.

As predicted by the theoretical model, relative economic power of lobbying coalitions has a statistically significant positive effect on interest group influence during the decision-making stage across both model specifications. A 1 percent increase in relative economic power of a lobbying coalition A, which implies a 1 percent decrease in relative economic power of its opposing lobbying coalition B, raises the chance of interest groups which belong to lobbying coalition A to influence the final legislative act by 2.1 percent (1.4 percent when control variables are included). Hence, interest groups belonging to a lobbying coalition that represents a large number of powerful economic actors which control business investments and job creation have a much better chance to influence decision-making by the Council, the EP, and the Commission than interest groups without the backing of important economic players. All model fit measures accordingly indicate that the inclusion of relative economic power has considerably improved the explanatory power of the statistical model. The full model furthermore suggests that the probability to succeed in lobbying the decision-making process significantly increases with the number of member states supporting the policy objective.

Table 7.5 Multilevel analysis examining the effect of economic power on interest group influence during the decision-making stage

Variables	Empty	Basic	Full
Fixed effects			
LOBBYING COALITION CHARACTERISTICS			
Rel. economic power		1.021***	1.014**
		(0.007)	(0.007)
CONTROLS: INTEREST GROUP LEVEL			
Type: Sectional group			1.079
			(0.363)
Rel. economic power			0.999
			(0.013)
CONTROLS: ISSUE LEVEL			
Salience			1.884
			(0.857)
Complexity			1.366
			(0.460)
Conflict			0.590
			(0.522)
Existence of EU SQ			0.530
			(0.271)
Legislative procedure: Codecision			3.928
			(4.044)
Voting rule: QM			0.582
			(0.985)
Member state support			1.037***
			(0.014)
Random effects			
Issue level variance	2.745	2.839	1.248
Model fit			
N / Issues	389 / 42	389 / 42	389 / 42
Log likelihood	−226	−221	−213
AIC	456	448	449
BIC	464	460	497
LR Test, Prob > Chi2		0.002	0.047

***$p \leq 0.01$,**$p \leq 0.05$,*$p \leq 0.10$, coefficients represent odds ratios, standard errors in parentheses, sectional and cause groups are compared to companies, Codecision is compared to Consultation, qualified majority voting is compared to unanimity, the reference model for the likelihood ratio test is the model left of the model in question

As a further illustration of the effect of economic power of lobbying coalitions during the decision-making stage, I also present simulated predicted probabilities for this effect (see figure 7.6). The solid line again indicates the point estimates for the predicted probabilities and the broken lines mark the 95 percent confidence interval. Relative economic power can vary from its minimum value (0) to its maximum value (100). The simulated probabilities

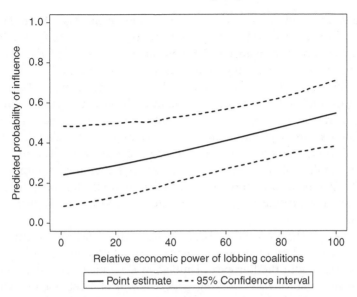

Fig. 7.6 Effect of relative economic power on interest group influence during the decision-making stage

Table 7.6 First differences: Effect of relative economic power on interest group influence during the decision-making stage

Change: Economic power	Change: Influence probability	95% Confidence interval	
0–25%	0.061	0.005	0.102
25–50%	0.075	0.006	0.134
50–75%	0.087	0.012	0.163
75–100%	0.088	0.004	0.163
0–100%	0.315	0.021	0.555

Note: Only lobbying coalition characteristic in question is changed; all other variables are held at their means

indicate that relative economic power of lobbying coalitions has a steady positive effect on the ability of interest groups to exert influence during the decision-making stage. A higher value of relative economic power is associated with a higher probability of lobbying success across the entire empirical range of relative economic power.

Finally, the size of the effect of relative economic power of lobbying coalitions is further illustrated drawing on simulated first differences that allow one to assess how the probability to influence European decision-making changes as relative economic power of lobbying coalitions varies (see table 7.6).

If relative economic power of a lobbying coalition increases from 25 to 50 percent, the predicted probability to influence the design of the final legislative act augments by approximately 7.5 percentage points. Similarly, if relative economic power of lobbying coalitions rises from 50 to 75 percent, the probability of lobbying success increases by on average 8.7 percentage points. Overall, the probability to successfully lobby decision-making in the European Union increases by 31.5 percentage points if economic power of lobbying coalitions rises from its minimum (0) to its maximum (100) value. The effect of economic power is therefore considerably smaller during the decision-making than during the policy formulation stage. At the same time, economic power and citizen support are more or less equally important for lobbying success at the decision-making stage while the effect of information supply is much smaller.

The policy debate on the revision of the energy labeling directive nicely illustrates the effect of economic power on interest group influence on decision-making in the European Union.[4] In December 2007, the European Commission published a working paper in which it set out its plans for a revision of the energy labeling directive. The policy initiative aimed to reform the existing energy labeling framework which had been in force since 1992. The European Commission proposed several policy measures to extend and reinforce the energy labeling directive such as extending the scope of the directive to additional household appliances or indicating the annual running costs of products on the energy label. The legislative initiative aimed at increasing the purchase of energy efficient products and to thereby reduce energy consumption in Europe. On the basis of the working paper, the European Commission launched a public consultation.

The publication of the Commission working paper led to considerable mobilization of interest groups. Two lobbying coalitions emerged that simultaneously lobbied the European institutions. The first coalition brought together a wide variety of industry representatives such as the European Committee of Domestic Equipment Manufacturers (CECED), Bosch, and the European Lamp Companies Federation (ELC). On the other side of the political spectrum was a coalition that united a variety of different environmental NGOs such as Greenpeace, Friends of the Earth, WWF, and the European Environmental Bureau. While the environmental groups strongly supported the policy initiative and demanded even more far-reaching measures, the industry groups lobbied decision-makers in order to dilute the proposed framework.

An important point of discussion between industry and environmental groups was the Commission's suggestion to indicate the annual running

---

[4] The following discussion is based on responses submitted to the Commission consultation on the revision of the energy labeling directive and the associated consultation document, legislative proposal (COM (2008) 778), and final legislative act (Directive 2010/30/EU).

costs of a product on the energy label. The environmental lobby supported the Commission's proposition to display the runnings costs. What is more, the environmental NGOs even went beyond the Commission's initiative by advocating for indicating the costs over an average product lifetime. It was argued that this information would enable consumers to quickly assess the average life-cycle costs. To estimate the costs, it was suggested to use average electricity prices. By contrast, the industry groups strongly opposed this idea. For instance, Bosch argued that it would be impossible to estimate average costs as these would depend on user habits and the climatic conditions. CECED furthermore stated that adding the running costs on the energy label would be impractical due to price differences of electricity providers within and across member states. Indicating the average costs would moreover be counterproductive since the pay-back time of higher investments would be longer than the expected energy savings during the use phase for the most energy efficient products.

After the public consultation, the European Commission adopted its proposal in November 2008 and in May 2010, the Council and the EP finally approved the directive. The industry groups were successful in lobbying the European institutions as neither the proposal nor the final directive includes any mention of indicating the running costs on the energy label. In this particular policy debate, business interests succeeded as they are economically powerful and control investments and jobs all over Europe. Even though environmental groups were supported by a few professional organizations, the industry coalition brought 83 percent of all the economic power of mobilized stakeholders in this debate to the table. At the same time, the levels of information supply and citizen support across the two lobbying coalitions were more or less equal since the industry coalition was partly supported by consumer groups. Accordingly, the crucial difference between the two lobbying coalitions was the supremacy of the industry coalition in terms of economic power. The debate about the revision of the energy labeling directive therefore constitutes a typical example of the power of business over citizen groups.

In conclusion, relative economic power of lobbying coalitions also has a positive effect on interest group influence during the decision-making stage. Hypothesis 3 has therefore not only been confirmed for lobbying during the policy formulation, but also for interest group lobbying during the decision-making stage. The size of the effect of economic power is, however, smaller than during the policy formulation stage suggesting that the Council and the European Parliament are less responsive to demands raised by powerful economic leaders than the European Commission. Moreover, during the decision-making stage citizen support and economic power are by and large equally important for lobbying success. By contrast, information supply still matters, but the size of the effect is considerably smaller than the magnitude of the effects of citizen support and economic power.

7.5 COLLECTIVE ACHIEVEMENT OR FREE-RIDING?

In the previous sections, it has been demonstrated that information supply, citizen support, and economic power of lobbying coalitions have a positive effect on the ability of interest groups to influence decision-making in the European Union. However, as argued in section 6.5, the aggregate analysis of lobbying coalitions alone does not tell us anything about how these effects come about. It has been suggested that there are two different explanations for lobbying coalition effects (see figure 6.5): First, it might be the case that one or just a few very powerful groups are responsible for the policy outcome while other coalition members were just lucky to have the same policy goal. Weak groups could therefore just free-ride on the pressure exerted by strong groups. Second, the positive coalition effects could also indicate that all coalition members simultaneously contribute to the attainment of the common policy objective.

In order to find out which of these explanations accounts for the coalition effects, the following observable implications have been developed (see section 6.5). If free-riding were really at play, one would find a systematic effect of information supply, citizen support, and economic power of individual groups if the strongest interest groups were analyzed separately because weak groups would no longer cancel out the effects. However, if one could not find any systematic relationship between individual information supply, citizen support, and economic power, one can conclude that coalition effects are not caused by the lobbying of a just a handful of powerful groups while others just free-ride on their success.

Table 7.7 presents descriptive information about the 15 percent strongest interest groups with regard to information supply, citizen support, and economic power. Out of the 648 strongest interest groups during the decision-making stage, only 53.40 percent were able to influence the final legislative act while also 47.34 percent of the weaker interest groups had an impact on the policy outcome. Accordingly, the Pearson correlation coefficient measuring the association between interest group influence and strength of individual interest groups also only amounts to 0.058. The descriptive statistics

Table 7.7 Lobbying success of the 15% strongest groups in the decision-making stage

Successful interest groups	Not successful interest groups
53.40% (Strongest groups)	46.60% (Strongest groups)
47.34% (Other groups)	52.66% (Other groups)

Pearson's r: 0.058, $p \leq 0.05$, N = 1,793

Table 7.8 Multilevel logistic regression testing the free-riding hypothesis for the decision-making stage

Variables	Information	Citizen support	Economic power
Relative information supply	0.983		
	(0.048)		
Relative citizen support		0.995	
		(0.011)	
Relative economic power			0.982
			(0.013)
Random effects			
Issue level variance	5.054	4.469	0.446
Model fit			
N / Issues	316 / 42	356 / 40	94 / 42
Log likelihood	−171	−178	−63
AIC	348	361	133
BIC	359	373	140
LR Test, Prob > Chi2	0.717	0.634	0.157
Pearson's r	−0.075	−0.120	−0.166

***$p \leq 0.01$,**$p \leq 0.05$,*$p \leq 0.10$, coefficients represent odds ratios, standard errors in parentheses

therefore do not provide any empirical support for the free-riding hypothesis as the strength of strong individual interest groups is not positively correlated with influence on policy-making.

In order find out whether free-riding can account for the detected coalition effects during the decision-making stage, I estimated multilevel logistic regression models solely based on the 15 percent strongest groups explaining interest group influence with individual information supply, citizen support, and economic power (see table 7.8). In line with the findings for the policy formulation stage, the multilevel analyses do not provide any empirical support for the free-riding hypothesis. Individual information supply, citizen support, and economic power do not have a statistically significant positive effect on interest group influence during the decision-making stage. What is more, the correlation coefficients indicated in the last row of table 7.8 do not even indicate a positive association between the amount of exchange goods of the strongest interest groups and their lobbying success. These analyses were repeated for different thresholds of strength and the results are robust across the different specifications. Hence, coalition effects during the decision-making stage cannot be explained by free-riding on a handful of very strong groups.

7.6 CONCLUSION

This chapter has demonstrated that the same factors that account for lobbying success during the policy formulation stage, also explain interest group influence in the decision-making stage. Lobbying in the European Union is an exchange relationship in which the European institutions trade influence for information, citizen support, and economic power provided by entire lobbying coalitions. While individual interest group characteristics do not have an effect on lobbying success, the aggregated information supply, citizen support, and economic power of issue-specific lobbying coalitions are decisive for interest group influence. This chapter has moreover corroborated the finding of the previous chapter that lobbying coalitions are not dominated by a few powerful groups while others just free-ride. What seems to matter are the collective efforts of all coalition members. In contrast to the policy formulation stage, this chapter has moreover shown that member state support is a crucial determinant of interest group influence during the decision-making stage. The likelihood that interest groups succeed in shifting the policy outcome towards their ideal points increases with the number of member states supporting their objective.

In line with the findings for the policy formulation stage, the analysis presented in this chapter indicates that the exchange goods are not equally important. Table 7.9 compares the effects of information supply, citizen support, and economic power during the policy formulation and the decision-making stage drawing on first differences (Mroz and Zayats 2008, see also page 130). It is indicated how the probability to influence policy formulation and decision-making changes when information supply, citizen support, and economic power change from their minimum (0) to their maximum (100) value. The effect of information supply is much smaller than the effects of citizen support and economic power. This finding suggests that even though information is demanded by the European institutions,

Table 7.9 Comparison of effect sizes at both stages

Change in supply of exchange good: 0–100%	Change: Influence probability	95% Confidence interval	
Policy formulation			
Information supply	0.555	0.451	0.643
Citizen support	0.797	0.716	0.864
Economic power	0.796	0.670	0.876
Decision-making			
Information supply	0.195	0.027	0.359
Citizen support	0.355	0.158	0.538
Economic power	0.315	0.021	0.555

interest groups are most importantly a source for the support of citizens and economically powerful actors. At the same time, there is no indication of a bias between different organized interests. Both citizen and economic interests have similar chances to influence decision-making in the European Union.

Finally, the empirical analysis demonstrated that the overall size of the effects varies across the two stages. The effects of relative information supply, citizen support, and economic power of lobbying coalitions on interest group influence are considerably larger during the policy formulation than during the decision-making stage. Interest groups are therefore well-advised to engage in lobbying activities as early as possible in order to have an impact on policy outcomes. It is much more difficult to shape the final policy outcome once a formal policy proposal is already on the table. As long as no policy proposal is formally adopted, interest groups can much more easily affect the content and the design of the legislative initiative.

8

Conclusion and Implications: Interest Groups, European Politics, and Democracy

Interest group influence is a central theme in the study of politics. The question of who wins and who loses is a recurring puzzle that has preoccupied generations of political scientists. A major objective of interest groups is to influence the political decision-making process in order to achieve a policy outcome that is close to their ideal points. The increasing number of interest groups that lobby legislators throughout the developed world is an indication of the extensive interest group pressure on legislators. It is therefore crucial to take into account interest group lobbying in order to understand the policy process and the decisions taken by politicians. The European Union provides a particularly promising opportunity structure to interest groups due to its multiple access points and its general openness towards interest groups which is driven by the desire to enhance the legitimacy of the European Union. Even though interest groups can easily gain access to the European institutions, not all interest groups can translate their access into influence. Despite the central importance of interest group influence for our understanding of the policy process and the democratic legitimacy of a political system, only few have studied it. As a result, it was unclear what made an interest group a winner or a loser. This book has therefore attempted to provide an answer to the question of why some interest groups are able to influence policy-making in the European Union while others are not.

Studying interest group influence is, however, not only of interest to the community of interest group researchers. Identifying the determinants of lobbying success is not only of intrinsic value, but it has major implications for our understanding of a political system. More specifically, analyzing interest group influence is crucial for two ongoing debates as pointed out in the introductory chapter. The first debate concerns the explanation of policy outcomes in the European Union. Legislative politics scholars have devoted considerable attention to explaining policy outcomes in the European Union (e.g. Tsebelis and Garrett 2000; Thomson et al. 2006; Schneider, Finke, and Bailer 2010; Thomson 2011). However, these studies have so far concentrated on the European Commission, the Council, and the European Parliament in order to explain why specific policies have been adopted. They have largely treated the European institutions as black boxes without any attention to their internal configuration and the processes of preference formation (for an exception, see Schneider, Finke, and Baltz 2007). Even though interest groups extensively lobby the European Commission, the Council, and the European Parliament, interest group pressure has largely been ignored in legislative politics research. Studying interest group influence can therefore shed light on the question of how policy outcomes in the European Union can be explained. What is even more important, the findings of this book also have major implications for the debate on the democratic legitimacy of the European Union. The European institutions have attempted to use interest group inclusion as a means to compensate for the democratic deficit often attributed to the European Union. However, interest group participation can only enhance the democratic legitimacy of a political system if public policy is not systematically biased in favor of some powerful interests while others are constantly losing. Analyzing interest group influence can therefore contribute to the assessment of the democratic potential of interest group participation in European policy-making.

In this concluding chapter I therefore first illustrate the contribution of this book to interest group research. In the light of the empirical findings, I then highlight the broader implications of this book for the study of policy outcomes and the debate on the democratic legitimacy of the European Union. Afterwards, I discuss what this book tell us about lobbying in other political systems before finally laying out open questions and directions for further research.

8.1 LESSONS FOR THE STUDY OF INTEREST GROUPS IN THE EUROPEAN UNION

This book provides three major contributions to the literature on interest groups. First, I have presented a coherent theoretical model that explains why some interest groups win and others lose by conceptualizing lobbying as an exchange between interdependent actors in which the European institutions trade influence for information, citizen support, and economic power provided by issue-specific coalitions of interest groups. Second, I have developed a new approach to measure interest group influence which allows one to overcome operationalization difficulties that have long plagued the study of interest group influence. Third, using this new measurement approach, I have tested my theoretical expectations across a wide variety of policy issues and interest groups which allows me to draw general conclusions about the determinants of interest group influence in the European Union. I explain the theoretical, methodological, and empirical contribution of this book and how it advances the current state of the literature on interest group politics in further detail below.

8.1.1 Theoretical, methodological, and empirical contribution

First, this book has presented a coherent theoretical model that combines explanatory variables on different levels of analysis to arrive at a better understanding of why some interest groups win and others lose. At the heart of the argument presented in this book is the notion that lobbying is an exchange between interdependent actors in which the supply of goods demanded by the European institutions determines the ability of interest groups to influence policy-making. Based on theoretical assumptions about the objectives of interest groups and the European institutions and by taking into account the institutional context in which they interact, I have derived propositions about the goods that are exchanged between interest groups and European institutions. I have theorized that interest groups demand influence from the European institutions whereas the European Commission, the Council, and the European Parliament request policy-relevant information, citizen support, and economic power from interest groups. I have furthermore argued that it is not sufficient to conceptualize lobbying as an individual endeavor, but that the contextual nature of lobbying has to be taken into account in order to arrive at a better understanding of lobbying success. Lobbying has to be conceptualized as a collective enterprise in which a multitude of interest groups is simultaneously lobbying the European institutions concerning a specific policy debate. It is therefore essential to analyze the issue-specific alignment of interest groups in the policy space to identify coalitions of interest groups which pursue the same policy objective. In order to understand why some interest groups succeed in their lobbying activities while others fail, I have therefore suggested that the exchange of goods has to be analyzed on the lobbying coalition, rather than on the individual interest group level. I have accordingly hypothesized that the aggregated information supply, citizen support, and economic power of lobbying coalitions determines the ability of interest groups to influence European policy-making. Finally, I have theorized that the intensity of the exchange relationship is affected by the issue context in which interest groups compete for influence. More precisely, I have suggested that the effect of information supply varies with issue complexity as the decision-makers' need for external information increases with the complexity of a policy issue.

Second, I have developed and tested a new measurement approach to interest group influence which allows interest group scholars to overcome the problem of operationalizing influence which has long prevented interest group researchers from studying interest group influence on policy-making. Drawing on recent developments in political methodology, I have used quantitative text analysis to extract policy preferences of interest groups from their submissions in public consultations launched by the European Commission. Based on a preliminary draft proposal setting out directions for a legislative framework, interest groups can submit comments for an eight-week consultation period before the European Commission adopts its final legislative proposal. The Commission consultations therefore provide a rich new data source for the measurement of interest group preferences which can be compared to the policy output at different stages of the legislative process in order to draw conclusions about the winners and the losers of the policy-making process. Chapter 3 has thoroughly tested this new measurement approach in a case study of one particular policy issue. The results of the case study are promising and text analysis proves to be a powerful tool to measure interest groups' policy positions, paving the way for the large-scale analysis of interest group influence carried out in this book.

Finally, by drawing on this new approach to influence measurement, I have been able to test my theoretical model across 56 policy issues and 2,696 interest groups. The sample of policy issues and interest groups covers a large number of policy areas and a wide variety of interest group types and therefore goes beyond the usual focus on one or just a few policy issues and a specific interest group type that characterizes previous studies. I enriched this large new dataset by gathering data on information supply, citizen support, and economic power of lobbying coalitions and by collecting data on several control variables on the interest group and issue level. The independent variables have been measured by a combination of several data sources, more specifically, by coding interest groups' websites, by a survey of all interest groups which participated in the consultations, and by information retrieved from the European Union databases *PreLex* and *EurLex*. This book therefore presents a unique empirical analysis of interest group influence on European policy-making which allows for drawing general conclusions about the determinants of interest group influence in the European Union.

8.1.2 Lobbying as an exchange relationship

The findings of the analysis carried out in this book largely confirm the hypotheses derived from the theoretical model. Information supply, citizen support, and economic power of lobbying coalitions have a positive effect on the ability of interest groups to exert influence during the policy formulation and the decision-making stage of the European legislative process. It can therefore be concluded that lobbying can indeed be conceptualized as an exchange relationship between interdependent actors. The European institutions trade influence for information, citizen support, and economic power. Thus, the key to lobbying success is providing the European institutions with these three goods. Variation in influence can therefore be explained by the amount of information, citizen support, and economic power that interest groups provide to the European Commission, the Council, and the European Parliament.

Information supply is important for two reasons. First, the European institutions require technical expertise in order to produce legislation that constitutes a technically appropriate solution to a given policy problem. In addition, they need information about the policy positions of affected societal interests in order to avoid opposition by major stakeholders. Moreover, the EU institutions' demand for citizen support and economic power is driven by the reelection objective of Members of the European Parliament and national governments in the Council. Interest groups that can help MEPs and national governments to get reelected are welcome interlocutors and their demands are thoroughly taken into account by the European Parliament and the Council. The European Commission is well aware of the electoral dependence of MEPs and national governments on interest groups with a high degree of citizen support and economic power, and therefore strategically rallies their support in order to gain the consent of the Council and the EP for its legislative proposals.

The importance of interest groups for the reelection of decision-makers depends on the number of citizens they represent and the number of economically powerful actors that interest groups assemble. The higher the number of citizens an interest group represents, the larger the number of voters it can mobilize for an election. In order to avoid electoral punishment for not adhering to their demands, the European institutions are therefore particularly attentive to the preferences of interest groups with a high degree of citizen support. As vote choice of citizens is strongly influenced by the overall state of the economy, the European institutions furthermore attempt to satisfy the demands of economically powerful actors since their investment and employment decisions largely affect economic performance and ultimately vote choice.

Whereas information supply, citizen support, and economic power all have a statistically significant positive effect on interest group influence, the effect of information supply is smaller than the effect of citizen support and economic power at both stages of the legislative process. Thus, while all three exchange goods are important for lobbying success, citizen support and economic power seem to be even more valuable to the European institutions than information supply. This indicates that the European institutions are more responsive to demands raised by interest groups which can have an effect on the reelection chances of national governments and MEPs than to interest groups which mainly rely on providing technical expertise. At the same time, the finding that citizen support and economic power have more or less equally strong effects on interest group influence signals that policy-making in the European Union is not biased in favor of economic interests. EU politics is not dominated by big business; citizen support is an equally important asset in the lobbying game.

8.1.3 Lobbying as a collective enterprise

I have moreover demonstrated that lobbying is a collective enterprise. Looking solely at the properties of individual interest groups disregards the fact that decision-makers are confronted with a plurality of interest groups that want to influence the outcome of a legislative debate. Policy issues raise the attention of numerous interest groups which are simultaneously lobbying the European Commission, the Council, and the European Parliament. It is therefore crucial to examine how interest groups align in the issue-specific policy space. Interest groups that pursue the same policy objective pull the European institutions in the same direction and can therefore be considered as a lobbying coalition.

In order to fully understand interest group influence on European policy-making, it is therefore necessary to take into account the aggregated information supply, citizen support, and economic power of these issue-specific lobbying coalitions rather than solely focusing on individual interest group characteristics. If an interest group supplies a considerable amount of information, represents a large number of citizens, and provides a high degree of economic power, but belongs to a lobbying coalition which only provides a small amount of these goods relative to its opposing coalition, the interest group has a very low chance to influence the decision-making process. By contrast, an interest group which only provides a medium amount of information, represents a medium number of citizens, and disposes of a medium degree of economic power can still have a good chance to be influential if it works together with other interest groups in a strong lobbying coalition that supplies more of these goods to the European institutions than its opposing coalition. Thus, the higher the relative information supply, citizen support, and economic power of a lobbying coalition as compared to the opposing lobbying team on a given policy issue, the higher the chance of its member interest groups to influence policy-making in the European Union.

I have furthermore demonstrated that the positive lobbying coalition effects are not due to the properties of a few powerful interest groups while other groups are just free-riding on their impact. There is no systematic pattern that links the characteristics of the most powerful individual interest groups with lobbying success. What seems to matter is therefore the sum of the characteristics of all coalition members rather than the individual properties of a few powerful interest groups. Accordingly, the empirical analysis does not provide any evidence that characteristics of individual interest groups can explain what makes an interest group a winner or a loser. Information supply, citizen support, and economic power of individual interest groups do not have a systematic effect on the ability of interest groups to influence European policy-making. Interest groups which provide a lot of information, citizen support, and economic power therefore do not automatically have a high chance to influence policy-making. They have to form a lobbying coalition with other powerful interest groups that provides a lot of information, citizen support, and economic power to the European institutions on the aggregate level. Hence, the same interest group can have a high chance to influence policy-making on one issue whereas its chances are very low on another issue depending on the aggregate characteristics of its issue-specific lobbying coalitions. In addition, interest group influence does also not vary systematically across interest group type as often argued in the literature (Schneider and Baltz 2003; Dür and De Bièvre 2007*a*). European policy-making is not systematically biased in favor of concentrated interests while diffuse interests are largely overruled. None of the individual interest group characteristics shows a systematic effect on the ability of interest groups to influence policy-making in the European Union across the large variety of policy issues analyzed in this book. Hence, interest group influence cannot be explained by merely looking at individual interest group properties.

In order to understand the nature of interest groups in the lobbying process, we need to change the way we think and talk about interest groups. Interest groups are not dangerous when encountered alone, but they generally travel in packs. Journalists usually report about individual interest groups and their impact on the policy process. As this book has shown, however, it is not sufficient to simply look at individual interest groups. A single corporation or advocacy group is not important, what matters are entire lobbying coalitions that collectively pressure decision-makers. The finding that individual interest groups are not decisive, but that issue-specific coalitions are the crucial players in the lobbying game has important implications for the effectiveness of lobbying regulations. Several countries have made efforts to regulate interest group lobbying. For instance, interest groups lobbying Members of Parliament in Germany have to register at the German Bundestag. Similarly, all lobbyists that enter the European Parliament need to be included in the European Parliament's accreditation registry. However, most of these registries only contain information about individual interest groups such as their organizational characteristics and the policy area they are working on. In the light of the findings of this book, these registers are not sufficient to monitor the lobbying process. What is needed are issue-specific registrations in which interest groups not only declare their resources and their lobbying expenses, but in which they indicate on which concrete issues they lobbied decision-makers and most importantly, which policy goals they pursued in these debates. Such a register would allow for assessing the strength of lobbying coalitions and to relate their activities to policy outcomes.

8.1.4 The contextual nature of lobbying

The importance of lobbying coalitions leads to another point: Most interest group scholars either analyzed one or just a few policy issues (e.g. Dür and De Bièvre 2007*a*; Michalowitz 2007; Woll 2007) or they investigated lobbying on the aggregate level without any attention to issue-specific differences (e.g. Bouwen 2004*a*; Eising 2007*b*). As this book has shown, however, the issue context plays a very important role for interest group influence. First of all, lobbying coalitions are issue-specific. Even though there might be formal and permanent networks among interest groups, it is important how interest groups align with others on a given policy issue. What counts are the aggregated characteristics of all interest groups which fight for the same policy objective, no matter whether they formally cooperate or not. As long as they have the same policy goal, they push the decision-makers in the same direction and one therefore has to take into account their aggregated characteristics.

Second, this book has furthermore demonstrated that the intensity of the exchange relationship between the European institutions and interest groups is considerably affected by the complexity of policy issues. The positive effect of information supply by lobbying coalitions varies with issue complexity. The higher the complexity of policy proposals, the stronger the effect of information supply as the information needs of the European institutions increase with the complexity of policy issues. Hence, lobbying coalitions which provide a lot of information to the European institutions should find it particularly easy to influence the decision-making process if a highly complex policy issue is debated. It is accordingly necessary to take into account the contextual nature of lobbying in order to understand variation in interest group influence.

With regard to the other policy issue characteristics incorporated as control variables in this study, the empirical analysis has not provided any empirical support for a systematic effect on lobbying success. Contrary to previous literature that suggests that lobbying success varies with issue-specific factors such as salience and conflict (Mahoney 2007*a*, 2008; Baumgartner et al. 2009), the empirical analysis presented in this book could not confirm these hypotheses. It is somewhat surprising that none of these factors displays any systematic effect. For instance, it is highly plausible that interest group influence should be particularly difficult if a policy debate is characterized by a high degree of conflict. If interest groups have strongly opposing views on what legislation should be adopted, decision-makers should find it very hard to just listen to one side. Similarly, if decisions in the Council have to be taken unanimously, it should be much more difficult for interest groups to influence the final legislative act as every single member state government has to approve a policy proposal. Given the plausibility of the explanatory approaches associated with the issue context, the empirical analysis presented here should be seen as a first starting point for the large-scale analysis of the effect of issue-level factors on interest group influence. Future research should further develop the theoretical arguments underlying the different issue-specific variables by for instance specifying cross-level interactions that might be at play and analyzing their effect on an even larger set of issues.

8.1.5 Lobbying and the policy-making cycle

Finally, this book has demonstrated that the ability of interest groups to influence European policy-making varies across different stages of the legislative process. The empirical analysis indicated that the effects of relative information supply, citizen support, and economic power of lobbying coalitions on interest group influence are considerably larger during the policy formulation than during the decision-making stage. Influencing policy-making is therefore most promising during the early stages of the policy-making process as no formal document has been adopted yet and changes to the legislative initiative can therefore be achieved much more easily. Interest groups that want to influence a policy debate in the European Union are therefore well-advised to start their lobbying activities as early as possible since changes to the legislative framework are more difficult to achieve once a formal policy proposal is already on the table. In order to assess the impact of interest group pressure on European policy-making, future research therefore needs to take into account that the ability to influence political decisions is also affected by the stage of the legislative process.

8.2 POLICY OUTCOMES IN THE EUROPEAN UNION: THE ROLE OF INTEREST GROUPS

This book provides important insights for the legislative politics literature that aims at explaining policy outcomes in the European Union. Legislative politics scholars have largely focused on the interaction between the Council, the European Parliament, and the European Commission in order to explain the emergence of policy outcomes in the European Union. Based on assumptions about the preferences of the three major institutions and taking into account the institutional procedures, these scholars make predictions about expected policy outcomes (e.g. Tsebelis 1994; Garrett and Tsebelis 1996; Tsebelis and Garrett 2000; Thomson et al. 2006; Thomson 2011). Early works have assumed a stable and uniform preference configuration that centers around a "degree of integration" dimension irrespective of the substance of the policy issue (e.g. Garrett and Tsebelis 1996; Tsebelis and Garrett 2000). Whereas such a broad distinction might be useful for the study of intergovernmental treaty bargaining, it is not meaningful when it comes to the day-to-day politics in the European Union (see also Rittberger 2000; Hörl, Warntjen, and Wonka 2005). It is not very plausible to believe that the configuration of policy preferences of the Council, the European Parliament, and the European Commission is stable across a diverse range of policy fields such as environmental policy, trade policy, or regional policy.

More recent studies have therefore started to empirically measure policy preferences of the three institutions on specific policy issues to arrive at a better understanding of the policy process at the European level (e.g. Thomson et al. 2006). However, even if policy preferences are allowed to vary across policy issues and are measured for each issue under consideration, we still do not have any knowledge about how these preferences actually come about. The European institutions are embedded in a complex environment with which they have to interact. They are politically dependent on other actors such as voters in the case of the Council and the EP, or member state governments in the case of the European Commission. Thus, even though they might have clear interests, they cannot single-handedly translate their interests into policy positions without taking into account their environmental constraints. In addition, the European Commission, the Council, and the European Parliament are by no means unitary actors. They are complex collective actors that are characterized by a high degree of vertical and functional differentiation. If we want to understand why a specific policy has emerged, it is necessary to find out what factors shape the preference formation of the European institutions and how internal decision-making can be explained. As Hörl, Warntjen, and Wonka (2005, 592) rightly stated, "future research needs to study mechanisms of preference formation and decision-making, i.e. aggregation of preferences, within EU legislative bodies."

The increasing number of interest groups that lobby political decision-makers on the European level can be taken as an indicator for the extensive interest group pressure that the European institutions are facing (Greenwood 2007b, 12; Wonka et al. 2010). Accordingly, Moravcsik (1993, 1998) argues that member state governments in the Council function as a transmission belt for societal interests. National governments do not pursue their own individual interests, but the preferences that they represent on the supranational level are determined through a process of national preference formation in which interest groups engage in a pluralist competition at the domestic level. The governments are considered to be agents of the dominant societal interests that prevail in the competition among national interest groups. Hence, according to Moravcsik (1993, 1998) preference formation within the Council of the European Union can be explained by the dependence of national governments on domestic interest groups.

Similarly, Stone Sweet and Sandholtz (1997) and Sandholtz and Stone Sweet (1998) argue that interest groups also have a considerable impact on the policy preferences and the behavior of the European Commission and the European Parliament. Due to costs emanating from cross-border activities, societal actors demand further integration from legislators. In order to achieve their objective, they not only lobby their own governments, but also engage in extensive exchanges with the European Commission and the European Parliament. While the grand European integration theories have clearly attributed a significant role to interest groups, systematic evidence on their impact on the decisions taken by the European institutions is scarce.

This book therefore contributes to our knowledge of preference formation within the European institutions by providing a thorough analysis of the exchange between interest groups and the European institutions and by specifying conditions under which interest groups are able to have an effect on the decision-making process. I have demonstrated that interest groups are actively seeking to influence European policy-making and that they engage in an exchange relationship with the European Commission, the Council, and the European Parliament. However, not all interest groups are equally able to influence preference formation within the European institutions. They need to provide the goods that are demanded by the European Commission, the Council, and the European Parliament in order to be able to have an impact on the decisions that they take.

All three institutions require policy-relevant information and interest groups which can provide this information are in a good position to shape the policy preferences expressed by the European institutions. In addition, national governments in the Council and Members of the European Parliament are dependent on voters in order to stay in office while the European Commission requires the approval of the Council and the European Parliament to successfully bring a new legislative initiative on its way. Member state governments and MEPs are therefore also attentive to the demands raised by interest groups that represent a large number of voters. Similarly, they also seek the support of interest groups that represent major economic players since their behavior crucially affects the overall economic performance which has a considerable impact on the electoral success of national governments and MEPs. The European Commission in turn can exploit the electoral dependence of MEPs and national governments. In order to make sure that the Council and the European Parliament approve a new legislative initiative, it can strategically rally the support of interest groups that enjoy the support of a large number of citizens and powerful economic actors. Thus, the European institutions and interest groups are interdependent actors who stand in an exchange relationship with each other. Whereas interest groups seek influence, the European institutions demand policy-relevant information, citizen support, and economic power from interest groups. By providing these goods, interest groups are able to influence the policy positions that the European institutions adopt concerning a specific policy initiative and to therefore shape the outcome of a legislative debate.

Hence, in order to understand the emergence of policy outcomes, one cannot solely look at the policy preferences of the three major institutions. To fully comprehend why a specific policy has been adopted, it is necessary to investigate how the policy preferences of the European Commission, the Council, and the European Parliament have been formed. Interest groups play an important role for the preference formation of political institutions as has been shown in the thorough analysis of interest group influence during the policy formulation and the decision-making stage of the European legislative process. Ignoring interest group pressure therefore constitutes an oversimplification of the policy-making process in the European Union. Future research therefore needs to systematically take into account interest group pressure when trying to explain the emergence of policy outcomes in the European Union.

8.3 INTEREST GROUPS AND DEMOCRACY IN THE EUROPEAN UNION

This book furthermore has important implications for the debate on the democratic legitimacy of the European Union. European integration has changed the role of the state dramatically. The deepening of the Single European Market, the establishment of the Economic and Monetary Union, and the increasing transfer of competences to the European Union has led to an internationalization of policy-making. More and more political decisions are taken not at the national but rather the European level. The authority of making legally binding decisions has partly been shifted away from democratically elected national parliaments to supranational institutions which have been severely criticized for a lack of democratic legitimacy and accountability (see e.g. Weiler, Haltern, and Mayer 1995; Bartolini 2005; Follesdal and Hix 2006).

Due to the constant criticism of the democratic deficit, the European institutions have recently started to consider interest group inclusion as a means to compensate for the representational deficit (see e.g. Kohler-Koch 2007; Saurugger 2010). Since the beginning of the 1990s, the Commission has therefore engaged in participatory engineering by taking various initiatives to increase the participation of interest groups such as the White Paper on European Governance or the Transparency Initiative (Kohler-Koch and Finke 2007). At the same time, democratic theory has debated the democratic potential of interest groups in bridging the gap between citizens and decision-makers (Finke 2007; Kohler-Koch and Finke 2007; Saurugger 2008). Under the heading of "associative democracy" these approaches have argued for a greater inclusion of interest groups in public policy-making since interest groups can simultaneously improve the efficiency of policy-making and assure citizen participation (Hirst 1994; Cohen and Rogers 1995; Schmalz-Bruns 1995).

There are consequently two dimensions to democratic legitimacy that scholars usually distinguish when analyzing the contribution of interest groups to the democratic quality of the European Union: input legitimacy and output legitimacy (Scharpf 1970; Rittberger 2003; Finke 2007). Scholars investigating the democratic potential from the input legitimacy perspective explore the ability of interest groups to ensure citizen participation in European policy-making. By contrast, scholars investigating the democratic potential of interest group inclusion from the output legitimacy perspective examine the contribution of interest groups to effective governance and problem-solving. In order to assess whether interest groups can enhance the input legitimacy of the European Union, it is important to look at the representation of interest groups at the European level and at the distribution of influence among different interest groups (Finke 2007, 9). In order to assess the contribution of interest groups to the output legitimacy of the European Union, it is necessary to discuss how interest groups can enhance the problem-solving capacity of the European institutions (Finke 2007, 4).

The Commission initiatives have provided open access to all sorts of interest groups, but having equal access in principle does not mean equal representation or equal influence (Kohler-Koch and Finke 2007, 216). In terms of representation, Persson (2007) found for instance that business interest groups are considerably better represented than cause groups in the consultation on the Commission proposal for a new European chemicals policy. This finding has been confirmed by the empirical analysis of 56 Commission consultations presented in this book. Of all 2,696 interest groups which participated in the 56 consultations, 66.50 percent were business associations or individual companies (see table 5.3). By contrast, only 20.07 percent were cause groups and only 1.04 percent of all consultation participants were trade unions. In terms of representation, it can therefore be concluded that there is a strong bias in favor of business interests.

Even though European policy-making provides a multitude of access points and the European institutions are actively seeking the input of interest groups, not all interest groups are able to make use of these access points. The European polity constitutes a complex institutional environment which is characterized by multiple levels of government, fragmentation of powers across different institutions, and a high degree of vertical and functional differentiation. This institutional environment creates a high amount of uncertainty since it is difficult to oversee policy developments. Interest groups which seek to participate in European policy-making must be able to effectively monitor the policy-making process in order to quickly respond to new policy initiatives. Thus, even though consultations are formally open to anyone interested in the policy issues, not all interest groups are equally able to seize this opportunity. Particularly business associations and companies have demonstrated that they have the capacities to use the access points offered by the European institutions whereas cause groups and trade unions find it very difficult to engage on the European level. Thus, business interest groups are better represented since they have the means that are necessary to exploit the access points offered by the European institutions. What is more, as Olson (1965) has pointed out, business interests find it rather easy to get organized in the first place as they represent primary economic interests of a small, clearly circumscribed group of actors. Diffuse interests by contrast find it very difficult to get organized, which is a precondition for effective lobbying, since they represent mainly secondary interests of a large, diffuse group of actors and therefore suffer from the free-rider problem.

However, when assessing the role of interest groups for the input legitimacy of the European Union, one cannot solely look at representation and access of interest groups. One also has to pay attention to the actual influence that represented interests can exert. Accordingly, Kohler-Koch and Finke (2007) distinguish between a "principled conception" and a "functional conception" that link participation to democracy. Whereas the "principled conception" is based on equal chances of access and equal representation, the "functional conception" of democracy is going further by requiring that citizens can effectively participate in decision-making processes and that political decisions are responsive to their demands (Kohler-Koch and Finke 2007, 214, 217). According to the "functional conception," discussing representation is not sufficient when assessing the democratic potential of interest group participation. It could in theory be the case that a specific actor type is very well represented, but that this actor type is hardly able to exert any influence. For instance, even though business interests are very well represented in consultations conducted by the European Commission, it does not mean that they are necessarily more influential than trade unions which are only poorly represented. So the question is how representation and access translate into influence. More specifically, what determines interest group influence?

This book has found that three characteristics in particular determine the ability of interest groups to exert influence: the provision of policy-relevant information to the European institutions, the number of citizens represented by interest groups, and the degree of economic power, that is the ability to control business investments and job creation. All three characteristics have a systematic positive effect on interest group influence. While information supply has a slightly smaller effect on interest group influence, citizen support and economic power have a more or less equally strong effect on lobbying success. This indicates that interest groups representing a large number of citizens and business associations speaking for a large number of companies are equally able to influence European policy-making. In addition, in order to control for interest group type, the empirical analysis presented in this book tested whether interest group influence systematically varies across companies, sectional groups, and cause groups. The findings indicate that lobbying success does not differ systematically across actor type so that European legislation is not systematically biased in favor of concentrated interests. It can therefore be concluded that influence is distributed fairly equally among different societal interests. Business interests have a good chance to influence policy-making in the European Union if they dispose of a high degree of economic power and provide a lot of information to the European Commission, the Council, and the European Parliament. Similarly, citizen associations also have a very good chance to influence policy-making if they represent a large number of citizens and supply policy-relevant information to the European institutions. Thus, one cannot say that business is running the European Union. Certainly, business associations have a good chance to shape policies, but only if they have a lot of economic power and provide policy-relevant information to the European institutions. The same is true for other organized interests: If they represent a high number of citizens and provide a lot of information to the European Commission, the Council, and the European Parliament, they also have a good chance to shape the outcome of a legislative debate.

Thus, in terms of representation, there is a clear bias in favor of business interests. They constitute by far the biggest group among the participants in Commission consultations. However, in terms of influence, the empirical evidence does not prove a systematic bias in favor of business interests. Even though economic power plays an important role, so do citizen support and information supply. If interest groups represent a large number of citizens, they have a good chance to influence policy-making. In addition, if interest groups provide a high amount of policy-relevant information to the European institutions, their chance to shape the outcome of a policy debate is also fairly high.

In conclusion, the results of the analysis carried out in this book lead me to draw a fairly optimistic picture of interest group participation in European policy-making. The positive effect of information supply indicates that interest groups enhance the output legitimacy of European policy-making. The European institutions do not simply produce policies in favor of specific interests. They demand policy-relevant information in order to develop technically appropriate solutions to given policy problems. Interest groups which supply such information to the European institutions have a fairly good chance to influence the legislative debate. Thus, interest group participation enhances the problem-solving capacity of European policy-making. The positive effect of economic power and citizen support indicates that interest group participation also enhances the input legitimacy of the European Union. The European institutions do not systematically favor business over other interests. Economic power surely plays a role, but not exclusively. Citizen support is also an important asset that increases the chance of interest groups to influence policy-making. Hence, in terms of input and output legitimacy, interest group participation indeed seems to enhance the democratic quality of the European Union.

8.4 IMPLICATIONS FOR INTEREST GROUP RESEARCH BEYOND THE EUROPEAN UNION

Finally, what does this book tell us about lobbying in other political systems? Some of the findings of this book are universal and apply to any political system. Other findings, however, have to be interpreted by taking into account the specific institutional design of the European Union (Hix 1994; Risse-Kappen 1996; Hix 1998). The European Union provides a particularly hard test case for some of the hypotheses while others are more likely to be confirmed in the EU than in other political systems. In the following, I will therefore discuss the implications of this book for the study of interest groups more generally.

The finding that lobbying is a collective enterprise is not restricted to the European Union. Policy issues usually raise the attention of more than just a single interest group. Numerous interest groups mobilize simultaneously and lobby decision-makers for their cause. The collective mobilization is a general phenomenon that applies to any political system in which interest groups engage in lobbying policy-makers. It is therefore universally important to consider how interest groups position themselves in a policy debate. Interest groups that fight for the same policy objective pull decision-makers in the same direction and can therefore be considered as one lobbying coalition. In order to better understand why some interest groups win and others lose, interest group scholars in any political system therefore have to take into account issue-specific lobbying coalitions.

In a similar vein, the major methodological contribution of this book is also universally applicable. In order to measure interest group influence, this book has introduced a new methodological approach that employs recently developed quantitative text analysis techniques to study legislative consultations. The quantitative text analysis allows for extracting policy preferences from interest group submissions to consultations held by the Commission and to compare them to the location of the policy output at different stages of the legislative process. I was therefore able to draw conclusions about the winners and the losers of the political decision-making process. This methodological approach can be applied in every political system in which consultations are held before a legislative act is adopted by the political institutions. For instance, the German Bundestag as well as the German federal ministries regularly launch consultations in which interest groups can express their views on a planned policy initiative. Open public consultations on new legislative initiatives are for instance similarly organized in the United Kingdom, the Netherlands, and Denmark. In addition, it would also be possible to apply the measurement approach to position papers released by interest groups on their websites without necessarily relying on a legislative consultation. The measurement approach introduced in this book therefore allows for studying interest group influence on a large empirical scale in a variety of different political systems.

With regard to citizen support, it has to be noted that citizen attention to EU politics is comparatively low. European Parliament elections have often been described as "second order" elections which are generally viewed as being of lesser importance since there is "less at stake" than in national elections (Reif and Schmitt 1980; van der Eijk and Franklin 1996). While national elections decide about the composition of the domestic governments, European Parliament elections are neither related directly to the composition of the European Commission nor do they affect membership in the Council. As a result, public salience and turnout is considerably lower than in national elections. Given the lack of direct electoral accountability of the European Commission and the Council, it should be particularly difficult to find an effect of citizen support on interest group influence. However, even despite the weak electoral ties between citizens and the European institutions, the empirical analysis presented in this book demonstrates that citizen support has an important effect on lobbying success in the European Union. Since the European Union is a particularly hard case for finding an effect of citizen support, it can be expected that citizen support should have an even stronger effect in other political systems in which political decision-makers are directly accountable to voters.

While the European Union constitutes a least likely case for finding an effect of citizen support, it constitutes a most likely case for the effect of information supply. The powers of the European Union have been considerably increased over the past decades. The European Union is responsible for a variety of policy areas such as trade policy, agricultural policy, and environmental policy. Despite its considerable decision-making powers and the high complexity of policy-making, the resources of the European institutions are fairly limited.

For instance, even though the European Commission is solely responsible for drafting new legislative proposals, it is notoriously understaffed (McLaughlin, Jordan, and Maloney 1993, 201; Marks and McAdam 1999, 105; Bouwen 2009, 20). Its staff resources are by and large comparable to those of a larger city administration. Even though information should be a valuable good for decision-makers in any political system as several scholars have pointed out (e.g. Potters and van Winden 1990, 1992; Austen-Smith 1993; Lohmann 1995, 1998), the informational needs of the European institutions should on average be higher than those of decision-makers in other institutional settings. For instance, while governments in national political systems can rely on their ministries to obtain necessary information, the European Commission largely lacks institutional alternatives and therefore heavily relies on information provided by interest groups. The effect of information supply should therefore be stronger in the European Union than in other political systems.

Finally, with regard to economic power there is no clear reason to believe that this effect should be systematically weaker or stronger in other institutional settings. On the one hand, the policy competences of the European Union largely revolve around the single market. As a result, one might argue that the European institutions might have particularly strong ties to the European institutions. Similarly, as discussed above, the European Union is largely insulated from public scrutiny which should make it particularly easy for business interests to push through their claims as their lobbying activities might be largely unnoticed by the general public. On the other hand, the European institutions actively support interest groups promoting diffuse interests such as consumer or environmental protection to balance the input of economic interests (Mahoney and Beckstrand 2011). As a result, there is no reason to expect that the effect of economic power should be weaker or stronger in the European Union than in any other political system.

8.5 FUTURE CHALLENGES

This book has analyzed interest group influence during the policy formulation and the decision-making stage of the European legislative process. During the policy formulation stage, the European Commission develops its legislative proposal on which basis the Council, the European Parliament, and the Commission negotiate the design of the final legislative act during the decision-making stage. Even though the policy formulation and the decision-making stage are crucial for the outcome of a legislative debate, further research has to extend the analysis to other stages of the policy-making process. More specifically, the analysis has to be extended to the agenda-setting and implementation stage of the European policy-making process.

The agenda-setting stage is crucial for any analysis of policy-making since it is determined here what policy issues are subject to formal decision-making at all. Since legislative attention is a limited good, decision-makers are forced to select a small subset of policy issues from a potentially infinite number of existing policy problems. The process of agenda-setting is therefore highly political since various actors are trying to place policy issues of their interest onto the legislative agenda while attempting to block the emergence of others. The European Commission plays a central role for agenda-setting in the EU. In the first pillar it enjoys the monopoly to formulate policy proposals so that it serves as a gate-keeper for policy-making. Only issues that attract the attention of the European Commission have the chance to be eventually translated into concrete policies. While agenda-setting processes in other political systems have received considerable attention (e.g. Cobb and Elder 1972; Kingdon 1984; Baumgartner and Jones 1993), the emergence of policy issues on the legislative agenda of the European Union has largely been neglected (for an exception, see Princen 2009). Future research should therefore extend the analysis of interest group pressure to the agenda-setting stage in order to study the first face of power, that is the ability of interest groups to place policy issues of their interest onto the legislative agenda (Bachrach and Baratz 1962).

While lobbying at later stages of the policy-making largely revolves around pushing decision-makers in a specific direction on a given policy issue, lobbying during the agenda-setting stage is more about raising the attention to a specific policy issue. I would therefore expect that the role of lobbying coalitions might be slightly different during the agenda-setting stage. Lobbying coalitions are clearly defined throughout the legislative process as interest group activities essentially boil down to directional lobbying. An issue is already on the agenda and the goal during these stages of the policy-making process is to achieve a policy outcome that is as close as possible to an interest group's ideal point. Hence, interest groups fighting for different policy goals with regard to a specific policy initiative come together in opposing lobbying coalitions. However, during the agenda-setting stage it is not about pushing the legislative act in a specific direction, it is about placing an issue on the legislative agenda in the first place. Interest groups might have opposing views on the design of a certain policy initiative, but they might share similar levels of attention to that issue. Hence, interest groups might agree that something has to be done about a certain issue without having necessarily the same policy objective. As a result, lobbying coalitions might play a different role during the agenda-setting stage. Future research should therefore extend the analysis to the agenda-setting stage to shed light on the role of lobbying coalitions for the second face of power.

In addition, it might also be very fruitful to go beyond the actual legislative debate which ends with the adoption of a legislative act. As compliance research has shown, not all legislative acts that have been adopted on the

European level are in fact implemented in member states (e.g. Börzel 2001; Falkner et al. 2005; König and Luetgert 2009; Steunenberg and Kaeding 2009). It is therefore plausible to expect that interest groups which did not manage to influence the actual "making" of policies at the European level, try to block the implementation of these policies at the national level. A full understanding of interest group influence in a political system therefore requires that one analyzes how interest groups are able to place a policy issue on the agenda, how they can influence the elaboration of a policy proposal on this issue, how they can affect the legislative decision on whether this policy proposal enters into force, and finally how interest groups can influence the implementation of this legislative act.

While this book has provided a thorough analysis of interest group influence on European policy-making by theorizing about the demands of the European Commission, the Council, and the European Parliament, internal institutional differences have not been considered. For the sake of analytical parsimony, I have conceptualized the European Commission as a unitary actor while I theorized that all MEPs and all national governments are driven by the same interests. I chose this approach in order to gain general insights into the incentives of the European institutions to engage in an exchange relationship with interest groups that allow the drawing of general conclusions concerning the determinants of interest group influence on European policy-making. Future research can build on these general insights, but might want to refine the analysis by focusing on the specificities of each European institution. For instance, it might be worthwhile to investigate whether particular DGs within the European Commission are more attentive to interest group demands than others. Moreover, it might be valuable to examine whether interest group influence on MEPs varies with their party affiliation or their committee membership. Finally, one could analyze whether interest group influence on national governments varies with the partisan composition of governments or the national origin of interest groups. Hence, while this book has provided important general insights that help us to better understand interest group influence on European policy-making, future research can extend the analysis to a more fine-grained investigation of interest group influence on specific European institutions that takes into account intra-institutional variation.

Another point which is worth further investigation is the issue of framing. Framing refers to the way a policy issue is understood and presented in a policy debate. A policy issue can be discussed in a variety of terms and actors can frame the debate in a particular direction by "selecting and highlighting some features of reality while omitting others" (Entman 1993, 53). The way a policy issue is framed can determine which interests mobilize, how many actors mobilize, and which institutional actors deal with the policy issues. Interest groups can therefore deliberately use a certain framing strategy to place an issue on the political agenda and to debate it in a way which favors their own standpoint. Thus, successful framing can dramatically improve the chances of interest groups to influence the political decision-making process in their favor.

Even though the importance of framing has long been known (e.g. Schattschneider 1960; Riker 1996), interest group scholars have so far not systematically analyzed framing strategies and their effect on interest group influence. This shortcoming can largely be explained by difficulties in operationalizing framing as it is methodologically challenging to identify issue-specific rhetorics employed by interest groups in an effort to influence policy outcomes. The measurement approach to interest group influence developed in this book also points at new opportunities to study framing processes empirically. I have demonstrated that quantitative text analysis can be used to extract interest groups' policy preferences from their submissions to Commission consultations. In addition, recent advances in quantitative text analysis offer promising tools for the study of framing processes (e.g. Schonhardt-Bailey 2008; Quinn et al. 2010). Future research should therefore make systematic use of quantitative text analysis and interest group documents to analyze framing strategies and their impact on interest group influence.

Concerning the contribution of interest group participation to democratic legitimacy, this study has provided important empirical evidence on the role of interest groups for the input and output legitimacy of the European Union. In terms of input legitimacy, I have demonstrated that interest group participation is biased towards business interests, but that this representational bias does not translate into an influence bias in favor of business groups. However, in order to truly enhance the input legitimacy of European policy-making, it is crucial how citizens participate in the internal decision-making processes of interest groups (e.g. Saurugger 2008, 1285–1286). In order to bridge the gap between citizens and the political system, interest groups must represent the interests of their members. However, it is largely unknown how interest groups arrive at their policy preferences. If decisions are largely taken by interest group elites without consulting their individual members, interest group inclusion in European policy-making can hardly be considered as a remedy for the democratic deficit. Several authors have accordingly contended that interest groups are not able to enhance citizen participation since their internal decision-making processes are fairly undemocratic (e.g. Warleigh 2001; Maloney 2008). However, so far we have no systematic evidence about the internal structure and the decision-making processes of European interest groups. Future research should therefore systematically analyze the internal decision-making and participation structure of interest groups in order to be able to assess whether interest group participation can truly link individual citizens to the policy-making process.

APPENDIX 1

Association Questionnaire

In the following, the questionnaire for the survey among associations is presented. I designed different questionnaires for associations and companies since they slightly differ in terms of question wording and some questions apply either only to associations or only to companies.

The questionnaire consists of two main parts. The first part contains questions concerning the characteristics of the associations such as resources, organizational structure, or founding date. The second part contains a battery of eight questions about characteristics of the policy issues the associations were lobbying on. These questions deal with issue-specific characteristics such as salience, conflict, or lobbying partners on specific issues. The battery of questions is repeated for every policy issue on which the associations participated in Commission consultations. For instance, if an association only participated in one consultation, it only responded to eight issue-specific questions. By contrast, if an association participated in five consultations, the battery of questions was repeated five times.

The repetition of these questions was triggered automatically by dummy variables that I coded "1" if the interest group participated in this consultation and that I coded "0" if the interest group did not participate in the consultation. The issue-specific questions only differed in terms of a description of the policy issue given at the beginning of the issue-specific part of the questionnaire and in terms of slight differences in the wording of some questions that contain a reference to the policy issue. However, since the issue-specific questions do not substantially change and since the entire association questionnaire is more than 240 pages long, I refrain from displaying the complete questionnaire and instead only present one set of issue-specific questions for the first policy issue.

Research Project: Interest Group Participation in EU Policy-Making

Dear Sir or Madam,

Thank you very much for participating in our online survey. The questionnaire consists of two parts: The first section contains several questions on the characteristics of your organization whereas the second section focuses on your experiences in the Commission consultations in which you participated.

The aim of this study is to better understand how interest groups can increase their participation and their impact on policy-making in the European Union. You were invited to this survey since your organization participated in consultations conducted by the European Commission. Your participation is crucial for the success of this research project and we are very grateful for your cooperation.

Please be assured that the collected data will only be used for **scientific purposes**. Your responses will be kept **confidential** and will be **anonymized** so that none of your answers can be traced back to you or your organization. The survey takes on average **10 minutes**.

After the completion of the research project we will be happy to provide you with a summary of our results. If you have any further questions please do not hesitate to contact us on **hkluever@mail.uni-mannheim.de** or **+49(0) 621 181 3725**.

Thank you again for your participation!

Yours sincerely,

Heike Klüver
University of Mannheim
Graduate School of Economic and Social Sciences
68131 Mannheim, Germany
Email: hkluever@mail.uni-mannheim.de
Phone: +49(0) 621 181 3725

Questions Concerning Interest Group Characteristics

Explanation:
These questions apply to all associations in the sample.

Page 1

1.1. When was your organization established?

Please indicate the year in which your organization was founded.

[＿＿＿＿]

1.2. According to your statute, who can become a member of your organization?

☐ Individuals

☐ Companies

☐ Other Associations

☐ Public Authorities

☐ Other [＿＿＿＿]

☐ Not applicable

Page 2: Filter - if question 1.2. "Individuals" = yes and "Other Associations" = no

2.1. How many individuals are members of your organization?

○ 0

○ up to 10,000

○ more than 10,000, up to 100,000

○ more than 100,000, up to 1 million

○ more than 1 million, up to 5 million

○ more than 5 million

Page 3: Filter - if question 1.2. "Companies" = yes and "Other Associations" = no

3.1. How many companies are members of your organization?

○ 0

○ up to 500

○ more than 500, up to 1,000

○ more than 1,000, up to 5,000

○ more than 5,000, up to 10,000

○ more than 10,000

Page 4: Filter - if question 1.2. "Public Authorities" = yes and "Other Associations" = no

4.1. How many public authorities are members of your organization?

○ 0

○ up to 50

○ more than 50, up to 100

○ more than 100, up to 1,000

○ more than 1,000, up to 5,000

○ more than 5,000

Page 5: Filter - if question 1.2. "Other Associations" = yes

5.1. How many individuals are members of your organization and its member organizations?

Please indicate the number of individual members that your organization and its member organizations have in total.

○ 0

○ up to 10,000

○ more than 10,000, up to 100,000

○ more than 100,000, up to 1 million

○ more than 1 million, up to 5 million

○ more than 5 million

5.2. How many companies are members of your organization and its member organizations?

Please indicate the number of corporate members that your organization and your member organizations have in total.

○ 0

○ up to 500

○ more than 500, up to 1,000

○ more than 1,000, up to 5,000

○ more than 5,000, up to 10,000

○ more than 10,000

5.3. How many public authorities are members of your organization and its member organizations?

Please indicate the number of public authority members that your organization and its member organization have in total.

○ 0

○ up to 50

○ more than 50, up to 100

○ more than 100, up to 1,000

○ more than 1,000, up to 5,000

○ more than 5,000

5.4. How many other actors are members of your organization and its member organizations?

Please indicate the number of other members that your organization and its member organization have in total.

○ 0

○ up to 500

○ more than 500, up to 1,000

○ more than 1,000, up to 5,000

○ more than 5,000, up to 10,000

○ more than 10,000

Page 6: Filter - if question 1.2. "Other" = yes and "Other Associations" = no

6.1. How many other members does you organization have?

○ 0

○ up to 500

○ more than 500, up to 1,000

○ more than 1,000, up to 5,000

○ more than 5,000, up to 10,000

○ more than 10,000

Page 7: Filter - if question 1.2. "Not applicable" = no and "Other Associations" = no

7.1. How many of the potential members are in fact members of your organization? Potential members are all actors who can become a member of your organization according to your organization's statute.

Please indicate the number of official members in percent of the total number of potential members.

○ 1–20%

○ 21–40%

○ 41–60%

○ 61–80%

○ 81–100%

Page 8: Filter - if question 1.2. "Not applicable" = no and "Other Associations" = yes

8.1. How many of the potential members are in fact members of your organization and its member organizations? Potential members are all actors who can become a member of your organization according to your organization's statute.

Please indicate the number of official members in percent of the total number of potential members.

○ 1 - 20%

○ 21 - 40%

○ 41 - 60%

○ 61 - 80%

○ 81 - 100%

Page 9: Filter - if question 1.2. "Not applicable" = no

9.1. How important are the following functions for your organization?

	not at all important				very important
Services to members	○	○	○	○	○
Influence on policy-making	○	○	○	○	○

9.2. In some associations, members prefer to completely delegate interest representation to their association. However, in other associations members actively seek to participate in internal decision-making. How much participation do members seek in your organization on average?

Members do not   Members strongly
seek participation   seek participation
   ○   ○   ○   ○   ○

Page 10

10.1. How many employees does your organization have?

Please indicate the number of employees including full-time and part-time employees as well as paid and unpaid interns/stagiaires.

- ○ 1–5
- ○ 6–10
- ○ 11–25
- ○ 26–50
- ○ more than 50

10.2. How many of these employees are dealing with monitoring and commenting on public policy at least half their working time?

Monitoring and commenting on public policy refers to all activities that aim at influencing legislation at the EU level such as participation in hearings and consultations, informal contacts with representatives of the EU institutions, demonstrations or media campaigns.

- ○ 1–5
- ○ 6–10
- ○ 11–25
- ○ 26–50
- ○ more than 50

Page 11

11.1. How many organizational units are dealing with monitoring and commenting on public policy? A unit is at least comprised of one employee devoting half her/his working-time to a function or subject within the broader task of monitoring and commenting on public policy (e.g. policy adviser for road safety).

- ○ 1–2
- ○ 3–5
- ○ 6–10
- ○ 11–20
- ○ more than 20

Page 12

12.1. Does your organization have an office in Brussels?

○ yes

○ no

12.2. Does your organization employ external consultants to monitor and comment on public policy?

○ yes

○ no

Page 13

13.1. How important are the following criteria when you recruit new staff to deal with monitoring and commenting on public policy ?

	not at all important				very important
Education	○	○	○	○	○
Professional experience	○	○	○	○	○
Commitment to goals of organization	○	○	○	○	○
Other _____	○	○	○	○	○

13.2. How does your organization employ the staff that deals with monitoring and commenting on public policy?

Please indicate the percentage of staff working as volunteers, as part-time or full-time employees and as paid or unpaid interns (Total = 100%)

Volunteers _____ %

Interns/Staigaires (unpaid) _____ %

Interns/Staigaires (paid) _____ %

Part-time employees _____ %

Full-time employees _____ %

Page 14

14.1. What is the highest level of education of your staff that deals with monitoring and commenting on public policy?

Please indicate how many percent of your staff have the following highest degree of education (Total = 100%)

PhD   [   ] %

Master   [   ] %

Bachelor   [   ] %

A-Levels/University-entrance diploma   [   ] %

less than A-Levels/University-entrance diploma   [   ] %

Page 15

15.1. How often do you offer additional training to your employees who deal with monitoring and commenting on public policy?

never   very often

  ○   ○   ○   ○   ○

15.2. On average, how many years of working experience do your employees who deal with monitoring and commenting on public policy have at the time when you hire them?

- ○ no experience
- ○ 1–2 years
- ○ 3–5 years
- ○ 6–10 years
- ○ more than 10 years

Page 16: Filter - if question 15.2. "no experience" = no

16.1. Where did these employees work before they joined your organization?

Please indicate the percentage of the total number of employees with prior working experience (Total = 100%)

European Institutions   [   ] %

Other Associations   [   ] %

National Political Institutions   [   ] %

Companies   [   ] %

Others   [   ] %

Page 17

17.1. Imagine the European Commission is launching a new policy initiative which is of high importance to your organization. How many people within your organization are actively involved in deciding on your organization's position concerning such a new policy initiative?

A policy initiative could be for example the release of a Green or White Paper in preparation for a policy proposal.

- ○ 1–2
- ○ 3–5
- ○ 6–10
- ○ 11–20
- ○ more than 20

17.2. How long does it take until your organization has decided on its position concerning such a policy initiative?

- ○ up to 1 week
- ○ more than 1 week, up to 2 weeks
- ○ more than 2 weeks, up to 3 weeks
- ○ more than 3 weeks, up to 1 month
- ○ more than 1 month

Page 18

18.1. What is the annual revenue of the sector you represent on average?

- ○ 0 EUR
- ○ up to 10 billion EUR
- ○ more than 10 billion, up to 50 billion EUR
- ○ more than 50 billion, up to 100 billion EUR
- ○ more than 100 billion, up to 500 billion EUR
- ○ more than 500 billion EUR

18.2. How many people does the sector that you represent employ?

- ○ 0
- ○ up to 50,000
- ○ more than 50,000, up to 100,000
- ○ more than 100,000, up to 500,000
- ○ more than 500,000, up to 1 million
- ○ more than 1 million

Page 19

19.1. What is your annual budget?

- ○ up to 100,000 EUR
- ○ more than 100,000 up to 500,000 EUR
- ○ more than 500,000, up to 1 million EUR
- ○ more than 1 million, up to 5 million EUR
- ○ more than 5 million EUR

19.2. How much do you spend on monitoring and commenting on public policy per year?

- ○ up to 50,000 EUR
- ○ more than 50,000, up to 100,000 EUR
- ○ more than 100,000, up to 500,000 EUR
- ○ more than 500,000, up to 1 million EUR
- ○ more than 1 million EUR

Page 20

20.1. How is your organization funded?

Please indicate the sources of your funding in percent of the total budget (Total = 100%)

Annual contributions of members	_____ %
EU Grants	_____ %
National Grants	_____ %
Donations	_____ %
Revenues from services	_____ %
Other	_____ %

PART II

Issue-Specific Questions

Explanation:
There are eight issue-specific questions that are repeated for all issues on which the associations have participated in Commission consultations. The issue-specific questions only differed in terms of a description of the policy issue given at the beginning of the issue-specific part of the questionnaire and in terms of slight differences in the wording of some questions that contain a reference to the policy issue. However, since the issue-specific questions do not substantially change and since the entire association questionnaire is more than 240 pages long, I refrain from displaying the complete questionnaire and instead only present one set of issue-specific questions for the first policy issue.

Page 21: Filter - only if interest group participated in this consultation

Consultation on advanced therapies

In May 2005, the European Commission invited stakeholders to submit comments on a draft regulatory framework for authorization, supervision, and post-authorization vigilance of advanced therapies (tissue engineering, cell and gene therapy) in preparation for a policy proposal on this issue.

Since your organization submitted a comment to this consultation, we are interested in your views and activities concerning this issue. The following questions therefore aim to investigate your opinion on the consultation draft and your activities surrounding this issue.

Please note that the questions refer to the consultation draft and not to the final policy proposal unless indicated.

Page 22: Filter - only if interest group participated in this consultation

22.1. How conflictual was the debate amongst stakeholders regarding this issue?
Please indicate the level of conflict.

no conflict at all   high level of conflict
  ○   ○   ○   ○   ○

22.2 How important was this policy issue to your organization?

not important   very important
  ○   ○   ○   ○   ○

22.3. Was there any interest group or company that had opposing views to you?
Please name one major opponent.

[   ]

Page 23: Filter - only if interest group participated in this consultation

23.1. In order to influence policy-making, interest groups have to rely on various strategies. How extensively did you use the following strategies in order to influence this proposal?

	not at all				extensively
Formal hearings, working groups, consultations	○	○	○	○	○
Informal contacts with decision-makers	○	○	○	○	○
Media Campaigns	○	○	○	○	○
Demonstrations/Protests	○	○	○	○	○
Other [ ]	○	○	○	○	○

23.2. In order to influence policy-making, interest groups also have to rely on various access channels. How extensively did you use the following channels to influence this particular policy proposal?

	not at all				extensively
European Commission	○	○	○	○	○
European Parliament	○	○	○	○	○
Council of the EU/Nat. government & ministries/ Permanent Representations	○	○	○	○	○
National Parliaments	○	○	○	○	○
Committee of the Regions/Economic and Social Committee	○	○	○	○	○

23.3 After the consultation had been closed, the European Commission reviewed the stakeholder comments and adopted its policy proposal for a regulation on advanced therapies in November 2005. How successful were you in shaping this policy proposal?

not at all successful   very successful

　　○　　　　　　　　○　　　　　　　　○　　　　　　　　○　　　　　　　　○

Page 24: Filter - only if interest group participated in this consultation

24.1. Interest groups often cooperate with other actors by coordinating their activities and exchanging information. With how many actors did your organization cooperate in order to influence this policy proposal?

Please indicate the total number of your cooperation partners

［＿＿＿＿＿＿＿＿＿＿］

24.2. Could you please provide the names of your five most important cooperation partners on this policy issue?

Please indicate the full name or official abbreviation of your cooperation partners in order of importance starting with the most important actor.

［＿＿＿＿＿＿＿＿＿＿］
［＿＿＿＿＿＿＿＿＿＿］
［＿＿＿＿＿＿＿＿＿＿］
［＿＿＿＿＿＿＿＿＿＿］
［＿＿＿＿＿＿＿＿＿＿］

PART III

Final Questions

Explanation:
These questions apply to all associations in the sample.

Page 245

245.1. Is your organization a member of another organization?

If yes, please indicate the name or official abbreviation of the organization(s) of which your organization is a member.

Page 246

246.1. Thank you very much, you have answered all questions. Do you have any additional comments or recommendations?

246.2. Do you wish to receive a summary of the results after the completion of the research project?

○ yes

○ no

Please only click "Next" if you have completed the whole questionnaire. After clicking on "Next" the questionnaire will be considered as completed and you cannot take part in the survey anymore.

Page 247

Thank you again for your participation!

Your responses have been saved, you can close your browser now.
For further questions and comments, please contact:

Heike Klüver
University of Mannheim
Graduate School of Economic and Social Sciences
68131 Mannheim, Germany
Email: hkluever@mail.uni-mannheim.de
Phone: +49(0) 621 181 3725

Company Questionnaire

In the following, the questionnaire for the survey among companies is presented. I designed different questionnaires for associations and companies since they slightly differ in terms of question wording and some questions apply either only to associations or only to companies.

The questionnaire consists of two main parts. The first part contains questions concerning the characteristics of the companies such as resources, organizational structure, or founding date. The second part contains a battery of eight questions about characteristics of the policy issues the companies were lobbying on. These questions deal with issue-specific characteristics such as salience, conflict, or lobbying partners on specific issues. The battery of questions is repeated for every policy issue on which the companies participated in Commission consultations. For instance, if a company only participated in one consultation, it only responded to eight issue-specific questions. By contrast, if a company participated in five consultations, the battery of questions was repeated five times.

The repetition of these questions was triggered automatically by dummy variables that I coded "1" if the interest group participated in this consultation and that I coded "0" if the interest group did not participate in the consultation. The issue-specific questions only differed in terms of a description of the policy issue given at the beginning of the issue-specific part of the questionnaire and in terms of slight differences in the wording of some questions that contain a reference to the policy issue. However, since the issue-specific questions do not substantially change and since the entire company questionnaire is more than 230 pages long, I refrain from displaying the complete questionnaire and instead only present one set of issue-specific questions for the first policy issue.

Research Project: Companies in EU Policy-Making

Dear Sir or Madam,

Thank you very much for participating in our online survey. The questionnaire consists of two parts: The first section contains several questions on the characteristics of your company whereas the second section focuses on your experiences in the Commission consultations in which you participated.

The aim of this study is to better understand how companies can increase their participation and their impact on policy-making in the European Union. You were invited to this survey since your company participated in consultations conducted by the European Commission. Your participation is crucial for the success of this research project and we are very grateful for your cooperation.

Please be assured that the collected data will only be used for **scientific purposes**. Your responses will be kept **confidential** and will be **anonymized** so that none of your answers can be traced back to you or your company. The survey takes on average **10 minutes**.

After the completion of the research project we will be happy to provide you with a summary of our results. If you have any further questions please do not hesitate to contact us on **hkluever@mail.uni-mannheim.de** or **+49 (0) 621-181-3725**.

Thank you again for your participation!

Yours sincerely,

Heike Klüver
University of Mannheim
Graduate School of Economic and Social Sciences
68131 Mannheim, Germany
Email: hkluever@mail.uni-mannheim.de
Phone: +49(0) 621 181 3725

PART I

Questions Concerning Interest Group Characteristics

Explanation:
These questions apply to all companies in the sample.

Page 1

1.1. When was your company established?

Please indicate the year in which your company was founded.

_____

1.2. In which country is your company's headquarter?

_____

1.3. In how many EU member states does your company have a branch?

_____

Page 2

2.1. How many employees does your company have?

Please indicate the number of employees including full-time and part-time employees as well as paid and unpaid interns/stagiaires.

○ up to 10,000

○ more than 10,000, up to 50,000

○ more than 50,000, up to 100,000

○ more than 100,000, up to 500,000

○ more than 500,000

2.2. Does your company have an office in Brussels?

○ yes

○ no

2.3. How are governmental affairs structured within your company?

Governmental affairs refer to all activities that aim at influencing legislation at the EU level such as participation in hearings and consultations, informal contacts with representatives of the EU institutions, demonstrations, or media campaigns.

☐ Governmental affairs are coordinated and directed by one single department

☐ The competence for governmental affairs is distributed across several departments

☐ Our company employs external consultants to deal with governmental affairs

Page 3: Filter - if question 2.3. "The competence for governmental affairs is distributed accross several departments" = yes

3.1. Are there any employees in the different departments who spend at least half their working-time with governmental affairs?

○ yes

○ no

Page 4: Filter - if question 2.3. "Governmental affairs are coordinated and directed by one single department" = yes or if question 2.3. "The competence for governmental affairs is distributed accross several departments" = yes and question 3.1. = yes

4.1. How many of your employees are dealing with governmental affairs at least half their working-time?

Please indicate the number of employees in governmental affairs including full-time and part-time employees as well as paid and unpaid interns/stagiaires.

○ 1–5

○ 6–10

○ 11–25

○ 26–50

○ more than 50

Page 5: Filter - if question 2.3. "Governmental affairs are coordinated and directed by one single department" = yes or if question 2.3. "The competence for governmental affairs is distributed accross several departments" = yes and question 3.1. = yes

5.1. How many organizational units deal with governmental affairs? A unit is at least comprised of one employee devoting half of his/her working-time to a function or subject within the broader task of governmental affairs (e.g. policy adviser for road safety).

○ 1–2

○ 3–5

○ 6–10

○ 11–20

○ more than 20

Page 6: Filter - if question 2.3. "Governmental affairs are coordinated and directed by one single department" = yes or if question 2.3. "The competence for governmental affairs is distributed accross several departments" = yes and question 3.1. = yes

6.1. How important are the following criteria when you recruit new staff to deal with governmental affairs?

	not at all important				very important
Education	○	○	○	○	○
Professional experience	○	○	○	○	○
Commitment to goals of your company	○	○	○	○	○
Other [____]	○	○	○	○	○

6.2. How does your company employ the staff that deals with governmental affairs?

Please indicate the percentage of staff working as volunteers, as part-time or full-time employees and as paid or unpaid interns (Total = 100%)

Volunteers   [_____] %

Interns/Staigaires (unpaid)   [_____] %

Interns/Staigaires (paid)   [_____] %

Part-time employees   [_____] %

Full-time employees   [_____] %

Page 7: Filter - if question 2.3. "Governmental affairs are coordinated and directed by one single department" = yes or if question 2.3. "The competence for governmental affairs is distributed accross several departments" = yes and question 3.1. = yes

7.1. What is the highest level of education of your staff that deals with governmental affairs?

Please indicate how many percent of your staff have the following highest degree of education (Total = 100%)

PhD   [_____] %

Master   [_____] %

Bachelor   [_____] %

A-Levels/University-entrance diploma   [_____] %

less than A-Levels/University-entrance diploma [_____] %

Page 8: Filter - if question 2.3. "Governmental affairs are coordinated and directed by one single department" = yes or if question 2.3. "The competence for governmental affairs is distributed accross several departments" = yes and question 3.1. = yes

8.1. How often do you offer additional training to your employees working on governmental affairs?

never   very often
○   ○   ○   ○   ○

8.2. On average, how many years of working experience do your governmental affairs employees have at the time when you hire them?

- ○ no experience
- ○ 1–2 years
- ○ 3–5 years
- ○ 6–10 years
- ○ more than 10 years

Page 9: Filter - if question 2.3. "Governmental affairs are coordinated and directed by one single department" = yes or if question 2.3. "The competence for governmental affairs is distributed accross several departments" = yes and question 3.1. = yes

9.1. Where did these employees work before they joined your company?

Please indicate the percentage of the total number of employees with prior working experience (Total = 100%)

European Institutions   [   ]   %

Other Associations   [   ]   %

National Political Institutions   [   ]   %

Companies   [   ]   %

Others   [   ]   %

Page 10

10.1. Imagine the European Commission is launching a new policy initiative which is of high importance to your company. How many people within your company are actively involved in deciding on your company's position concerning such a new policy initiative?

A policy initiative could be for example the release of a Green or White Paper in preparation for a policy proposal.

○ 1–2

○ 3–5

○ 6–10

○ 11–20

○ more than 20

10.2. How long does it take until your company has decided on its position concerning such a policy initiative?

○ up to 1 week

○ more than 1 week, up to 2 weeks

○ more than 2 weeks, up to 3 weeks

○ more than 3 weeks, up to 1 month

○ more than 1 month

Page 11

11.1. What is the annual revenue of your company on average?

○ up to 5 billion EUR

○ more than 5 billion, up to 10 billion EUR

○ more than 10 billion, up to 50 billion EUR

○ more than 50 billion, up to 100 billion EUR

○ more than 100 billion EUR

Page 12

12.1. What is your annual budget?

○ up to 100,000 EUR

○ more than 100,000, up to 500,000 EUR

○ more than 500,000, up to 1 million EUR

○ more than 1 million, up to 5 million EUR

○ more than 5 million EUR

12.2. How much do you spend on governmental affairs per year?

○ up to 50,000 EUR

○ more than 50,000, up to 100,000 EUR

○ more than 100,000, up to 500,000 EUR

○ more than 500,000, up to 1 million EUR

○ more than 1 million EUR

PART II

Issue-Specific Questions

Explanation:
There are eight issue-specific questions that are repeated for all issues on which the companies have participated in Commission consultations. The issue-specific questions only differed in terms of a description of the policy issue given at the beginning of the issue-specific part of the questionnaire and in terms of slight differences in the wording of some questions that contain a reference to the policy issue. However, since the issue-specific questions do not substantially change and since the entire company questionnaire is more than 230 pages long, I refrain from displaying the complete questionnaire and instead only present one set of issue-specific questions for the first policy issue.

Page 13: Filter - only if interest group participated in this consultation

Consultation on advanced therapies

In May 2005, the European Commission invited stakeholders to submit comments on a draft regulatory framework for authorization, supervision, and post-authorization vigilance of advanced therapies (tissue engineering, cell and gene therapy) in preparation for a policy proposal on this issue.

Since your company submitted a comment to this consultation, we are interested in your views and activities concerning this issue. The following questions therefore aim to investigate your opinion on the consultation draft and your activities surrounding this issue.

Please note that the questions refer to the consultation draft and not to the final policy proposal unless indicated.

Page 14: Filter - only if interest group participated in this consultation

14.1. How conflictual was the debate amongst stakeholders regarding this issue?
Please indicate the level of conflict.

no conflict at all   high level of conflict

   ○   ○   ○   ○   ○

14.2. How important was this policy issue to your company?

not important   very important

   ○   ○   ○   ○   ○

14.3. Was there any interest group or company that had opposing views to you?
Please name one major opponent.

Page 15: Filter - only if interest group participated in this consultation

15.1. In order to influence policy-making, companies have to rely on various strategies. How extensively did you use the following strategies in order to influence this proposal?

	not at all				extensively
Formal hearings, working groups, consultations	○	○	○	○	○
Informal contacts with decision-makers	○	○	○	○	○
Media campaigns	○	○	○	○	○
Demonstrations/protests	○	○	○	○	○
Other [_____]	○	○	○	○	○

15.2. In order to influence policy-making, companies also have to rely on various access channels. How extensively did you use the following channels to influence this particular policy proposal?

	not at all				extensively
European Commission	○	○	○	○	○
European Parliament	○	○	○	○	○
Council of the EU/Nat. government & ministries/ Permanent Representations	○	○	○	○	○
National Parliaments	○	○	○	○	○
Committee of the Regions/Economic and Social Committee	○	○	○	○	○

15.3. After the consultation had been closed, the European Commission reviewed the stakeholder comments and adopted its policy proposal for a regulation on advanced therapies in November 2005. How successful were you in shaping this policy proposal?

not at all successful   very successful

○   ○   ○   ○   ○

Page 16: Filter - only if interest group participated in this consultation

16.1. Companies often cooperate with other actors by coordinating their activities and exchanging information. With how many actors did your company cooperate in order to influence this policy proposal?

Please indicate the total number of your cooperation partners

[   ]

16.2. Could you please provide the names of your five most important cooperation partners on this policy issue?

Please indicate the full name or official abbreviation of your cooperation partners in order of importance starting with the most important actor.

[   ]
[   ]
[   ]
[   ]
[   ]

PART III

Final Questions

Page 237

237.1. Is your company a member of another organization?

If yes, please indicate the name or official abbreviation of the organization(s) of which your company is a member.

┌──────────
├──────────
├──────────
├──────────
└──────────

Page 238

238.1. Thank you very much, you have answered all questions. Do you have any additional comments or recommendations?

┌──────────
├──────────
├──────────
├──────────
└──────────

238.2. Do you wish to receive a summary of the results after the completion of the research project?

○ yes

○ no

Please only click "Next" if you have completed the whole questionnaire. After clicking on "Next" the questionnaire will be considered as completed and you cannot take part in the survey anymore.

Page 239

Thank you again for your participation!

Your responses have been saved, you can close your browser now.
For further questions and comments, please contact:

Heike Klüver
University of Mannheim
Graduate School of Economic and Social Sciences
68131 Mannheim, Germany
Email: hkluever@mail.uni-mannheim.de
Phone: +49(0) 621 181 3725

Bibliography

Adams, James, Michael Clark, Lawrence Ezrow, and Garrett Glasgow. 2006. "Are Niche Parties Fundamentally Different from Mainstream Parties? The Causes and the Electoral Consequences of Western European Parties' Policy Shifts, 1976-1998." *American Journal of Political Science* 50(3): 513-529.

Aguilar Fernández, Susana. 1997. *El Reto Del Medio Ambiente*. Madrid: Alianza Universidad.

Alexa, Melina and Cornelia Züll. 2000. "Text Analysis Software: Commonalities, Differences and Limitations: The Results of a Review." *Quality and Quantity* 34(3): 299-321.

Allison, Paul D. 2000. "Multiple Imputation for Missing Data." *Sociological Methods and Research* 28(3): 301-309.

—— 2002. *Missing Data*. Thousand Oaks: Sage.

Aspinwall, Mark and Justin Greenwood. 1998. Conceptualising Collective Action in Europe. In *Collective Action in Europe: Interests and the New Politics of Associability*, ed. Justin Greenwood and Mark Aspinwall. London: Routledge, pp. 1–30.

Austen-Smith, David. 1987. "Interest Groups, Campaign Contributions, and Probabilistic Voting." *Public Choice* 54(2): 123-139.

—— 1993. "Information and Influence: Lobbying for Agendas and Votes." *American Journal of Political Science* 37(4): 799-833.

Austen-Smith, David and John R. Wright. 1994. "Counteractive Lobbying." *American Journal of Political Science* 38(1): 25-44.

Austin, Peter C. 2002. "A Brief Note on Overlapping Confidence Intervals." *Journal of Vascular Surgery* 36: 194-195.

Bachrach, Peter and Morton S. Baratz. 1962. "Two Faces of Power." *American Political Science Review* 56(4): 947-952.

Bailer, Stefanie. 2004. "Bargaining Success in the European Union: The Impact Of Exogenous and Endogenous Power Resources." *European Union Politics* 5(1): 99-123.

Bakker, Ryan, Erica Edwards, and Catherine E. de Vries. 2006. "Fickle Parties or Changing Dimensions? Testing the Comparability of the Party Manifesto Data Across Time." Paper presented at the 64th National Conference of the Midwest Political Science Association, Chicago, 20–23 April 2006.

Balme, Richard and Didier Chabanet. 2002. Action collective et représentation des intérêts dans l'Union européenne. In *L'action collective en Europe [Collective Action in Europe]*, ed. Richard Balme, Didier Chabanet and Vincent Wright. Paris: Presses de Sciences Po, pp. 21–122.

Balme, Richard, Didier Chabanet, and Vincent Wright, eds. 2002. *L'Action collective en Europe [Collective Action in Europe]*. Paris: Presses de Sciences Po.

Barry, Brian. 1980a. "Is it Better to be Powerful or Lucky? Part 1." *Political Studies* 28(2): 183-194.

Barry, Brian. 1980*b*. "Is it Better to be Powerful or Lucky? Part 2." *Political Studies* 28(3): 338–352.

—— 2002. "Capitalists Rule Ok? Some Puzzles About Power." *Politics, Philosophy & Economics* 1(2): 155–184.

Bartolini, Stefano. 2005. *Restructuring Europe: Centre Formation, System Building and Political Structuring between the Nation-State and the European Union*. Oxford: Oxford University Press.

Bauer, Michael W. 2002. "Limitations to Agency Control in European Union Policy-Making: The Commission and the Poverty Programmes." *Journal of Common Market Studies* 40(3): 381–400.

Baumgartner, Frank R. and Bryan D. Jones. 1993. *Agendas and Instability in American Politics*. Chicago: University of Chicago Press.

Baumgartner, Frank R. and Beth Leech. 1998. *Basic Interests: The Importance of Groups in Politics and in Political Science*. Princeton: Princeton University Press.

Baumgartner, Frank R., Jeffrey M. Berry, Marie Hojnacki, David C. Kimball, and Beth Leech. 2009. *Lobbying and Policy Change: Who Wins, Who Loses, and Why*. Chicago: University of Chicago Press.

Benoit, Kenneth and Michael Laver. 2003*a*. "Estimating Irish Party Policy Positions Using Computer Wordscoring." *Irish Political Studies* 18(1): 97–107.

—— 2003*b*. "Extracting Policy Positions From Political Texts Using Phrases As Data: A Research Note." Paper presented at the 61st National Conference of the Midwest Political Science Association, Chicago, 3–6 April 2003.

—— 2006. *Party Policy in Modern Democracies*. London: Routledge.

Benoit, Kenneth, Michael Laver, Christine Arnold, Paul Pennings, and Madeleine O. Hosli. 2005. "Measuring National Delegate Positions at the Convention on the Future of Europe using Computerized Word Scoring." *European Union Politics* 6(3): 291–313.

Benoit, Kenneth, Michael Laver, and Slava Mikhaylov. 2009. "Treating Words as Data with Error: Uncertainty in Text Statements of Policy Positions." *American Journal of Political Science* 53(2): 495–513.

Berelson, Bernard and Paul F. Lazarsfeld. 1948. *The Analysis of Communication Content*. Chicago: University of Chicago Press.

Berkhout, Joost and David Lowery. 2008. "Counting Organized Interests in the European Union: A Comparison of Data Sources." *Journal of European Public Policy* 15(4): 489–513.

Bernhagen, Patrick. 2007. *The Political Power of Business Structure and Information in Public Policymaking*. London: Routledge.

—— 2012. "Who Gets What in British Politics – and How? An Analysis of Media Reports on Lobbying around Government Policies, 2001–7." *Political Studies* 60(3): 557–577.

Bernhagen, Patrick and Thomas Bräuninger. 2005. "Structural Power and Public Policy: A Signaling Model of Business Lobbying in Democratic Capitalism." *Political Studies* 53(1): 43–64.

Bernhagen, Patrick and Neil J. Mitchell. 2009. "The Determinants of Direct Corporate Lobbying in the European Union." *European Union Politics* 10(2): 155–176.

Berry, Jeffrey M. 1997. *The Interest Group Society*. 3rd edn. New York: Longman.

Beyers, Jan. 2002. "Gaining and Seeking Access: The European Adaptation of Domestic Interest Associations." *European Journal of Political Research* 41(5): 585–612.

—— 2004. "Voice and Access: Political Practices of European Interest Associations." *European Union Politics* 5(2): 211–240.

—— 2008. "Policy Issues, Organisational Format and the Political Strategies of Interest Organisations." *West European Politics* 31(6): 1188–1211.

Beyers, Jan and Bart Kerremans. 2007. "Critical Resource Dependencies and the Europeanization of Domestic Interest Groups." *Journal of European Public Policy* 14(3): 460–481.

—— 2012. "Domestic Embeddedness and the Dynamics of Multilevel Venue Shopping in Four EU Member States." *Governance* 25(2): 263–290.

Beyers, Jan, Rainer Eising, and William Maloney. 2008. "Researching Interest Group Politics in Europe and Elsewhere: Much We Study, Little We Know?" *West European Politics* 31(6): 1103–1128.

Borgatta, Edgar F. and George W. Bohrnstedt. 1980. "Level of Measurement: Once Over Again." *Sociological Methods and Research* 9(2): 147–160.

Bouwen, Pieter. 2002. "Corporate Lobbying in the European Union: The Logic of Access." *Journal of European Public Policy* 9(3): 365–390.

—— 2003. "A Theoretical and Empirical Study of Corporate Lobbying in the European Parliament." *European Integration Online Papers* 7(11): 1–17.

—— 2004a. "Exchanging Access Goods for Access: A Comparative Study of Business Lobbying in the European Union Institutions." *European Journal of Political Research* 43(3): 337–369.

—— 2004b. "The Logic of Access to the European Parliament: Business Lobbying in the Committee on Economic and Monetary Affairs." *Journal of Common Market Studies* 42(3): 473–495.

—— 2009. The European Commission. In *Lobbying in the European Union: Institutions, Actors, and Issues*, ed. David Coen and Jeremy Richardson. Oxford: Oxford University Press, pp. 19–38.

Bouwen, Pieter and Margaret McCown. 2007. "Lobbying versus Litigation: Political and Legal Strategies of Interest Representation in the European Union." *Journal of European Public Policy* 14(3): 422–443.

Brambour, Thomas, William Roberts Clark, and Matt Golder. 2006. "Understanding Interaction Models: Improving Empirical Analysis." *Political Analysis* 14(1): 63–82.

Broscheid, Andreas and David Coen. 2003. "Insider and Outsider Lobbying of the European Commission: An Informational Model of Forum Politics." *European Union Politics* 4(2): 165–189.

—— 2007. "Lobbying Activity and Fora Creation in the EU: Empirically Exploring the Nature of the Policy Good." *Journal of European Public Policy* 14(3): 346–365.

Börzel, Tanja A. 2001. "Non-compliance in the European Union: Pathology or Statistical Artefact?" *Journal of European Public Policy* 8(5): 803–824.

Buckley, Walter. 1967. *Sociology and Modern Systems Theory*. Englewood Cliffs: Prentice Hall.

Budge, Ian and Judith Bara. 2001. Introduction: Content Analysis and Political Texts. In *Mapping Policy Preferences: Estimates for Parties, Electors, and Governments 1945–1998*, ed. Ian Budge, Hans-Dieter Klingemann, Andrea Volkens, Judith Bara, and Eric Tanenbaum. Oxford: Oxford University Press, pp. 1–16.

Budge, Ian, Hans-Dieter Klingemann, Andrea Volkens, Judith Bara, and Eric Tanenbaum. 2001. *Mapping Policy Preferences: Estimates for Parties, Electors, and Governments 1945–1998*. Oxford: Oxford University Press.

Buholzer, René. 1998. *Legislatives Lobbying in der Europäischen Union: Ein Konzept für Interessengruppen*. Bern: Haupt.

Butt Philip, Alan. 1985. "Pressure Groups in the European Community." *UACES Occasional Paper* 2.

Clinton, Joshua, Simon Jackman, and Douglas Rivers. 2004. "The Statistical Analysis of Roll Call Voting." *American Political Science Review* 98(2): 355–370.

Cobb, Roger W. and Charles D. Elder. 1972. *Participation in American Politics: The Dynamics of Agenda-Building*. Boston: Allyn and Bacon.

Coen, David. 1997. "The Evolution of the Large Firm as a Political Actor in the European Union." *Journal of European Public Policy* 4(1): 91–108.

—— 1998. "The European Business Interest and the Nation State: Large-Firm Lobbying in the European Union and Member States." *Journal of Public Policy* 18(1): 75–100.

—— 2009. Business Lobbying in the European Union. In *Lobbying the European Union: Institutions, Actors, and Issues*, ed. David Coen and Jeremy Richardson. Oxford: Oxford University Press, pp. 145–168.

Coen, David and Charles Dannreuther. 2003. Differentiated Europeanisation: Large and Small Firms in the EU Policy Process. In *The Politics of Europeanisation*, ed. Kevin Featherstone and Claudio M. Radaelli. Oxford: Oxford University Press, pp. 255–275.

Coen, David and Jeremy Richardson. 2009a. Learning to Lobby the European Union: 20 Years of Change. In *Lobbying the European Union: Institutions, Actors, and Issues*, ed. David Coen and Jeremy Richardson. Oxford: Oxford University Press, pp. 3–15.

—— eds. 2009b. *Lobbying the European Union: Institutions, Actors and Issues*. Oxford: Oxford University Press.

Coen, David, Wyn Grant, and Graham K. Wilson. 2010a. *The Oxford Handbook of Business and Government*. Oxford: Oxford University Press.

—— 2010b. Political Science: Perspectives on Business and Government. In *The Oxford Handbook of Business and Government*, ed. David Coen, Wyn Grant, and Graham K. Wilson. Oxford: Oxford University Press, pp. 9–34.

Cohen, Joshua and Joel Rogers. 1995. Secondary Association and Democratic Governance. In *Associations and Democracy: The Real Utopias Project*, ed. Joshua Cohen, Joel Rogers, and Erik Olin Wright. London: Verso, pp. 7–98.

Coleman, James Samuel. 1990. *Foundations of Social Theory*. Cambridge, MA: Belknap Press.

Cowles, Maria Green. 1995. "Setting the Agenda for a New Europe: The ERT and EC 1992." *Journal of Common Market Studies* 33(4): 501–526.

—— 2001. The Transatlantic Business Dialogue and Domestic Business–Government Relations. In *Transforming Europe: Europeanization and Domestic Change*, ed. Maria Green Cowles, James A. Caporaso, and Thomas Risse. Ithaca, NY: Cornell University Press, pp. 159–179.

Cox, Eli P. 1980. "The Optimal Number of Response Alternatives for a Scale: A Review." *Journal of Marketing Research* 17(4): 407–422.

Crombez, Christophe. 1997. "The Co-Decision Procedure in the European Union." *Legislative Studies Quarterly* 22(1): 97–119.

—— 2002. "Information, Lobbying and the Legislative Process in the European Union." *European Union Politics* 3(7): 7–32.

Dahl, Robert Alan. 1957. "The Concept of Power." *Behavioral Science* 2(3): 201–215.

—— 1989. *Democracy and its Critics*. New Haven, CT: Yale University Press.

Däubler, Thomas, Kenneth Benoit, Slava Mikhaylov, and Michael Laver. 2012. "Natural Sentences as Valid Units for Coded Political Texts." *British Journal of Political Science* 42(4): 937–951.

Döring, Holger. 2007. "The Composition of the College of Commissioners: Patterns of Delegation." *European Union Politics* 8(2): 207–228.

Dowding, Keith. 1991. *Rational Choice and Political Power*. Aldershot: Edward Elgar.

—— 1996. *Power*. Buckingham: Open University Press.

—— 2003. "Resources, Power and Systematic Luck: A Response to Barry." *Politics, Philosophy & Economics* 2(3): 305–322.

Downs, Anthony. 1957. *An Economic Theory of Democracy*. New York: Harper.

Duch, Raymond M. and Randolph T. Stevenson. 2005a. "Context and the Economic Vote: A Multilevel Analysis." *Political Analysis* 13(4): 387–409.

—— 2005b. *The Economic Vote: How Political and Economic Institutions Condition Election Results*. Cambridge: Cambridge University Press.

Dür, Andreas. 2008a. "Bringing Economic Interests Back into the Study of EU Trade Policy-Making." *British Journal of Politics and International Relations* 10(1): 27–45.

—— 2008b. "Interest Groups in the European Union: How Powerful Are They?" *West European Politics* 31(6): 1212–1230.

—— 2008c. "Measuring Interest Group Influence in the EU: A Note on Methodology." *European Union Politics* 9(4): 559–576.

Dür, Andreas and Dirk De Bièvre. 2007a. "Inclusion Without Influence? NGOs in European Trade Policy." *Journal of Public Policy* 27(1): 79–101.

—— 2007b. "The Question of Interest Group Influence." *Journal of Public Policy* 27(1): 1–12.

Dür, Andreas and Gema Mateo. 2009. "Interest Group Politics in the EU: The National Level." Paper presented at the 5th General Conference of the European Consortium of Political Science: Potsdam, 10–12 September.

Egdell, Janet M. and Kenneth J. Thomson. 1999. "The Influence of UK NGOs on the Common Agricultural Policy." *Journal of Common Market Studies* 37(1): 121–131.

Eising, Rainer. 2004. "Multilevel Governance and Business Interests in the European Union." *Governance* 17(2): 211–245.

—— 2007a. "The Access of Business Interests to EU Institutions: Towards Élite Pluralism?" *Journal of European Public Policy* 14(3): 384–403.

—— 2007b. "Institutional Context, Organizational Resources and Strategic Choices: Explaining Interest Group Access in the European Union." *European Union Politics* 8(3): 329–362.

—— 2008. "Interest Groups in EU Policy-Making." *Living Reviews in European Governance* 3(4): 1–32.

—— 2009. *The Political Economy of State–Business Relations in Europe: Interest Mediation, Capitalism and EU Policy-Making*. London: Routledge.

Eising, Rainer and Beate Kohler-Koch, eds. 2005. *Interessenpolitik in Europa*. Baden-Baden: Nomos.

Entman, Robert M. 1993. "Framing: Toward Clarification of a Fractured Paradigm." *Journal of Communication* 43(4): 51–58.

European Commission. 2000. *The Commission and Non-governmental Organisations: Building a Stronger Partnership*. COM (2000) 11 final, URL (consulted April 2010): http://ec.europa.eu/civil_society/ngo/docs/communication_en.pdf.

—— 2002. *Towards a Reinforced Culture of Consultation and Dialogue: General Principles and Minimum Standards for Consultation of Interested Parties by the Commission*. COM(2002) 704 final, URL (consulted April 2010): http://ec.europa.eu/governance/docs/comm_standards_en.pdf.

European Parliament. 2009. *Codecision and Conciliation: A Guide to How the Parliament Co-legislates under the Treaty of Lisbon*. URL (consulted March 2011): http://www.europarl.europa.eu/code/information/guide_en.pdf.

European Round Table of Industrialists. 1987. *Internal Market Support Committee*. Press release: 24 June 1987.

Evans, Joel R. and Anil Mathur. 2005. "The Value of Online Surveys." *Internet Research* 15(2): 195–219.

Falkner, Gerda, Miriam Hartlapp, Simone Leiber, and Oliver Treib. 2005. Die Kooperation der Sozialpartner im Arbeitsrecht: Ein europäischer Weg? In *Interessenpolitik in Europa*, ed. Rainer Eising and Beate Kohler-Koch. Baden-Baden: Nomos, pp. 341–362.

Finke, Barbara. 2007. "Civil Society Participation in EU Governance." *Living Reviews in European Governance* 2(2): 1–31.

Follesdal, Andreas and Simon Hix. 2006. "Why There is a Democratic Deficit in the EU: A Response to Majone and Moravcsik." *Journal of Common Market Studies* 44(3): 533–562.

Fordham, Benjamin O. and Timothy J. McKeown. 2003. "Selection and Influence: Interest Groups and Congressional Voting on Trade Policy." *International Organization* 57(3): 519–549.

Fox, John. 1991. *Regression Diagnostics*. Newbury Park: Sage.

—— 2005. *Applied Regression Analysis, Linear Models, and Related Methods*. Thousand Oaks: Sage.

Franchino, Fabio. 2007. *The Powers of the Union: Delegation in the EU*. Cambridge: Cambridge University Press.

Frieden, Jeffrey A. 2002. "Real Sources of European Currency Policy: Sectoral Interest and European Monetary Integration." *International Organization* 56(4): 831–860.

Gabel, Matthew J. and John D. Huber. 2000. "Putting Parties in their Place: Inferring Party Left–Right Ideological Positions from Party." *American Journal of Political Science* 44(1): 94–103.

Garrett, Geoffrey and George Tsebelis. 1996. "An Institutional Critique of Intergovernmentalism." *International Organization* 50(2): 269–299.

Gelman, Andrew and Jennifer Hill. 2007. *Data Analysis Using Regression and Multilevel/Hierarchical Models*. Cambridge: Cambridge University Press.

Gerber, Elisabeth R. 1999. *The Populist Paradox: Interest Group Influence and the Promise of Direct Legislation*. Princeton: Princeton University Press.

Goldstein, Kenneth M. 1999. *Interest Groups, Lobbying, and Participation in America*. Cambridge: Cambridge University Press.

Görg, Holger and Aoife Hanley. 2004. "Does Outsourcing Increase Profitability?" *Economic and Social Review* 35(3): 267–288.

Gornitzka, Åse and Ulf Sverdrup. 2008. "Who Consults? The Configuration of Expert Groups in the European Union." *West European Politics* 31(4): 725–750.

Grant, Robert M. 1991. *Contemporary Strategy Analysis: Concepts, Techniques, Applications*. Oxford: Basil Blackwell.

Grant, Wyn. 1997. *The Common Agricultural Policy*. Basingstoke: Macmillan.

Gray, Virginia and David Lowery. 1996. "A Niche Theory of Interest Representation." *Journal of Politics* 58(1): 91–111.

—— 1998. "To Lobby Alone or in a Flock: Foraging Behavior among Organized Interests." *American Politics Research* 26(5): 5–34.

Greenwood, Justin. 2002. *Inside the EU Business Associations*. Basingstoke: Palgrave Macmillan.

—— 2007a. *Interest Representation in the European Union*. 2nd edn. Basingstoke: Palgrave Macmillan.

—— 2007b. "Review Article: Organized Civil Society and Democratic Legitimacy in the European Union." *British Journal of Political Science* 37(2): 333–357.

Grossman, Gene M. and Elhanan Helpman. 2001. *Special Interest Politics*. Cambridge, MA: MIT Press.

Hagemann, Sara and Bjorn Høyland. 2008. "Parties in the Council?" *Journal of European Public Policy* 15(8): 1205–1221.

Hall, Peter A. and Rosemary C. R. Taylor. 1996. "Political Science and the Three New Institutionalisms." *Political Studies* 44(5): 936–957.

Hall, Richard L. and Alan Deardorff. 2006. "Lobbying as Legislative Subsidy." *American Political Science Review* 100(1): 69–84.

Hannan, Michael T. and John Freeman. 1977. "The Population Ecology of Organizations." *American Journal of Sociology* 82(5): 929–964.

Hansen, John Mark. 1991. *Gaining Access: Congress and the Farm Lobby, 1919–1981*. Chicago: University of Chicago Press.

Hartlapp, Miriam, Julia Metz, and Christian Rauh. 2010a. "The Agenda Set by the EU Commission: The Results of Balanced or Biased Aggregation of Positions?" *LSE Europe in Question Discussion Paper* 21: 1–29.

—— 2010b. "How External Interests Enter the European Commission: Mechanisms at Play in Legislative Position Formation." *WZB Discussion Paper* SP IV 2010(501): 1–37.

Hayes-Renshaw, Fiona. 2006. The Council of Ministers. In *The Institutions of the European Union*, ed. John Peterson and Michael Shackleton. Oxford: Oxford University Press, pp. 60–80.

—— 2009. Least Accessible but not Inaccessible: Lobbying the Council and the European Council. In *Lobbying the European Union: Institutions, Actors, and Issues*, ed. David Coen and Jeremy Richardson. Oxford: Oxford University Press, pp. 70–88.

Heclo, Hugh. 1978. Issue Networks and the Executive Establishment. In *The New American Political System*, ed. Anthony King. Washington, DC: American Enterprise Institute for Public Policy, pp. 87–124.

Henning, Christian H. C. A. 2000. *Macht und Tausch in der europäischen Agrarpolitik: Eine positive Theorie kollektiver Entscheidungen.* Frankfurt/Main: Campus.

Hirst, Paul. 1994. *Associative Democracy: New Forms of Economic and Social Governance.* Amherst: University of Massachussetts Press.

Hix, Simon. 1994. "The Study of the European Community: The Challenge to Comparative Politics." *West European Politics* 17(1): 1–30.

—— 1998. "The Study of the European Union II: The 'New Governance' Agenda and its Rival." *Journal of European Public Policy* 5(1): 38–65.

—— 2002. "Parliamentary Behavior with Two Principals: Preferences, Parties, and Voting in the European Parliament." *American Journal of Political Science* 46(3): 688–698.

—— 2005. *The Political System of the European Union.* 2 edn. Basingstoke: Palgrave Macmillan.

Hix, Simon and Bjorn Høyland. 2011. *The Political System of the European Union.* 3rd edn. Basingstoke: Palgrave Macmillan.

Hojnacki, Marie. 1997. "Interest Groups' Decisions to Join Alliances or Work Alone." *American Journal of Political Science* 41(1): 61–87.

—— 1998. "Organized Interests' Advocacy Behavior in Alliances." *Political Research Quarterly* 51(2): 437–459.

Hooghe, Liesbet and Neill Nugent. 2006. The Commission's Services. In *The Institutions of the European Union,* ed. John Peterson and Michael Shackleton. 2nd edn. Oxford: Oxford, pp. 147–168.

Hörl, Björn, Andreas Warntjen, and Arndt Wonka. 2005. "Built on Quicksand? A Decade of Procedural Spatial Models on EU Legislative Decision-Making." *Journal of European Public Policy* 12(3): 592–606.

Huber, John and Ronald Inglehart. 1995. "Expert Interpretations of Party Space and Party Locations in 42 Societies." *Party Politics* 1(1): 73–111.

Hug, Simon and Tobias Schulz. 2007. "Left–Right Positions of Political Parties in Switzerland." *Party Politics* 13(3): 305–330.

Hula, Kevin W. 1999. *Lobbying Together: Interest Group Coalitions in Legislative Politics.* Washington, DC: Georgetown University Press.

Hull, Robert. 1993. Lobbying Brussels: A View from Within. In *Lobbying in the European Community,* ed. Sonia Mazey and Jeremy Richardson. Oxford: Oxford University Press, pp. 82–92.

Imai, Kosuke, Gary King, and Olivia Lau. 2006. *Zelig: Everyone's Statistical Software.* Version 3.4–8, URL (consulted March 2010): http://gking.harvard.edu/zelig.

Imig, Doug. 2002. "Contestation in the Streets: European Protest and the Emerging Euro-Polity." *Comparative Political Studies* 35(8): 914–933.

Imig, Doug and Sidney Tarrow. 2000. "Political Contention in a Europeanising Polity." *West European Politics* 23(4): 73–93.

Kaeding, Michael. 2006. "Determinants of Transposition Delay in the European Union." *Journal of Public Policy* 26(3): 229–253.

Kampen, Jarl and Marc Swyngedouw. 2000. "The Ordinal Controversy Revisited." *Quality and Quantity* 34(1): 87–102.

Kau, James B. and Paul H. Rubin. 1979. "Public Interest Lobbies: Membership and Influence." *Public Choice* 34(1): 45–54.

Kiewiet, D. R. and Mathew D. McCubbins. 1991. *The Logic of Delegation: Congressional Parties and the Appropriations Process*. Chicago: University of Chicago Press.

King, Gary, Robert O. Keohane, and Sidney Verba. 1994. *Designing Social Inquiry: Scientific Inference in Qualitative Research*. Princeton: Princeton University Press.

King, Gary, Michael Tomz, and Jason Wittenberg. 2000. "Making the Most of Statistical Analyses: Improving Interpretation and Presentation." *American Journal of Political Science* 44(2): 341–355.

Kingdon, John W. 1984. *Agendas, Alternatives, and Public Policies*. Boston: Little, Brown.

Kitschelt, Herbert P. 1986. "Political Opportunity Structures and Political Protest: Anti-Nuclear Movements in Four Democracies." *British Journal of Political Science* 16(1): 57–85.

Klemmensen, Robert, Sara Binzer Hobolt, and Martin Ejnar Hansen. 2007. "Estimating Policy Positions Using Political Texts: An Evaluation of the Wordscores Approach." *Electoral Studies* 26(4): 746–755.

Klingemann, Hans-Dieter, Andrea Volkens, Judith Bara, Ian Budge, and Michael McDonald. 2006. *Mapping Policy Preferences II: Estimates for Parties, Electors, and Governments in Eastern Europe, European Union, and OECD 1990–2003*. Oxford: Oxford University Press.

Kluger Rasmussen, Maja. 2011. The Lobbying See-saw: Who Tips the Scales in the European Parliament? Paper presented at the 12th Biennial International Conference of the European Union Studies Association: Boston, 3–5 March 2011.

Klüver, Heike. 2009. "Measuring Interest Group Influence Using Quantitative Text Analysis." *European Union Politics* 10(4): 535–549.

—— 2010. "Europeanization of Lobbying Activities: When National Interest Groups Spill Over to the European Level." *Journal of European Integration* 32(2): 175–191.

—— 2011. "The Contextual Nature of Lobbying: Explaining Lobbying Success in the European Union." *European Union Politics* 12(4): 483–506.

—— 2012. "Informational Lobbying in the European Union: The Effect of Organisational Characteristics." *West European Politics* 35(3): 491–510.

—— 2013. "Lobbying as a Collective Enterprise: Winners and Losers of Policy Formulation." *Journal of European Public Policy* 20(1).

Knill, Christoph, Marc Debus, and Stephan Heichel. 2010. "Do Parties Matter in Internationalised Policy Areas? The Impact of Political Parties on Environmental Policy Outputs in 18 OECD Countries, 1970–2000." *European Journal of Political Research* 49(3): 301–336.

Knoke, David and David Prensky. 1984. "What Relevance Do Organization Theories Have for Voluntary Associations?" *Social Science Quarterly* 65(3): 3–20.

Kohler-Koch, Beate. 1997. "Organized Interests in the EC and the European Parliament." *European Integration Online Papers* 1(9).

—— 2007. The Organization of Interests and Democracy in the European Union. In *Debating the Democratic Legitimacy of the European Union*, ed. Beate Kohler-Koch and Berthold Rittberger. Lanham: Rowman & Littlefield, pp. 255–271.

Kohler-Koch, Beate and Rainer Eising, eds. 1999. *The Transformation of Governance in the European Union*. London: Routledge.

Kohler-Koch, Beate and Barbara Finke. 2007. "The Institutional Shaping of EU–Society Relations: A Contribution to Democracy via Participation?" *Journal of Civil Society* 3(3): 205–221.

Kollman, Ken. 1998. *Outside Lobbying: Public Opinion and Interest Group Strategies.* Princeton: Princeton University Press.

König, Thomas and Brooke Luetgert. 2009. "Troubles with Transposition? Explaining Trends in Member-State Notification and the Delayed Transposition of EU Directives." *British Journal of Political Science* 39(1): 163–194.

Kraft, Kornelius. 1991. "The Incentive Effects of Dismissals, Efficiency Wages, Piece-Rates and Profit-Sharing." *The Review of Economics and Statistics* 73(3): 451–459.

Krippendorff, Klaus. 2004. *Content Analysis: An Introduction to Its Methodology.* 2nd edn. Thousand Oaks: Sage.

Landis, Richard J. and Gary G. Koch. 1977. "The Measurement of Observer Agreement for Categorical Data." *Biometrics* 33(1): 159–174.

Lasswell, Harold D. 1936. *Politics: Who Gets What, When, How.* New York: McGraw-Hill.

Laver, Michael and John Garry. 2000. "Estimating Policy Positions from Political Texts." *American Journal of Political Science* 44(3): 619–634.

Laver, Michael, Kenneth Benoit, and John Garry. 2003. "Extracting Policy Positions from Political Texts Using Word as Data." *American Political Science Review* 97(2): 311–331.

Leech, Beth, Frank R. Baumgartner, Jeffrey M. Berry, Marie Hojnacki, and David C. Kimball. 2007. "Does Money Buy Power? Interest Group Resources and Policy Outcomes." Paper presented at the 65th National Conference of the Midwest Political Science Association: Chicago, 12–15 April 2007.

Lehmann, Wilhelm. 2009. The European Parliament. In *Lobbying the European Union: Institutions, Actors, and Issues*, ed. David Coen and Jeremy Richardson. Oxford: Oxford University Press, pp. 39–69.

Lewis, Jordan D. 1990. *Partnerships for Profit: Structuring and Managing Strategic Alliances.* New York: The Free Press.

Lewis-Beck, Michael S. and Mary Stegmaier. 2000. "Economic Determinants of Electoral Outcomes." *Annual Review of Political Science* 3(1): 183–219.

Lindblom, Charles Edward. 1977. *Politics and Markets: The World's Political-Economic Systems.* New York: Basic Books.

Linhart, Eric and Susumu Shikano. 2007. "Die Generierung von Parteipositionen aus vorverschlüsselten Wahlprogrammen für die Bundesrepublik Deutschland (1949–2002)." *Working Paper, Mannheim Centre for European Social Research* 98: 1–30.

Lipsky, Michael. 1968. "Protest as a Political Resource." *American Political Science Review* 62(4): 1144–1158.

Lohmann, Susanne. 1993. "A Signaling Model of Informative and Manipulative Political Action." *American Review of Political Science* 87(2): 319–333.

—— 1995. "Information, Access, and Contributions: A Signaling Model of Lobbying." *Public Choice* 85(3/4): 267–284.

—— 1998. "An Information Rationale for the Power of Special Interests." *American Political Science Review* 92(4): 809–827.

Long, J. Scott and Jeremy Freese. 2001. *Regression Models for Categorical Dependent Variables Using STATA*. College Station: Stata Press.

Long, Tony. 1995. "Shaping Public Policy in the European Union: A Case Study of the Structural Funds." *Journal of European Public Policy* 2(4): 672–679.

Lowe, Will. 2003. *Software for Content Analysis – A Review*. Technical Report for the Identity Project: Weatherhead Center for International Affairs, Harvard University.

—— 2008. "Understanding Wordscores." *Political Analysis* 16(4): 356–371.

—— 2009a. *Jfreq*. Version 0.2.2, URL (consulted February 2009): http://www.williamlowe.net/software.

—— 2009b. *Yoshikoder*. Version 0.6.3., URL (consulted May 2009): http://www.yoshikoder.org.

Lowe, Will, Ken Benoit, Slava Mikhaylov, and Michael Laver. 2011. "Scaling Policy Positions from Coded Units of Political Texts." *Legislative Studies Quarterly* 36(1): 123–155.

Lowery, David. 2007. "Why Do Organized Interests Lobby? A Multi-goal, Multi-context Theory of Lobbying." *Polity* 39(1): 29–54.

Lowi, Theodore J. 1964. "American Business, Public Policy, Case-Studies, and Political Theory." *World Politics* 16(4): 677–715.

Lukes, Steven. 1974. *Power: A Radical View*. Basingstoke: Macmillan.

McCarthy, John D. and Mayer N. Zald. 1977. "Resource Mobilization and Social Movements: A Partial Theory?" *American Journal of Sociology* 82(6): 1212–1241.

McCubbins, Mathew D., Roger G. Noll, and Barry R. Weingast. 1987. "Administrative Procedures as Instruments of Political Control." *Journal of Law, Economics and Organization* 3(2): 243–277.

McLaughlin, Andrew M., Grant Jordan, and William A. Maloney. 1993. "Corporate Lobbying in the European Community." *Journal of Common Market Studies* 31(2): 191–212.

Mahoney, Christine. 2004. "The Power of Institutions: State and Interest Group Activity in the European Union." *European Union Politics* 5(4): 441–466.

—— 2007a. "Lobbying Success in the United States and the European Union." *Journal of Public Policy* 27(1): 35–56.

—— 2007b. "Networking vs. Allying: The Decision of Interest Groups to Join coalitions in the US and the EU." *Journal of European Public Policy* 14(3): 366–383.

—— 2008. *Brussels versus the Beltway: Advocacy in the United States and the European Union*. Washington, DC: Georgetown University Press.

Mahoney, Christine and Michael Joseph Beckstrand. 2011. "Following the Money: EU Funding of Civil Society Organizations." *Journal of Common Market Studies* 49(6): 1339–1361.

Majone, Giandomenico. 1996a. The European Commission as Regulator. In *Regulating Europe*, ed. Giandomenico Majone. London: Routledge, pp. 61–79.

—— 1996b. Regulatory Legitimacy. In *Regulating Europe*, ed. Giandomenico Majone. London: Routledge, pp. 284–301.

—— 2001. "Two Logics of Delegation: Agency and Fiduciary Relations in EU Governance." *European Union Politics* 2(1): 103–121.

Maloney, William A. 1999. Contracting out the Participation Function: Social Capital and Cheque-book Participation. In *Social Capital and European Democracy*, ed. Jan W. van Deth. London: Routledge, pp. 100–110.

Maloney, William A. 2008. "The Professionalization of Representation: Biasing Participation." *CONNEX Report Series* 5: 69–85.

Maniadis, Zacharias. 2009. "Campaign Contributions as a Commitment Device." *Public Choice* 139(3–4): 301–315.

March, James G. and Johan P. Olsen. 1984. "The New Institutionalism: Organizational Factors in Political Life." *American Political Science Review* 78(3): 734–749.

Marks, Gary and Doug McAdam. 1996. "Social Movements and the Changing Structure of Political Opportunity in the European Community." *West European Politics* 18(2): 249–278.

—— 1999. On the Relationship of Political Opportunities to the Form of Collective Acrion: The Case of the European Union. In *Social Movements in a Globalizing World*, ed. Donatella Della Porta, Hanspeter Kriesi, and Dieter Rucht. Basingstoke: Macmillan, pp. 97–111.

Marks, Gary, Liesbet Hooghe, Moira Nelson and Erica Edwards. 2006. "Party Competition and European Integration in the East and West: Different Structure, Same Causality." *Comparative Political Studies* 39(2): 155–175.

Marks, Gary, Liesbet Hooghe, Marco R. Steenbergen and Ryan Bakker. 2007. "Crossvalidating data on party positioning on European integration." *Electoral Studies* 26(1): 23–38.

Marshall, David. 2010. "Who to Lobby and When: Institutional Determinants of Interest Group Strategies in European Parliament Committees." *European Union Politics* 11(4): 553–575.

Martin, Lanny W. and Georg Vanberg. 2008. "A Robust Transformation Procedure for Interpreting Political Text." *Political Analysis* 16(1): 93–100.

—— 2011. *Parliaments and Coalitions: The Role of Legislative Institutions in Multiparty Governance*. Oxford: Oxford University Press.

Mattila, Mikko. 2004. "Contested Decisions: Empirical Analysis of Voting in the European Union Council of Ministers." *European Journal of Political Research* 43(1): 29–50.

Mayhew, David R. 1974. *Congress: The Electoral Connection*. New Haven, CT: Yale University Press.

Mazey, Sonia and Jeremy Richardson. 1992. "British Pressure Groups in the European Community: The Challenge of Brussels." *Parliamentary Affairs* 45(1): 92–107.

—— 1993. Environmental Groups and the EC: Challenges and Opportunities. In *A Green Dimension for the European Community: Political Issues and Processes*, ed. David Judge. London: Frank Cass, pp. 109–128.

Messer, Anne, Joost Berkhout, and David Lowery. 2010. "The Density of the EU Interest System: A Test of the ESA Model." *British Journal of Political Science* 41(1): 161–190.

Michalowitz, Irina. 2004. *EU Lobbying: Principals, Agents and Targets—Strategic Interest Intermediation in EU Policy-making*. Münster: LIT.

—— 2007. "What Determines Influence? Assessing Conditions for Decision-making Influence of Interest Groups in the EU." *Journal of European Public Policy* 14(1): 132–151.

Mikhaylov, Slava, Michael Laver, and Kenneth Benoit. 2012. "Coder Reliability and Misclassification in the Human Coding of Party Manifestos." *Political Analysis* 20(1): 78–91.

Moe, Terry M. 1980. *The Organization of Interests: Incentives and the Internal Dynamics of Political Interest Groups*. Chicago: University of Chicago Press.

—— 1990. The Politics of Structural Choice: Towards a Theory of Public Bureaucracy. In *Organization Theory: From Chester Barnard to the Present and Beyond*, ed. Olivier E. Williamson. Oxford: Oxford University Press, pp. 116–153.

Mood, Carina. 2010. "Logistic Regression: Why We Cannot Do What We Think We Can Do, and What We Can Do About It." *European Sociological Review* 26(1): 67–82.

Moravcsik, Andrew. 1993. "Preferences and Power in the European Community: A Liberal Intergovernmentalist Approach." *Journal of Common Market Studies* 31(4): 473–524.

—— 1997. "Taking Preferences Seriously: A Liberal Theory of International Politics." *International Organization* 51(4): 513–553.

—— 1998. *The Choice for Europe: Social Purpose and State Power from Rome to Maastricht*. Ithaca, NY: Cornell University Press.

Mosteller, Frederick and David L. Wallace. 1964. *Inference and Disputed Authorship: The Federalist*. Reading: Addison-Wesley.

Mroz, Thomas A. and Yaraslau V. Zayats. 2008. "Arbitrarily Normalized Coefficients, Information Sets, and False Reports of 'Biases' in Binary Outcome Models." *Review of Economics and Statistics* 90(3): 406–413.

Müller, Wolfgang and Kaare Strøm. 2000. *Coalition Governments in Western Europe*. Oxford: Oxford University Press.

Nagel, Jack H. 1975. *The Descriptive Analysis of Power*. New Haven, CT: Yale University Press.

Naoi, Megumi and Ellis Krauss. 2009. "Who Lobbies Whom? Special Interest Politics under Alternative Electoral Systems." *American Journal of Political Science* 53(4): 874–892.

Neuendorf, Kimberly A. 2002. *The Content Analysis Guidebook*. Thousand Oaks: Sage.

Niskanen, William A. 1971. *Bureaucracy and Representative Government*. Chicago: Aldine Atherton.

—— 1975. "Bureaucrats and Politicians." *Journal of Law and Economics* 18(3): 617–643.

North, Douglass C. 1990. *Institutions, Institutional Change and Economic Performance*. Cambridge: Cambridge University Press.

Nugent, Neill. 2001. *The European Commission*. Basingstoke: Palgrave Macmillan.

Olson, Mancur. 1965. *The Logic of Collective Action: Public Goods and the Theory of Groups*. Cambridge, MA: Harvard University Press.

Pappi, Franz U. and Christian H. C. A. Henning. 1999. "The Organization of Influence on the EC's Common Agricultural Policy: A Network Approach." *European Journal of Political Research* 36(2): 257–281.

—— and Nicole M. Seher. 2009. "Party Election Programmes, Signalling Policies and Salience of Specific Policy Domains: The German Parties from 1990 to 2005." *German Politics* 18(3): 403–425.

Payton, Mark E., Matthew H. Greenstone, and Nathaniel Schenker. 2003. "Overlapping Confidence Intervals or Standard Error Intervals: What Do They Mean in Terms of Statistical Significance?" *Journal of Insect Science* 34(3): 1–6.

Peltzman, Sam. 1985. "An Economic Interpretation of the History of Congressional Voting in the Twentieth Century." *American Economic Review* 75(4): 656–675.

Peltzman, Sam, Michael E. Levine, and Roger G. Noll. 1989. "The Economic Theory of Regulation after a Decade of Deregulation." *Brookings Papers on Economic Activity. Microeconomics* 1989: 1–59.

Persson, Thomas. 2007. "Democratizing European Chemicals Policy: Do Consultations Favour Civil Society Participation?" *Journal of Civil Society* 3(3): 223–238.

Peterson, John. 1991. "Technology Policy in Europe: Explaining the Framework Programme and Eureka in Theory and Practice." *Journal of Common Market Studies* 29(3): 269–290.

Pfeffer, Jeffrey and Gerald R. Salancik. 1978. *The External Control of Organizations: A Resource Dependence Perspective*. New York: Harper & Row.

Pijnenburg, Bert. 1998. "EU Lobbying by Ad Hoc Coalitions: An Exploratory Case Study." *Journal of European Public Policy* 5(2): 303–21.

Plotnick, Robert D. 1986. "An Interest Group Model of Direct Income Redistribution." *Review of Economics and Statistics* 68(4): 594–602.

Pollack, Mark A. 1997*a*. "Delegation, Agency, and Agenda-Setting in the European Community." *International Organization* 51(1): 99–134.

—— 1997*b*. "Representing Diffuse Interests in EC Policy-making." *Journal of European Public Policy* 4(4): 572–590.

—— 2003. *The Engines of European Integration: Delegation, Agency, and Agenda-Setting in the EU*. Oxford: Oxford University Press.

Polsby, Nelson W. 1960. "How to Study Community Power: The Pluralist Alternative." *Journal of Politics* 22(3): 474–484.

Poole, Keith. 2005. *Spatial Models of Parliamentary Voting*. Cambridge: Cambridge University Press.

Porst, Rolf. 2008. *Fragebogen: Ein Arbeitsbuch*. Wiesbaden: VS Verlag für Sozialwissenschaften.

Porter, Michael E. 1980. *Competitive Strategy: Techniques for Analyzing Industries and Competitors*. New York: Free Press.

Potters, Jan and Randolph Sloof. 1996. "Interest Groups: A Survey of Empirical Models That Try to Assess Their Influence." *European Journal of Political Economy* 12(3): 403–442.

Potters, Jan and Frans van Winden. 1990. "Modelling Political Pressure as Transmission of Information." *European Journal of Political Economy* 6(1): 61–88.

—— 1992. "Lobbying and Asymmetric Information." *Public Choice* 74(3): 269–292.

Princen, Sebastiaan. 2007. "Advocacy Coalitions and the Internationalization of Public Health Policies." *Journal of Public Policy* 27(1): 13–33.

—— 2009. *Agenda-Setting in the European Union*. Basingstoke: Palgrave Macmillan.

Proksch, Sven-Oliver and Jonathan B. Slapin. 2008. *WORDFISH: Scaling Software for Estimating Political Positions from Texts*. Version 1.3., URL (consulted January 2009): http://www.wordfish.org.

—— 2009*a*. "How to Avoid Pitfalls in Statistical Analysis of Political Texts: The Case of Germany." *German Politics* 18(3): 323–344.

—— 2009*b*. *WORDFISH Manual*. Version 1.3, URL (consulted Sept. 2009): http://www.wordfish.org.

—— 2010. "Position Taking in European Parliament Speeches." *British Journal of Political Science* 40(3): 587–611.

Przeworski, Adam and Michael Wallerstein. 1988. "Structural Dependence of the State on Capital." *American Political Science Review* 82(1): 11–29.

Quinn, Kevin M., Burt Monroe, Michael Colaresi, Michael Crespin, and Drago Radev. 2010. "How to Analyze Political Attention with Minimal Assumptions and Costs." *American Journal of Political Science* 54(1): 209–228.

Quittkat, Christine. 2006. *Europäisierung der Interessenvermittlung: Französische Wirtschaftsverbände zwischen Beständigkeit und Wandel.* Wiesbaden: VS Verlag für Sozialwissenschaften.

—— 2011. "The European Commission's Online Consultations: A Success Story?" *Journal of Common Market Studies* 49(3): 653–674.

Quittkat, Christine and Barbara Finke. 2008. "The EU Consultation Regime." *CONNEX Report Series* (5): 183–222.

Rabe-Hesketh, Sophia and Anders Skrondal. 2008. *Multilevel and Longitudinal Modeling Using Stata.* 2nd edn. College Station: Stata Press.

Radaelli, Claudio M. 1999. "The Public Policy of the European Union: Whither Politics of Expertise?" *Journal of European Public Policy* 6(5): 757–774.

Reif, Karlheinz and Hermann Schmitt. 1980. "Nine Second-Order National Elections: A Conceptual Framework for the Analsyis of European Election Results." *European Journal of Political Research* 8(1): 3–44.

Richardson, Jeremy. 2000. "Government, Interest Groups and Policy Change." *Political Studies* 48(5): 1006–1025.

Richardson, Jeremy and David Coen. 2009. Institutionalizing and Managing Intermediation in the EU. In *Lobbying in the European Union: Institutions, Actors, and Issues,* ed. David Coen and Jeremy Richardson. Oxford: Oxford University Press, pp. 337–350.

Riker, William. 1996. *The Strategy of Rhetoric: Campaigning for the American Constitution.* New Haven, CT: Yale University Press.

Riker, William Harrison. 1962. *The Theory of Political Coalitions.* New Haven, CT: Yale University Press.

Risse-Kappen, Thomas. 1996. "Exploring the Nature of the Beast: International Relations Theory and Comparative Policy Analysis Meet the European Union." *Journal of Common Market Studies* 34(1): 53–80.

Rittberger, Berthold. 2000. "Impatient Legislators and New Issue-Dimensions: A Critique of the Garrett-Tsebelis Standard Version of Legislative Politics." *Journal of European Public Policy* 7(4): 554–575.

—— 2003. "The Creation and Empowerment of the European Parliament." *Journal of Common Market Studies* 41(2): 203–225.

—— 2005. *Building Europe's Parliament: Democratic Representation Beyond the Nation-State.* Oxford: Oxford University Press.

Rittberger, Berthold and Frank Schimmelfennig. 2006. "Explaining the constitutionalization of the European Union." *Journal of European Public Policy* 13(8): 1148–1167.

Roberts, Carl W. 2000. "A Conceptual Framework for Quantitative Text Analysis: On Joining Probabilities and Substantive Inferences about Texts." *Quality and Quantity* 34(3): 259–274.

Royston, Patrick. 2004. "Multiple Imputation of Missing Values." *The Stata Journal* 4(3): 227–241.

Sabatier, Paul A. 1988. "An Advocacy Coalition Framework of Policy Change and the Role of Policy-Oriented Learning Therein." *Policy Sciences* 21(2/3): 129–168.

Safire, William. 1993. *Safire's New Political Dictionary: The Definitive Guide to the New Language of Politics*. New York: Random House.

Salisbury, Robert H., John P. Heinz, Edward O. Laumann, and Robert L. Nelson. 1987. "Who Works with Whom? Interest Group Alliances and Opposition." *American Political Science Review* 81(4): 1217–1234.

Sánchez-Salgado, Rosa. 2007. "Giving a European Dimension to Civil Society Organizations." *Journal of Civil Society* 3(3): 253–269.

Sandholtz, Wayne. 1992. "ESPRIT and the Politics of International Collective Action." *Journal of Common Market Studies* 30(1): 1–21.

Sandholtz, Wayne and Alec Stone Sweet. 1998. *European Integration and Supranational Governance*. Oxford: Oxford University Press.

Sandholtz, Wayne and John Zysman. 1989. "1992: Recasting the European Bargain." *World Politics* 42(1): 95–128.

Saurugger, Sabine. 2002. "L'expertise: une forme de participation des groupes d'intérêt au processus décisionnel communautaire." *Revue française de Science Politique* 52(4): 375–401.

—— 2003. *Européansiser les intérêts*. Paris: Harmattan.

—— 2008. "Interest Groups and Democracy in the European Union." *West European Politics* 31(6): 1274–1291.

—— 2009. COREPER and National Governments. In *Lobbying the European Union: Instituions, Actors, and Issues*, ed. David Coen and Jeremy Richardson. Oxford: Oxford University Press, pp. 105–127.

—— 2010. "The Social Construction of the Participatory Turn: The Emergence of a Norm in the European Union." *European Journal of Political Research* 49(4): 471–495.

Scharpf, Fritz W. 1970. *Demokratietheorie zwischen Utopie und Anpassung*. Konstanz: Universitätsverlag.

—— 1999. *Governing in Europe: Effective and Democratic?* Oxford: Oxford University Press.

Schattschneider, Elmer E. 1960. *The Semisovereign People: A Realist's View of Democracy in America*. New York: Holt.

Schendelen, Marinus P. C. M. van, ed. 1993. *National Public and Private EC Lobbying*. Aldershot: Dartmouth.

Schenker, Nathaniel and Jane F. Gentleman. 2001. "On Judging the Significance of Differences by Examining the Overlap Between Confidence Intervals." *The American Statistician* 55(3): 182–186.

Schimmelfennig, Frank. 2001. "The Community Trap: Liberal Norms, Rhetorical Action, and the Eastern Enlargement of the European Union." *International Organization* 55(1): 47–80.

—— 2003. *The EU, NATO and the Integration of Europe: Rules and Rhetoric*. Cambridge: Cambridge University Press.

Schimmelfennig, Frank, Berthold Rittberger, Alexander Bürgin, and Guido Schwellnus. 2006. "Conditions for EU Constitutionalization: A Qualitative Comparative Analysis." *Journal of European Public Policy* 13(8): 1168–1189.

Schmalz-Bruns, Rainer. 1995. *Reflexive Demokratie: Die demokratische Transformation moderner Politik*. Baden-Baden: Nomos.

Schmidt, Vivien A. 1996. "Loosening the Ties that Bind: The Impact of European Integration on French Government and its Relationship to Business." *Journal of Common Market Studies* 34(2): 223–254.

Schmitt, Ralf. 2008. "Die politikfeldspezifische Auswertung von Wahlprogrammen am Beispiel der deutschen Bundesländer." *Working Paper, Mannheim Centre for European Social Research* 114: 1–25.

Schmitter, Philippe C. and Wolfgang Streeck. 1999. "The Organization of Business Interests: Studying the Associative Action of Business in Advanced Industrial Societies." *MPIfG Discussion Paper* 99(1): 1–95.

Schneider, Carsten Q. and Claudius Wagemann. 2007. *Qualitative Comparative Analysis and Fuzzy Sets.* Opladen: Barbara Budrich.

Schneider, Gerald and Konstantin Baltz. 2003. "The Power of Specialization: How Interest Groups Influence EU Legislation." *Rivista di Politica Economica* 93(1–2): 253–283.

—— 2004. Specialization Pays Off: Interest Group Influence on EU Pre-negotiations in Four Member States. In *Governance in Europe*, ed. Andreas Warntjen and Arndt Wonka. Baden-Baden: Nomos, pp. 130–147.

—— 2005. "Domesticated Eurocrats: Bureaucratic Discretion in the Legislative Pre-negotiations of the European Union." *Acta Politica* 40: 1–27.

Schneider, Gerald, Daniel Finke, and Konstantin Baltz. 2007. "With a Little Help from Your State: Interest Intermediation in the Pre-Negotiations of EU Legislation." *Journal of European Public Policy* 14(3): 444–459.

Schneider, Gerald, Daniel Finke, and Stefanie Bailer. 2010. "Bargaining Power in the European Union: An Evaluation of Competing Game-Theoretic Models." *Political Studies* 58(1): 85–103.

Schonhardt-Bailey, Cheryl. 2008. "The Congressional Debate on Partial-Birth Abortion: Constitutional Gravitas and Moral Passion." *British Journal of Political Science* 38(3): 383–410.

Selck, Torsten J. and Bernard Steunenberg. 2004. "Between Power and Luck: The European Parliament in the EU Legislative Process." *European Union Politics* 5(1): 25–46.

Slapin, Jonathan and Sven-Oliver Proksch. 2008. "A Scaling Model for Estimating Time Series Policy Positions from Texts." *American Journal of Political Science* 52(8): 705–722.

Smith, Mark A. 2000. *American Business and Political Power: Public Opinion, Elections, and Democracy.* Chicago: University of Chicago Press.

Smith, Richard A. 1995. "Interest Group Influence in the U.S. Congress." *Legislative Studies Quarterly* 20(1): 89–139.

Steenbergen, Marco R. and Bradford S. Jones. 2002. "Modeling Multilevel Data Structures." *American Journal of Political Science* 46(1): 218–237.

Steunenberg, Bernard. 1994. "Decision-making under Different Institutional Arrangements: Legislation by the European Community." *Journal of Institutional and Theoretical Economics* 150(4): 642–669.

Steunenberg, Bernard and Michael Kaeding. 2009. "'As time goes by': Explaining the Transposition of Maritime Directives." *European Journal of Political Research* 48(3): 432–454.

Stewart, John David. 1958. *British Pressure Groups: Their Role in Relation to the House of Commons*. Oxford: Clarendon Press.

Stigler, George J. 1971. "The Theory of Economic Regulation." *Bell Journal of Economics and Management Science* 2(1): 3–21.

Stone Sweet, Alec and Neil Fligstein. 2002. "Constructing Polities and Markets: An Institutionalist Account of European Integration." *Americal Journal of Sociology* 107(5): 1206–1243.

Stone Sweet, Alec and Wayne Sandholtz. 1997. "European Integration and Supranational Governance." *Journal of European Public Policy* 4(3): 297–317.

Tallberg, Jonas. 2002. "Delegation to Supranational Institutions: Why, How and With What Competences?" *West European Politics* 25(1): 23–46.

Thomson, Robert. 2011. *Resolving Controversy in the European Union: Legislative Decision-Making Before and After Enlargement*. Cambridge: Cambridge University Press.

Thomson, Robert and Madeleine O. Hosli. 2006. Explaining Legislative Decision-making in the European Union. In *The European Union Decides*, ed. Robert Thomson, Frans N. Stokman, Christopher H. Achen, and Thomas König. Cambridge: Cambridge University Press, pp. 1–24.

Thomson, Robert, Frans N. Stokman, Christopher H. Achen, and Thomas König. 2006. *The European Union Decides*. Cambridge: Cambridge University Press.

Tsebelis, George. 1994. "The Power of the European Parliament as a Conditional Agenda Setter." *American Political Science Review* 88(1): 128–142.

Tsebelis, George and Geoffrey Garrett. 2000. "Legislative Politics in the European Union." *European Union Politics* 1(1): 9–36.

van der Eijk, Cees and Mark N. Franklin. 1996. *Choosing Europe? The European Electorate and National Politics in the Face of Union*. Ann Arbor: University of Michigan Press.

van Winden, Frans. 2003. Interest group behavior and influence. In *Encyclopedia of Public Choice*, ed. Charles K. Rowley and Friedrich Schneider. Dordrecht: Kluwer, pp. 118–129.

Volkens, Andrea. 2005. *Manifesto Dataset MDS2005 Handbook*. Comparative Manifestos Project/Manifesto Research Group, URL (consulted March 2010): http://www.wzb.eu/zkd/dsl/pdf/manifesto-project.pdf.

Wallace, Helen and Alasdair R. Young, eds. 1997. *Participation and Policy-Making in the European Union*. Oxford: Clarendon Press.

Warleigh, Alex. 2000. "The Hustle: Citizenship Practice, NGOs and 'policy Coalitions' in the European Union—the Cases of Auto Oil, Drinking Water and Unit Pricing." *Journal of European Public Policy* 7(2): 229–243.

—— 2001. "'Europeanizing' Civil Society: NGOs as Agents of Political Socialization." *Journal of Common Market Studies* 39(4): 619–639.

Warntjen, Andreas, ed. 2004. *Governance in Europe: The Role of Interest Groups*. Baden-Baden: Nomos.

Weiler, J. H. H., Ulrich R. Haltern, and Franz C. Mayer. 1995. "European Democracy and its Critique." *West European Politics* 18(3): 4–39.

Whiteley, Paul and Stephen J. Winyard. 1987. *Pressure for the Poor: The Poverty Lobby and Policy Making*. London: Methuen.

Woll, Cornelia. 2007. "Leading the Dance? Power and Political Resources of Business Lobbyists." *Journal of Public Policy* 27(1): 57–78.

—— 2008. *Firm Interests: How Governments Shape Business Lobbying on Global Trade.* Ithaca, NY: Cornell University Press.

Wonka, Arndt. 2007. "Technocratic and Independent? The appointment of European Commissioners and its Policy Implications." *Journal of European Public Policy* 14(2): 169–189.

Wonka, Arndt, Frank R. Baumgartner, Christine Mahoney and Joost Berkhout. 2010. "Measuring the Size of the EU Interest Group Population." *European Union Politics* 11(3): 463–476.

Zimmer, Christina, Gerald Schneider, and Michael Dobbins. 2005. "The Contested Council: Conflict Dimensions of an Intergovernmental EU Institution." *Political Studies* 53(2): 403–422.

Index

advocacy coalition 12
agenda-setting 31, 156, 219–220

CMP *see* Comparative Manifesto
College of Commissioners 31, 72, 156
Comparative Manifesto Project 65–66, 67,
   69, 74–75, 87
concentrated interests 13, 15, 208, 216
content analysis 65–67, 69, 71–72, 75, 77,
   91–92 *see also* text analysis
Coreper 42
corporatist 9

democratic deficit 1, 34, 37, 203, 213, 222
democratic governance 34, 47–49
diffuse interests 13, 15, 140, 208, 215, 219
Directorate General 103, 132, 134–135,
   155–156, 221

economic voting 49–52
electorate 39, 44–47, 49, 51
environmental groups 2, 6, 55, 63, 72, 76–77,
   80–90, 151, 166, 171, 185, 196–197
ESPRIT program 43, 51
EurLex 16, 21, 106, 121,122, 205
expert survey 64, 68–69, 87
expertise 12, 30, 33, 39–45, 58, 107, 136,
   160–162, 170, 186, 206–207

free-ride 23, 172, 173, 175, 198, 200, 215

governments 18, 29–30, 33–35, 37–54, 121,
   206–207, 211–212, 218–219, 221

health check 103, 133, 135–136, 170

influence
   attributed influence 16, 61–62
   definition 7–9
   face of power 7, 220
   luck 7–9, 63, 172, 198
   preference attainment 16, 20–21, 61–64,
      90, 93, 98, 176
   process-tracing 16, 61, 63
institutional context 10–11
interest group
   actor type 13
   cause group 119, 139–140, 143–144,
      147–148, 214–216

chamber 6, 27, 139,
company 110, 111, 149–150
definition 5–6
information 14–15, 40–45
members 26–27
non-governmental organizations
   (NGOs) 2, 5, 55, 95, 139, 147, 160, 166,
   170–171, 185–186, 191–192, 197
non-permanent characteristics 13–15
permanent characteristics 12–13
population 9, 14–16, 22, 95, 108–110, 131,
   138–144, 152, 154, 192
professional association 6, 139, 143,
   147–148
representation 26, 139–141, 148, 152,
   214–216
resources 13
sectional group 119, 140, 216
territorial origin 140–141, 152
trade union 6, 27, 46, 139–143, 147–148,
   214–215
issue
   complexity 19, 57–59, 101, 120,
      122–125, 136–137, 152, 155–157,
      161–163, 168, 176, 182–183, 186–189,
      194, 204, 209
   conflict 11, 22, 101, 103, 120, 122–124,
      131–153, 157, 163, 168, 182, 189, 194,
      209
   distributive 12, 152
   issue network 54
   redistributive 12
   regulatory 12, 135, 152
   salience 11, 48, 101, 103, 119–120, 136,
      152, 209
   scope 11, 102
   status quo 117, 120–123

left–right 63, 67
legislative instrument
   directive 94, 102–104, 133–134, 138,
      191–192, 196–197
   regulation 31, 72, 81–82, 85–88, 90, 94,
      102–104, 138
legislative procedure
   Codecision 32, 33, 34, 35, 36, 40, 44, 71,
      102, 103, 123, 133, 138, 157, 163, 168,
      175, 178, 179, 180, 181, 182, 189, 194,
      199